Georgia Atlas & Gazetteer

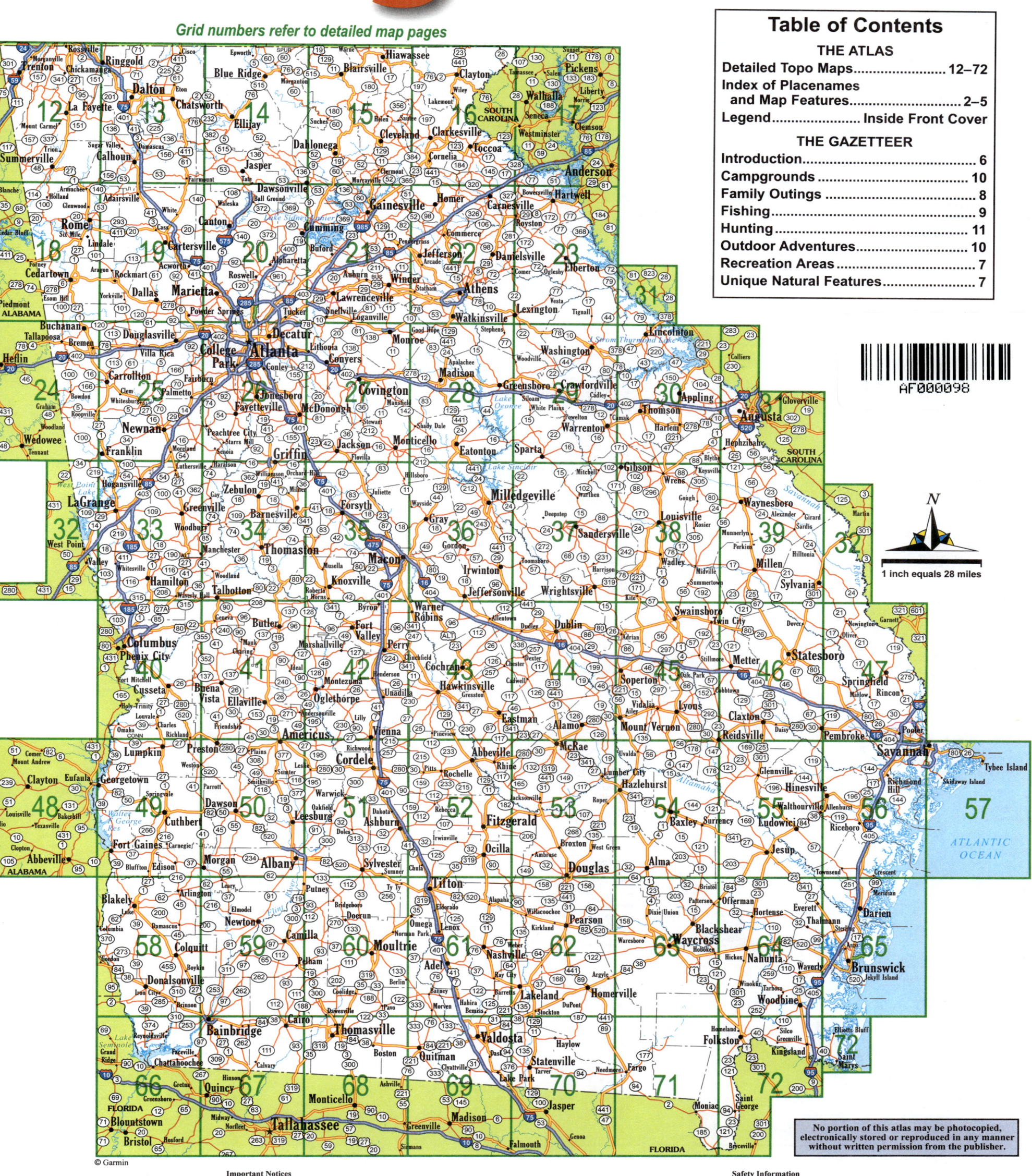

Grid numbers refer to detailed map pages

Table of Contents

THE ATLAS
- Detailed Topo Maps 12–72
- Index of Placenames and Map Features 2–5
- Legend .... Inside Front Cover

THE GAZETTEER
- Introduction 6
- Campgrounds 10
- Family Outings 8
- Fishing 9
- Hunting 11
- Outdoor Adventures 10
- Recreation Areas 7
- Unique Natural Features 7

AF000098

1 inch equals 28 miles

No portion of this atlas may be photocopied, electronically stored or reproduced in any manner without written permission from the publisher.

Important Notices
Garmin has made reasonable efforts to provide you with accurate maps and related information, but we cannot exclude the possibility of errors or omissions in sources or of changes in actual conditions. GARMIN MAKES NO WARRANTIES OF ANY KIND, EITHER EXPRESS OR IMPLIED, INCLUDING MERCHANTABILITY AND FITNESS FOR A PARTICULAR PURPOSE. GARMIN SHALL NOT BE LIABLE TO ANY PERSON UNDER ANY LEGAL OR EQUITABLE THEORY FOR DAMAGES ARISING OUT OF THE USE OF THIS PUBLICATION, INCLUDING, WITHOUT LIMITATION, FOR DIRECT, CONSEQUENTIAL OR INCIDENTAL DAMAGES.

Nothing in this publication implies the right to use private property. There may be private inholdings within the boundaries of public reservations. You should respect all landowner restrictions.

Some listings may be seasonal or may have admission fees. Please be sure to confirm this information when making plans.

Safety Information
To avoid accidents, always pay attention to actual road, traffic and weather conditions while you are operating a vehicle. Please consult local authorities for the most current information on road and other travel-related conditions.

Do not use this publication for marine or aeronautical navigation, as it does not depict navigation aids, depths, obstacles, landing approaches and other information necessary to performing these functions safely.

California Prop 65 Warning
⚠ WARNING: Cancer and Reproductive Harm - www.p65warnings.ca.gov

EIGHTH EDITION
Copyright © 2024 Garmin Ltd. or its Affiliates. All rights reserved.   2 DeLorme Dr. Suite 200, Yarmouth, Maine 04096
www.garmin.com/DeLormeAtlas   Printed in Canada.

Index of Placenames and Map Features

ABOUT THE INDEX

This index contains over 4,400 Georgia placenames and map features. Names are listed alphabetically with map page(s) and grid coordinates to help locate them. The grid coordinates correspond to the letters (A–E) and numbers (1–10) along the top and outside edges of all map pages.

Guidelines for using this index:

- Placenames appear in boldface type, such as **Richland** 40 E5
- Drainage names (e.g., lakes, reservoirs, rivers, creeks, springs) appear in italic type, such as *Savannah River* 23 A9
- All geographic features (e.g., mountains, canyons, valleys) appear in regular type, such as Howard Mountain 16 A2

A

23d Street Swamp 59 A8
42d Street Swamp 59 A8
Aaron Mountain 14 C3
Abbeville 52 A3
Abe Mountain 15 C6
Abercorn Creek 47 D10
Aboothlacoosta Creek 27 E7
Abraham Point 72i D4
Abram Mountain 16 C3
Abrams Creek 51 D7,9
Acheson Hill 40 D3
Acorn Creek 25 D7
Acree 51 E7
Acworth 19 C10
Adairsville 19 A7
Adam Springs 52 A4
Adams Bald 15 C8
Adams Island 34 D3
Addie Gap 16 A4
Adel 61 D7
Adgateville 35 A10
Adrian 45 B6
African Island 65 E6
Ailey 45 E6
Alabaha River 63 B9,10; 52 A1;B1;C2;D2;E3; 61 A8,9;B10; 62 C-E1; 70 A-C1
Alaculsy Gap 14 B1
Alaculsy Valley 13 A10
Alapaha 61 A9
Alapahoochee River 69 B10; 70 C1
Albany 50 E5
Albany Lake 50 D3
Alcovy Mountain 27 A9
Alcovy River 21 D7;E8,9; 27 A9;B9;D8
Alec Mountain 14 C5; 16 C1
Aleck Island 64 A5
Alex Creek 55 E10; 64 A4
Alex Mountain 16 A3
Alexander 39 B8
Alexander Creek 25 D10
Alisons Creek 54 C4
Allatoona Creek 19 D10
Allen Creek 21 B9,10; 25 B6
Allen Mountain 16 E2
Allen Mountain 15 A9
Allen Shoals 27 D8
Allen Spring Gap 12 B2
Allenhurst 56 C1
Allentown 43 A9
Alligator Bay 56 A3
Alligator Bays 64 B4
Alligator Creek 36 E3; 53 A10;B6,7; 54 A2; 59 B6; 63 D7,8; 70 C2; 71 A6
Alligator Swamp 64 B4
Allison Mountain 15 C8
Allison Ridge 15 B8
Allisons Creek 35 A10
Alma 54 E2
Almand Creek 27 B6
Almon 27 B7
Alpharetta 20 C3
Alpine Creek 12 E2
Alston 54 A2
Altamaha River 54 B2-3,5; 55 C6,8;D9;E10; 65 A6;B7,8
Altamaha Sound 65 B9
Alto 16 E1
Alvaton 34 A1
Ambrose 53 E7
Americus 50 A4
Amicalola Creek 14 D4,E4; 20 A5
Anderson Cave Spring 12 C2
Anderson Creek 14 D4
Anderson Knob 15 A7
Anderson Mill Creek 23 E9; 29 A10
Andersonville 20 C2
Andersonville 41 E10
Andrews Hill 36 E1
Andrews Island 65 D7
Andy Gap 15 A10
Andy Mountain 25 A8
Angelica Creek 41 E9
Ann Gap 16 C1
Apalachee 28 B2
Apalachee River 21 D7,8;E9,10; 22 E1; 28 A2;B3
Appling 30 C4
Arabi 51 C9
Arabia Swamp 62 D3
Aragon 19 D6
Arcade 22 C1
Archers Lakes 37 B10
Arco 65 C6
Arcola 47 C6
Argyle 62 D5
Argyle Island 47 D10
Arkaqua Creek 15 B8
Arlington 58 A4
Armstrong Branch 29 A9
Armstrong Mountain 19 A6
Armuchee Creek 12 E5; 18 A5
Arnold Creek 61 A6
Arnold Mill 20 C3
Arnoldsville 22 E5
As Knob 16 A1
Ash Branch 47 D6
Ash Mountain 15 C9
Ash Ridge 15 D8
Ashburn 51 D10
Ashburn Branch 51 D10
Athens 22 D3
Atkins Knob 15 A7
Atkinson 64 C3
Atlanta 26 A2
Atlantic Ocean 57 D8; 65 D9; 72 E5

Attapulgus 67 B7
Attapulgus Creek 67 A7;B7
Aubrey Lake 19 B9
Auburn 21 D8
Auchumpkee Creek 34 D5;E4
Aucilla River 68 A3;B3,4
Augusta 31 D7
Austell 25 A10
Austin Gap 15 B10
Avera 38 A1
Avery Creek 35 E6
Avondale Estates 26 A4
Axson 62 B4
Aycocks Creek 58 C3;D4

B

Back River 56 E3; 65 C7
Back Swamp 55 D9
Back Valley Ridge 18 A2
Backbone Ridge 24 E5
Baconton 59 B10
Bad Prong 46 C2
Baden 69 B6
Bagley Creek 40 D4
Bailey Branch 41 E10
Baileys Branch 72 A2
Bainbridge 67 A6
Baker Creek 40 A5
Baker Island 64 B4
Baker Knob 15 B10
Baker Mountain 15 C7
Baker Swamp 56 C2
Balance Rock 28 B3
Bald Mountain 12 E3
Bald Ridge 15 B10
Baldwin 16 E1
Ball Creek 14 D1; 52 B3
Ball Ground 20 A3
Ball Mountain 15 C6
Ballard Gap 15 A7
Ballard Mountain 15 A7
Bancroft 58 A3
Banks Creek 46 A3
Banks Lake 62 E1
Banks Mountain 21 A7
Bannister Creek 20 A5
Baptist Creek 42 B3
Barber Creek 21 D10; 22 E1
Barbers Creek 64 B2
Barbour Island River 56 D4
Bardman Hill 40 C4
Barfield Creek 34 E3
Bark Camp Creek 38 D5
Barkeley Ridge 40 C2
Barkers Swamp 64 D5
Barn Mountain 13 C7
Barnard Mill 46 E3
Barnes Creek 33 E7
Barnes Gap 14 A2
Barnesville 34 B5
Barnesville Reservoir 34 B5
Barnetts Creek 59 E10; 68 A1
Barney 61 E6
Barney Bluff 31 E8
Barnum Branch 63 E6; 71 A6
Barr Bluff 53 C8
Barrel Head Swamp 65 E6
Barrett Mountain 15 A10
Barretts 61 E10
Barrow Creek 22 E5; 28 A4
Bart Top 14 B3
Bartletts Ferry Lake 33 E6
Bartow 38 D2
Barwick 68 A4
Basin Creek 34 C3
Basin Pond 59 B8
Bass Island 66 B4
Battle Branch 29 D7
Battle Creek 55 A6
Baugh Mountain 13 D6
Baxley 54 C3
Bay Branch 39 E7; 43 A10; 49 E9; 60 A3
Bay Creek 21 E8; 42 B3;B4; 54 B3;
Bay Gall Creek 42 A5; 46 A3
Bay Island 63 D8
Bay Pole Branch 60 C2; 59 D9
Bay Pole Sink 59 D9
Beach 63 A7
Beach Creek 24 A4
Beach Hammock 56 E5
Bear Bay 62 D3
Bear Branch 50 A4; 49 E9; 63 E6; 70 B4
Bear Creek 12 B2; 22 D1; 25 B9;C9;C10; 26 E3; 33 A9,10;B8; 42 E5; 43 E6; 45 D6; 53 E7; 47 D10; 49 A10; 50 B1,3; 53 E7,10; 60 C5;D5; 61 D6,8
Bear Den Mountain 14 B2
Bear Gap 16 C2
Bear Island 56 C5
Bear Island 63 D9
Bear Mountain 19 A10
Bear River 56 C5
Bearden Mountain 14 C5
Beards Creek 55 B8; 55 A7;C7
Bearmeat Gap 15 A9
Bearpen Island 63 D8
Beasley Knob 15 B7
Beaver Creek 23 D6; 34 A1; 35 E7; 36 C4; 41 A10; 42 A1,2;B1,4;C2; 45 D10; 49 B9
Beaver Dam Creek 38 B5
Beaver Knob 14 B5
Beaver Mountain 13 B10
Beaver Ruin Creek 20 E5
Beaverdam Bay 70 B2
Beaverdam Creek 16 D1; 21 E9; 22 B2;D5; 23 B6;C8; 28 A2;B4;C5;E1;

29 A8;B9;D8;E6,7;C7,9; 32 C1; 35 C9; 39 B9;C6,8,9;D10
Becky Bay 69 A10
Bee Bait Mountain 16 A5
Bee Bay 70 A2
Bee Gap 12 B1
Bee Gum Lake 71 C10
Bee Mountain 15 A10
Bee Pond Flats 62 D2
Beebait Knob 15 B6
Beech Creek 18 A4;B3; 21 D10; 22 D1; 33 B7,8
Beech Island 31 D7
Beechtree Creek 30 E1
Beechwood Swamp 42 B1
Belfast River 56 C4
Bell Creek 34 D3
Bell Knob 15 A9
Bellcamp Ridge 14 B4
Belle Isle 56 C4
Bells Mill Creek 54 A4
Bellville 46 E2
Belmont 26 A5
Belmont Mountain 12 B5
Belvedere Park 26 A4
Bemiss 61 E9
Ben Creek 62 D2
Ben Gap 15 A10
Ben Mountain 16 A3
Benevolence 49 B9
Bennett Bay 63 C6
Bennett Bay 62 E2
Bent Ridge 16 A4
Bentley Creek 24 A5
Benton Branch 30 C4
Berkeley Lake 20 D5
Berlin 60 D5
Berry Spring 59 A10
Bertram Creek 23 D9
Bethel Creek 33 D9
Bethlehem 21 E10
Bettes Gap 20 B5
Betts Mountain 34 C1
Betty Gap 14 B1
Betty Mountain 14 B1
Bettys Branch 30 C5
Betz Creek 57 A7
Bevel Creek 69 C9
Bexley Bay 70 B3
Bibbs Lake 25 D8
Big Alligator Creek 63 C6
Big Arm 70 B3
Big Battleground Creek 38 E1
Big Bay 47 C7; 56 E1; 63 D6; 64 E2
Big Bay Island 63 D6
Big Beech Creek 35 E6
Big Bend Falls 16 A5
Big Branch 33 D6; 37 E9; 39 C10; 43 E9; 46 B2;D3; 51 D9; 71 B6; 59 E10; 60 C2; 61 C6; 70 A4;B5; 71 A6
Big Branch Horse Creek 53 A6
Big Cedar Creek 18 C3; 36 A2; 37 D9;E10
Big Cedar Mountain 15 C7
Big Clouds Creek 22 D5
Big Cotton Indian Creek 27 C6
Big Creek 20 C5
Big Creek 16 A5;18 E4; 20 B5;C4;D4; 22 E4; 28 A4; 30 C1; 37 A10;E9; 38 A-C3; 42 C4;D5; 43 D6,7; 52 C3;D2; 60 D1,2,4;E2,3; 62 D1; 63 C10
Big Creek Gap 14 C4
Big Cypress 71 C6
Big Cypress Camp Island 71 B10
Big Cypress Creek 58 B5; 59 C6
Big Cypress Lake 59 A9
Big Cypress Swamp 64 A4
Big Drain 58 D5
Big Dry Creek 18 A4
Big Face 16 A2
Big Flat Creek 21 E8; 27 A8,9
Big Grassy Knob 15 B7
Big Grocery Creek 43 B6
Big Haynes Creek 27 A7;B7
Big Indian Creek 28 B1;C1;D2; 42 B2,3;C5; 43 C6
Big Island 64 B5
Big Island 71 A6
Big John Dick Mountain 14 C5
Big Leatherwood Creek 16 E3
Big Long Creek 38 D5;E4
Big Mortar Swamp 56 E2
Big Mountain 16 A4 ; 29 A6
Big Rock Sink 59 D8
Big Sandy Creek 27 A10;E6; 28 B2; 35 A8; 36 C2;D2,3;E4,5; 37 E6,7
Big Satilla Creek 54 C1;D2,3;E4; 63 A10; 64 A1
Big Shoal Mountain 16 C3
Big Shoals 16 A4
Big Sink 39 D6
Big SI 59 E6
Big Slough 59 C9
Big Spring 13 E8; 19 B9
Big Spring Branch 12 B1
Big Swamp 56 B1
Big Texas Valley 18 A4
Big Towaliga Creek 34 B5
Big Water Lake 63 E9
Big Water Prairie 71 A8
Biger Creek 22 D4
Bill Cove 15 C7
Bill Hunter Mountain 14 A5
Bill Mountain 16 A5
Bill Ridge 14 B4
Billy Branch 39 D8
Billy Mountain 16 A2
Billys Island 71 A8

Birch Creek 26 D5; 34 A3;B2
Bird Gap 15 C7
Bird Mountain 14 D4
Bird Sand Hill 138 ft 71 A6
Bishop 28 A2
Bishop Creek 54 D2
Bivins Bay 70 C5
Black Branch 70 B5
Black Calico 55 D9
Black Creek 22 B3; 36 C4,5; 32 E1,2; 37 C6;D6; 40 E4; 41 A7,8;B6; 47 D9;E7,10; 59 E9
Black Falls 15 D6
Black Hammock 56 D5; 63 D8; 65 D6
Black Island 56 D2
Black Island 65 B8
Black Jack Mountain 24 B4
Black Mill Creek 21 A6
Black Mountain 15 C6 ; 16 A1;C3
Black Point 72i D4
Black River Island 63 D8
Black Swamp 55 C8
Black Water Creek 54 C3
Blackbeard Shoal 65 A10
Blackjack Branch 38 B3
Blackjack Island 71 C9
Blackjack Lake 71 B9,10
Blackjack Mountain 15 A6; 24 D4
Blackman Branch 41 A6
Blackrock Mountain 16 A2
Blacks Creek Knob 16 A3
Blackshear 63 B9
Blackshear Branch 41 D8
Blackwell Creek 27 D10
Blackwells 20 D2
Bladen Creek 49 A7
Blairsville 15 B7
Blakely 58 B2
Blalock Lake 25 E7
Blalock Mountain 13 D10
Blalock Reservoir 26 C4
Blitchton 47 E7
Blocker Creek 55 A8
Blood Mountain 15 C7
Bloomingdale 47 E8
Blowing Spring 12 D2
Blue Creek 15 D10; 33 A8; 58 B3
Blue Hole Spring 19 C7
Blue Knob 15 C9
Blue Mountain 13 B6 ; 15 B9
Blue Ridge 14 B3
Blue Ridge 14 A1;B5; 15 B10
Blue Ridge Lake 14 B4
Blue Rock 15 A8
Blue Spring 51 A8; 59 B7
Blue Spring Branch 13 E6
Blue Springs 32 C1; 39 D6
Blue Springs Creek 13 D7
Blue Sprs 43 E7
Bluebird Gap 12 C3
Bluestone Creek 22 C5
Bluff Cove 15 A10
Bluff Creek 20 A2; 37 C6; 43 C7
Bluff Springs Branch 49 A8
Bluffton 49 E8
Bluffy Creek 19 E7
Blythe 30 E5
Board Tree Creek 20 B4
Boat Landing Island 63 E10
Bobtail Creek 45 C6
Bogan Mountain 18 B2
Bogart 22 E1
Boggy Bay 63 C8; 70 B2
Boggy Branch 41 D10; 50 B5; 53 E7
Boggy Creek 54 D5; 55 D6;E6; 58 A5
Boggy Gall 65 B6
Boggy Gall Swamp 65 A8
Boggy Gut 39 C9
Boggy Gut Creek 30 D4; 38 C2; 39 A8
Boggy Head Bay 56 A1
Boiling Spring 38 C4
Bolingbroke 35 C9
Bonaire 43 B6
Bonanza 26 D3
Boneville 30 D2
Boney Creek 53 C6
Bonner Creek 36 C1
Bonnet Bay 56 A1
Boone Creek 72 C1
Boston 68 B4
Boston Creek 19 B10
Bostwick 28 A2
Bow Creek 13 D6
Bowden Creek 28 C5; 29 C6
Bowdens Pond No 1 30 E3
Bowdon 24 C4
Bowdon Junction 24 B5
Bowers Gap 12 B2
Bowers Mountain 15 B7
Bowersville 23 A6
Bowling Knob 15 A7
Bowman 23 B6
Box Creek 52 D5
Box Springs 40 B5
Boyd Branch 40 A4
Boyds Creek 23 B7
Boykin 58 D5
Boyle Lake No 5 27 D9
Brackett Knob 15 B6
Bradford Gap 12 B2
Bradley Pt 57 C6
Bradley River 57 C6
Brady Branch 47 A6
Brailey Swamp 64 D4
Bramlet Ridge 15 B10
Brandy Pt 65 D7
Brannen Bay 47 D6
Brannen Lake 46 D2
Brantley Creek 50 C3
Braselton 21 C9
Brasstown Creek 15 A8;D10
Braswell Creek 62 A1
Brawley Mountain 14 B5
Bray Branch 36 C1
Brazells Creek 45 E10
Breastworks Branch 58 A2
Bremen 24 A5
Brewert Bay 55 C9
Brewster Mountain 18 E3
Brewton Creek 20 A5
Briar Branch 60 A4
Briar Creek 14 B3; 28 B3; 54 E3; 63 A8
Briar Island 63 B7
Briardam Swamp 65 A7

Brickhill River 72 D4
Bridge Creek 16 B1; 60 B-D2
Bridgeboro 60 A2
Brier Bay 56 A1
Brier Creek 30 D1,2;E2-4; 32 C1;D2; 38 A5; 39 A6;B7,9;C10
Bright Spring 58 A1
Brinson 58 E4
Bristol 63 A10
Brittens Creek 33 A10
Broach Creek 40 E4
Broad River 22 B5;C5; 23 C6;D8,10
Broadhurst 64 A3
Bronwood 50 C3
Brookfield 61 A8
Brooklet 46 C5
Brooklyn 40 E4
Brooks 26 E2
Brooks Creek 22 E5; 25 A6
Brooks Mountain 34 C2
Brookwood 20 C5
Broom Branch 39 A7
Broomstraw Island 71 C9
Brotherton Creek 12 B3
Broughton Island 65 B7
Brown Branch 27 E6
Brown Island 64 B5
Brown Mountain 16 A4
Brown Pond 69 C9
Brown Sprs 38 D4
Browns Creek 25 D9
Broxton 53 D8
Broxton Creek 53 D8;E8
Bruce Creek 29 D6
Bruce Top 14 A2
Brumbley Creek 59 E10; 67 A10
Brunswick 65 C6
Brunswick River 65 D7
Brush Creek 22 C4,5; 32 A5; 37 B,C7
Brushy Branch 60 B2
Brushy Creek 35 A6; 38 A2,4; 43 D8; 52 A2;D5; 61 B7;C8; 63 A6
Brushy Fork 27 A7
Brushy Island 46 E5
Brushy Knob 15 C7
Brushy Mountain 19 D7
Brushy Mountain 14 C5
Brushy Top 13 C10
Bryan Bay 46 E5
Bryant Creek 14 E1
Bryant Spr 12 E4
Bryants Swamp 42 B2
Bryson Gap 14 C5
Buchanan 24 A5
Buck Branch 36 E2
Buck Creek 13 C9; 25 B6; 32 D1,2; 37 D6; 36 B5; 34 A5; 35 A10; 41 C8;D9,10; 42 C1; 43 A9;C6; 62 E2; 67 B9; 70 A2
Buck Hill Swamp 56 E2
Buck Hole 58 E3
Buck Island 55 D9; 64 B5;C1; 71 C7
Buck Knob 13 C10; 14 A2; 15 A9,10;B6C7
Buck Lake 71 B10
Buck Ridge 15 A8
Buck Trail Island 71 B6
Buckeye Creek 37 E8
Buckeye Gap 15 B7
Buckeye Knob 15 B7
Buckeye Mountain 14 A1;C4
Buckhead 20 E3
Buckhead 28 C3
Buckhead Creek 38 B4;C5; 39 C6;D7
Buckhorn Branch 37 D6
Buckhorn Creek 45 E7; 43 B10
Buckhorn Mountain 21 A8
Buena Vista 41 C7
Buffalo Creek 21 C10; 23 E6; 24 C5; 29 A6;E7; 64 D1,2
Buffalo Swamp 64 B5; 65 A7
Bufford Mountain 19 B9
Buford 21 C7
Bug Bluff 55 E10
Bug Island 55 E10
Bugaboo Island 71 B9
Bull Branch 38 D4
Bull Creek 15 E8; 29 C10; 34 B3; 40 A3;B3; 46 E1-3; 60 C5; 61 D6
Bull Gap 16 A1
Bull Island 64 A5
Bull Mountain 14 D5
Bull River 57 B7
Bull Town Swamp 56 D1
Bull Trail Mountain 34 C3
Bullard 43 A7
Bullards Creek 54 B2
Bullhead Creek 72 A3
Bulloch Bay 46 E4
Bunkle Bay 62 E5
Burgess Gap 14 B5
Burkhalter Gap 12 A2
Burks Mountain 30 B4
Burned Out Prairie 63 D8
Burnham Bay 52 A3
Burnham Branch 42 C5
Burnt Island 63 E7
Burnt Mountain 14 E3
Burnt Ridge 15 C8
Burnt Scrub Swamp 64 B4
Burrell Mountain 16 A5
Burroughs 56 A4
Burt Creek 15 E6
Bush Creek 24 A5
Bush Head Shoals 25 E6
Bush Hill 40 C5
Bush I 63 E8
Bushnell 53 E7
Buss Creek 59 E9
Busseys Pond 52 D1
Bustahatchee Creek 49 A6
Butler 41 B9
Butler Creek 19 D10; 23 B6; 30 D5
Butler Island 65 B7
Butler River 65 B7
Buttermilk Sound 65 B8
Buttlers Creek 35 C10
Buzzard Bay 53 C8
Buzzard Island 70 C2
Buzzard Knob 16 A1
Buzzard Mountain 34 B2
Buzzard Mountain 15 C8
Buzzard Roost 52 B4
Buzzard Roost 14 C4

Buzzard Roost 34 C1
Byrd Mountain 20 B2
Byromville 42 D2
Byron 42 A4

C

Cabbage Island 57 B7
Cabbage Island Spit 57 B7
Cabin Creek 18 A3; 26 E4; 35 A6
Cabretta Island 65 A9
Cadley 29 C10
Cagle Mountain 20 A1
Cairo 67 A10
Calbeck Mountain 13 E6
Calhoun 13 E7
Calhoun Gap 13 D6
Callahan Mountain 14 B2
Calls Creek 22 E2
Calvary 67 B8
Camak 29 D10
Cambers Island 65 B7
Camilla 59 C9
Camp Bay 62 B2
Camp Bend 18 B3
Camp Branch 70 A4
Camp Creek 16 D1; 20 E5; 25 B10; 26 B1;D1,5; 27 C6; 36 B4;C3; 41 C9,10;D9,10; 42 D1,5
Camp Flats 59 E7
Camp Island 71 A8
Campbell Creek 27 C10
Campbell Hill 19 B10
Campbell Mountain 15 D6
Campbellton 25 B10
Campton 21 E9
Candler Creek 21 A10; 22 B1
Cane Break Island 63 E7
Cane Creek 12 D4; 15 D6;E7; 34 C1; 62 D4,5; 63 A6;E6
Cane Creek Falls 15 D7
Cane Creek Structure No 2 Lake 33 C10
Cane Swamp 72 A5;D3
Cane Water Pond 59 E7
Caney Bay 56 A1; 64 C1
Caney Branch 49 D7
Caney Creek 25 C7;E7; 32 B5; 35 B10; 59 A6
Caney Fork 27 E7
Caney Swamp 72 A5
Canoe Pond 45 B10
Canoe Swamp 64 E5
Canon 23 A6
Canoochee Creek 38 E4; 45 B9; 55 A9;B10
Canoochee River 55 A10; 45 C10; 46 C1;E2,4; 56 A1-3
Canton 20 B2
Canton Creek 20 B2
Canton Mills Lake 20 B2
Cape Charlotte 57 B7
Cape May 57 B7
Captain Fleming Swamp 56 C1
Carden Branch 43 C7
Carlan Creek 22 A2,3
Carlisle Gap 33 E10
Carlton 23 D6
Carmichel Lake 25 B9
Carnegie 49 D9
Carnesville 22 A4
Carnigan River 65 A8
Carr Mountain 18 B2
Carr Spring 58 E2
Carrol Mountain 16 A5
Carroll Branch 68 A5
Carrollton 25 C6
Carrs I 65 B7
Carrs Neck 56 D3
Carrs Neck Creek 56 D4
Carson Hill 40 D3
Carsonville 34 E4
Cartbody Creek 25 C6
Cartecay Mountain 14 C3
Cartecay River 14 C3;D2
Carter Creek 19 B9; 49 C9;D9
Carter Island 36 B5
Carter Island 55 D8
Carter Lake 62 E1
Carter Mountain 13 E10
Carters Creek 23 C8
Carters Mill Creek 37 B8
Carters Prairie 63 E10
Cartersville 19 C8
Cascade Falls 33 D10
Case Cavern 12 B2
Casey Mountain 18 E3
Cass 19 B8
Cass Mountain 15 C8
Cassville 19 B8
Cassville Mountain 19 A8
Castle Rock 12 A1
Cat Branch 30 D3
Cat Creek 53 B6; 61 D9;E9; 62 A5; 68 B5
Cataula 40 A3
Cathead Creek 65 A7
Cathey Creek 15 D9
Catlett Gap 12 C3
Catna Creek 42 C5
Cattle Hammock 56 D4
Cave Spring 13 A6
Cavender Gap 15 C6
Cavender Mountain 15 C6
Cavender Ridge 15 C6
Cay Creek 56 B2;C3
Cecil 61 D8
Cedar Bay 55 B10
Cedar Cliff 16 A5
Cedar Cliff Knob 16 A1
Cedar Creek 13 E9; 16 D3; 19 A8; 21 D9; 23 A8;D7; 24 E5; 25 C8,9; 27 E10; 35 A10; 36 E4; 37 E6; 41 B7;C8,10; 43 D6;E7,8; 46 D1;E2; 51 B8
Cedar Hammock 56 E4; 71 A10
Cedar Hammocks 64 E1
Cedar Knob 15 A9
Cedar Man 15 C6
Cedar Mountain 15 B8;C7; 25 A8
Cedar Point 56 D5
Cedar Point 12 E2
Cedar Springs 58 C1
Cemochechobee Creek 49 D7,8
Center Post 12 D3
Centerville 42 A5

Centerville Branch 23 E8; 29 A7
Centralhatchee 25 D6
Centralhatchee Creek 24 D4,5
Chamblee 20 E3
Chamblee Gap 20 B5
Champion Creek 14 E3; 36 B5
Champney Island 65 B7
Chancey Mill Creek 58 B1
Chandlers Creek 25 D10
Chapel Creek 55 A7
Chapman Creek 34 B3
Chapman Lake 41 C7
Chappel Creek 12 D4
Charing 41 B8
Charles 40 E3
Charles Creek 56 B5
Charles Island 71 B9
Charlie Mountain 16 B1
Charlies Creek 16 A1
Chase Mountain 14 A3
Chase Prairie 71 A9
Chatsworth 13 C9
Chattahoochee Bay 21 B7
Chattahoochee Plantation 20 E2
Chattahoochee River 15 D10;E10; 20 D4; 25 B9;C9;D6-8; 26 A1; 32 D5; 40 C2;D2; 49 B6;C6;E6; 58 B1;D2;C1;E2; 66 B2
Chattanooga Valley 12 A3
Chattanooga Valley 12 B3
Chattooga River 12 D3;E3; 16 A5;B4;C3; 18 A2
Cheatam Creek 20 B5
Chelsea Creek 12 E2
Chenocetah Mountain 16 E1
Chenube Creek 50 C1
Cherokee Creek 30 A3
Cherokee Ridge 13 A6
Cherry Creek 69 A9
Cherry Log 14 B3
Cherry Log Creek 14 B3
Chesser Island 71 B10
Chesser Prairie 71 B10
Chestatee Bay 21 B7
Chestatee River 15 D7,8
Chester 43 C10
Chestnut Knob 13 C10; 15 A7;D7; 16 A1
Chestnut Mountain 21 C8
Chestnut Mountain 15 C6
Chestnut Mountain 13 D6
Chestnut Ridge 14 B2; 15 C6; 16 A1,3
Chestnut Top 15 A7
Chew Mill Creek 39 D6
Chickamauga 12 B3
Chickamauga Creek 15 C10
Chickasaw Creek 23 A6
Chickasawhatchee Creek 50 C3;E2; 59 A7,8
Chicken Coop Gap 13 A10
Chicken Creek 13 C9
Chicopee 21 B8
Chief McIntosh Lake 35 A7
Chigoe Creek 30 B4
Chimney Mountain 15 B10
Chimney Top 15 A9
Chimneytop Mountain 15 B8
Chinquapin Ridge 15 B10
Chisholm Swamp 65 A7
Choctahatchee Creek 41 E8; 50 A2
Chokee Creek 51 B6,7
Chokeelagee Creek 50 B3
Christie Prairie 71 A10
Christmas Branch 40 E5
Chuck Shoals 15 E6
Chula 52 E1
Cisco 13 A9
Clark Creek 23 E9; 29 A8
Clark Mountain 14 C4
Clarkdale 25 A10
Clarkesville 16 D1
Clarks Bluff 65 A6
Clarks Creek 16 E5; 18 A3; 23 A6
Clarks Fork 28 D3
Clarks Island 64 D4
Clarkston 26 A4
Claxton 46 E2
Clay Creek 15 D6
Clay Creek Falls 15 D6
Clayhole Swamp 65 B6
Clayton 16 B3
Clayton Co Res 26 C5
Clear Creek 14 D3; 19 B8; 25 E7; 36 D3,4; 49 A10; 50 A1; 63 B7
Clegborn Spring 12 C5
Clem 25 C6
Clements Creek 52 B3
Clements Mountain 15 B6
Clermont 15 E9
Cleveland 15 D9
Clewis Island 63 E8
Cliff Creek 16 B3
Cliff Mountain 16 B3
Cliff Ridge 15 C6
Clifton Bluff 55 A10
Climax 67 A7
Clinchfield 42 C5
Clothespole Bay 62 E2
Cloughs Bay 63 C7
Clyatt Mill Creek 69 C8
Clyattville 69 B8
Clyde Creek 56 A2,3
Clyo 47 B9
Coahulla Creek 13 B7;C8
Coal Mountain 21 B6
Coat Creek 38 C2
Cobb 51 B7
Cobb Creek 45 E7; 54 A3
Cobb Mountain 18 E5
Cobb Mountain 15 A6
Cobbtown 45 D10
Cochran 43 C8
Cochran Creek 18 E5; 24 A5
Cochrans Creek 14 E5
Cochrans Falls 14 D4
Coffee Bluff 53 C8
Coffee Branch 53 C7; 53 C8
Coffey Mountain 15 B6
Coffman Spring 12 C4
Cogburn Creek 20 A5
Cogdell 62 C5
Coheelee Creek 58 B1
Cohutta 13 A7
Cohutta Mountain 14 B1
Colbert 22 D4
Colbert Mountain 14 C4
Cold Creek 37 C9
Cold Mountain 13 C3

Cold Spring 13 C10
Cold Spring Mountain 13 C10
Cold Springs Gap 15 B9
Coldwater Creek 23 B7,8
Cole City Creek 12 A1
Cole Eddy 55 D9
Coleman 49 D8
Coleman Creek 33 A9,10; 46 A4
Coleman River 16 A2
Colemans Creek 54 D4;E5; 55 E6
Coleoatchee Creek 34 D2
College Creek 64 C4
College Park 26 B2
Collins 46 E1
Collins Bay 62 D5
Collins Mill Creek 49 C10
Collins Mountain 14 B2; 15 D8; 19 A8
Colochee Creek 40 E3
Colonels Island 56 D4; 65 D6
Colquitt 58 C4
Colston Mountain 19 B7
Columbia Mountain 15 C7
Columbia Ridge 15 C7
Columbia Top 14 C3
Columbus 40 B2
Comer 22 D5
Commerce 22 B2
Commissioner Creek 36 C2,3;D4,5; 37 D7
Commodore Island 65 A9
Conasauga River 13 A8;C7;D7
Concord 34 B2
Concord Creek 12 C5
Concord Shoal 56 E5
Conley 26 B3
Conn Creek 20 A4
Connell Creek 68 B4
Conner Mountain 15 D6
Connesena Creek 19 B7
Connesena Mountain 19 B7
Connesena Spring 19 B7
Conrad Hill 40 C3
Constitution 26 B3
Contentment Bluff 56 E4
Conyers 27 B7
Coody Creek 23 D10; 31 A8
Cook Mountain 15 B8
Cooks Island 47 D6
Cool Spring 13 B9
Cooleewahee Creek 50 E4; 59 A9;B8
Coolidge 60 E3
Coon Creek 41 C8; 60 E2; 69 A6
Coon Mountain 22 E3
Cooper Creek 15 C6
Cooper Heights 12 B3
Coopers Pr 46 A1
Coosa Bald 15 B7
Coosa Creek 15 B7
Coosa River 18 B2,4
Coosawattee River 13 D8,9;E6,7; 14 C1
Copeland Creek 29 D6
Copperhill 14 A3
Coppermine Gap 14 D5
Corbin Creek 15 B10
Cordele 51 B9
Cordell Mountain 14 A4
Corinth 33 A7
Corncob Island 63 D10
Cornelia 16 E1
Cornhouse Creek 72 C1
Cornish Creek 27 A8
Cornish Mountain 27 B8
Cotton 60 C1
Couch Cove 14 A2
Council 71 C7
Courthouse Gap 16 A3
Cove Gap 13 B6
Covena Branch 45 B7
Coverdale 51 D9
Covington 27 C8
Cow Creek 62 E2; 64 E3; 70 A2
Coward Lake Prairie 71 C10
Cowart Gap 16 A1
Cowart Lake 26 B1
Cowarts Mill Pond 45 B10
Cowhouse Branch 70 B5
Cowhouse Island 63 D9
Cowpen Branch 47 B8
Cowpen Creek 37 A8
Cowpen Mountain 14 A1
Cowpen Swamp 65 B6
Cowtail Branch 33 B10
Cox Creek 14 E3; 40 A4;B4; 63 B7
Cox Mountain 14 E4
Cox Prairie 71 A7
Crabapple 20 C3
Craig Gap 15 B8
Craig Hill 40 C2
Crandall 13 B9
Cravens Hammock 71 A7
Crawfish Creek 12 B4; 33 C8
Crawford 22 E5
Crawford Top 15 A8
Crawfordville 29 C8
Crawley Gap 15 B7
Crawley Mountain 15 B7
Creighton Island 56 E3
Crescent 56 E3
Crescent River 56 E3
Crevasse Pond 69 A6
Crews Creek 25 C7
Crews Island 70 A5
Cribb Bay 63 D6
Crispen Island 65 C6
Croaker Island 63 D8
Crockett Creek 22 A3
Crooked Creek 22 B2; 28 D4;E4; 36 C2; 38 E2; 39 E9; 43 B7,9;E10; 45 A7,8; 49 C7,9; 52 A4,5; 53 A10; 54 A1; 63 A9; 72 A5;D3,4
Cross Bay 47 E6; 71 C7
Cross Branch 71 C9
Cross Creek 43 E9; 62 C1
Cross Swamp 63 B10; 64 D2
Cross Tide Creek 56 D4
Crossroads Bay 61 C8
Crossway Branch 46 B2
Crow Gap 15 A8
Crow Harbor Island 64 E5
Crow Mountain 16 B1;C1
Crown Mountain 15 E7
Crumbly Knob 15 C9
Culberson 14 A5
Culloden 35 D6
Culpepper Spring 59 B9

Culvert Swamp 56 A4
Culverton 29 E8
Cumberland Island 72 D5
Cumberland River 65 E7; 72 D4
Cumberland Sound 72 D4
Cumming 20 B5
Cunningham Shoals 23 D6
Currahee Mountain 16 E3
Curry Creek 22 C1,2
Curry Hill 66 B5
Curry Hill 67 B6
Curry Hill 59 E8
Cusseta 40 D4
Cut Locust Gap 15 B9
Cuthbert 49 C9
Cypress Bay 47 E6
Cypress Branch 45 E6
Cypress Creek 37 E10; 39 D6; 45 D6; 52 B4; 58 C4; 61 B8; 71 C6,7
Cypress Flat Creek 46 D1
Cypress Lake 46 C3
Cypress Swamp 64 A3

D

Dacula 21 D7
Dahlonega 15 E7
Daisy 46 E3
Dakota 51 C10
Dale Branch 53 C9
Dallas 19 E8
Dally Gap 14 A1
Dalton 13 B7
Damascus 13 D7
Damascus 58 B5
Dames Ferry 35 B9
Dan Bland Bay 53 C8
Dan Mountain 14 A5
Daniel Creek 12 B2
Daniel Shoals 25 E6
Daniel Springs 29 B7
Daniels Branch 39 B8
Daniels Creek 51 D9;E10
Daniels Mill Creek 38 E3
Daniels Pond 61 D8
Danielsville 22 C4
Danville 43 A9
Darien 65 B7
Dark Bay 62 B2
Dark Thick 63 D10
Dasher 69 B10
Dasher Creek 47 D9
Davenport Knob 14 A5
Davenport Mountain 15 A6
Davenport Mountain 14 B4
Daves Creek 20 C5
Davidson Creek 16 C3
Davidson Hill 40 C2
Davis Hill 34 D4
Davis Mountain 15 C6
Davis Ridge 15 B8
Davis Swamp 56 C1
Davisboro 38 C1
Dawesville 60 E2
Daws Knob 14 B5
Dawson 50 C2
Dawsonville 14 E5
Day Creek 49 A8
Day Knob 15 A10
Dead Man Hammock 57 B7
Dead Oak Creek 26 E1
Deaden Branch 52 B4
Deadennen Mountain 14 B5
Deadline Ridge 14 B3
Dean Cove 15 A8
Dean Creek 15 D9; 34 D3
Dean Gap 15 A6
Dean Mountain 15 D10
Dearing 30 D3
Deaton Creek 21 C8
Decatur 26 A4
Deenwood 63 C8
Deep Creek 16 C2;D2; 23 C7; 35 E8; 37 D8;E7; 38 A1;E5; 51 B10;C10; 52 C1;D2
Deep Gap 15 C6
Deep Gap 16 A3
Deepstep 37 B7
Deepstep Creek 37 B7
Deer Creek 24 D4; 35 C8,9; 41 D9;E8
Defoor Walters Lake 13 E9
Delbos Bay 55 B7
Delegal Creek 57 B6
Demorest 16 D1
Demps Mountain 14 B1
Denson Marsh 36 E1
Denton 53 D10
Devereux 37 A6
Devils Bay 62 D2;E5
Devils Branch 47 B7
Devils Den 59 D9
Dewitt 59 A10
Dewy Rose 23 C7
Dick Creek 12 C5; 20 C5
Dick Ridge 12 D5
Dickey Mountain 14 A4
Dickinson Creek 56 C4
Dicks Creek 16 B1;E3
Dicks Knob 16 A1
Dickson Spring 12 C3
Dicksons Mill Creek 53 D6
Dillard 16 A3
Dillard Creek 65 C6
Dinkins Bay 55 B6
Dirtseller Mountain 18 A2
Dismal Knob 15 B10
Ditney Knob 14 B5
Dividing Ridge 14 A4
Dixie 68 B5
Dixie Union 63 B7
Dixon Mountain 34 C1
Doboy I 65 A8
Doboy Sound 65 A8,9
Doctors Creek 55 C9;D10
Doctortown 55 D8
Dodge Lake 43 E10
Doe Eddy 55 D9
Doerun 60 B3
Dog Hammock 56 E4
Dog Hammock Spit 56 E4
Dog Island 63 E8
Dog River 25 B8,9
Doles 51 D8
Dominy Branch 51 A6
Donalsonville 58 E2
Donovan 37 E9
Doogan Hole 14 C5
Doogan Mountain 13 A10
Dooley Branch 39 C7
Dopson Branch 53 C8
Doraville 20 E4
Dorster Mountain 34 C2
Double Branch 22 A5; 23 B8; 43 C7; 67 B8
Double Gap 15 C9
Double Head 15 C9
Double Hogpen 14 B2
Double Knob 14 B2; 16 A2,3
Double O Bay 71 B10
Double Run Creek 52 B1;C2
Double Run Swamp 71 C6
Double Springs 59 B9
Double Top 14 B1
Double Yellow Bluff 55 E10
Dougherty Gap 12 D2
Douglas 53 E8
Douglas Mountain 14 B2
Douglasville 25 A9
Dove Creek 23 C7;D7
Dover 46 A4
Dover Creek 65 E7
Dowdell Creek 33 E9
Dowdell Knob 33 D9
Downing Creek 69 A6
Downing Island 64 A4
Dozier Branch 30 A2
Dozier Creek 19 A6; 40 B4
Drag Nasty Creek 49 C6
Drakies Bluff 47 E10
Drawhorn Creek 37 A6
Dripping Rocks 34 C2
Dripping Spring 19 A10
Drive Ridge 16 A2
Drizzell Bluff 72i D3
Drowning Creek 21 D8
Druid Hills 26 A3
Drum Point Island 72i E4
Dry Bone Creek 36 D1
Dry Branch 36 D2
Dry Branch 36 D5; 38 B5; 39 C9;D6; 46 B3;C3; 54 D4
Dry Branch Creek 36 E1; 51 B6
Dry Creek 12 B5;C4; 13 C6;D6,9; 18 C4;D3; 19 A7;C7; 19 A8; 29 E8; 37 E7; 38 C3,4; 40 D5; 41 E6; 43 C6; 46 D2; 55 D6;E6; 58 A3;B3,4;D2-4; 60 A1,2; 62 A5
Dry Fork 23 D8; 36 D4
Dry Fork Creek 23 E7; 29 A6,7; 30 A2
Dry Lake Creek 68 A5
Dry Pond Mountain 20 A1
Dryden Creek 63 B7
Duboise Bay 63 C8
Duck Creek 12 C3
Duck Island 71 B10
Duck Knob 15 B8
Dug Gap 13 C7
Dug Mountain 13 C6
Dugdown Mountain 18 E4
Duhart Creek 38 A2;B2
Dukes Creek 15 C9
Duluth 20 D5
Dunagan Mountain 14 B5
Dunaway Gap 12 E5
Dunbar Mountain 33 A7
Duncan Ridge 15 B6
Dunsmore Mountain 15 B6
Dunwoody 20 E3
Duplin River 65 A9
DuPont 62 E3
Dutch Island 57 A6
Dyer Gap 14 B2
Dyer Mountain 16 A5
Dyer Mountain 14 A1
Dyers Creek 37 D8
Dykes Creek 19 B6

E

Eagle Cliff 12 A3
Eagle Creek 56 E4
Eagle Knob 15 B9
Eagle Mountain 15 A10
Eagle Neck 56 D4
Easley Gap 12 B1
East Armuchee Creek 12 D5
East Armuchee Valley 12 D5
East Bear Creek 27 C9
East Branch Barnetts Creek 60 D1;E1
East Branch Long Swamp Creek 14 E3
East Channel 56 C4
East Chickamauga Creek 12 C5
East Ellijay 14 C2
East Fork Little River 15 E9
East Fork Pond Fork 21 B10
East Fork Suwannee River 71 A9
East Fork West Fork Little River 12 D2
East Mountaintown Creek 14 B1
East Point 26 B2
East Sandy Creek 22 D3
Eastanollee 16 E4
Eastanollee Creek 16 D3;E4,5
Eastland Heights 26 B3
Eastman 43 E10
Eastman Mountain 16 B3
Eatonton 28 E3
Ebenezer Creek 47 C9,10
Echeconnee Creek 34 C5; 35 D6,8;E10
Eddards Creek 53 A9
Eden 47 E8
Edie Creek 34 A5
Edison 49 E9
Edmondson Gap 15 C6
Edwards Creek 34 E1; 41 A6
Egg Island 65 B9
Egg Island Shoal 57 C6
Egg Islands 57 C6
Eightmile Creek 35 A7; 38 C5
Elberton 23 C8
Elbow Swamp 56 B4
Eldorado 61 B7
Eldorendo 58 D5
Elijah Mountain 27 B6
Elisha Mountain 16 A2
Elizabeth 20 D1
Elkins Creek 34 A3;B2,3
Elko 42 C5
Elko Creek 42 C4
Ella Island 57 B6
Ellabelle 47 E8
Ellaville 41 D9
Ellenton 61 C6
Ellenwood 26 B4
Eller Gap 15 A10
Ellerslie 40 A3
Ellicotts Mound 113 ft 71 D10
Ellijay 14 C2
Ellijay River 14 C2
Elliotts Bluff 72i D3
Ellis Knob 14 A3
Ellison's Cave 12 C3
Elmodel 59 B7
Elsberry Mountain 19 E8
Emerson 19 C9
Emmalane 39 E6
Empire 43 C9
Eneck Bay 47 A7
Enigma 61 A8
Ennis Branch 46 E2
Epsey Bay 62 E3
Epworth 14 A3
Esom Slough 18 D3
Estatoah Falls 16 A3
Estelle Spring 13 A8
Etna Mountain 18 D3
Eton 13 B9
Etowah River 15 D6;E6; 19 B6,7;C8; 20 A3-5;B1,2;C1; 21 A6
Eubank Lake 19 E6
Euharlee Creek 19 C7;D6
Euharlee Creek 19 D6
Evans 30 C5
Everett 64 A5
Everett Mountain 18 E5
Everett Springs 18 D5
Evergreen Creek 43 B8
Excelsior 46 D2
Experiment 26 E4
Experiment Shoal 56 E5

F

Faceville 66 B5
Factory Creek 29 C10
Factory Creek 58 A1
Fain Mountain 14 B3
Fair Oaks 20 E1
Fairburn 26 C1
Fairmount 13 E9
Fall Creek 14 E3
Falling Creek 23 C8;D8; 28 A5; 35 A10;B9; 50 D1
Falls Mountain 15 D6; 16 B1
Fancy Hill 13 A9
Fargo 71 B6
Farmer Mountain 16 E3
Farmington 28 A2
Fayetteville 26 D2
Fearnside Lake 69 B7
Featherbed Bay 62 C2
Featherfield Lake 50 D2
Ferry Branch 47 A7
Fields Cut 57 A7
Fifteenmile Creek 46 A1;B1
Fifty Dollar Bay 62 C2
Fightingtown Creek 14 A2;B2,3
Fincher Bluff 13 C8
Fish Branch 62 E2
Fish Creek 18 D5
Fish Pond Bay 62 E1
Fisher Creek 14 E2
Fishhole Swamp 64 B5
Fishing Creek 28 B5; 29 A9,10; 31 B8;C8; 36 B3,4; 53 B9; 54 E4; 63 A9
Fishpond Dr 58 D3
Fishpond Drain 58 E3; 66 A3
Fitz Branch 39 B7
Fitzgerald 52 D4
Fivemile Branch 50 B5
Fivemile Creek 34 C3; 55 C6; 61 B10
Flanders Shady Bluff 64 C3
Flat Branch 14 C1; 39 E8
Flat Creek 14 D1; 15 E9; 21 B8; 26 D1;E1; 33 A7,9; 34 A2; 36 E2; 42 C4; 43 A7; 45 A7,9;D6; 49 E7; 58 C2; 61 C9
Flat Creek Mountain 16 C1
Flat Shoal Creek 33 C7-9;D6
Flat Shoals 34 B1
Flat Shoals Creek 23 A7
Flat Top 16 A4
Flat Top Mountain 14 B2
Flat Wood Creek 24 A4
Flatrock Point 12 C3
Fleming 56 B2
Flint Knob 16 A4
Flint River 26 B3;D3;E2; 34 A2;B1;C1;D2;E3; 35 E6; 42 A-E1; 51 C7;D6; 59 A10;B10;C7,8;E6; 66 A5;B4
Flintstone 12 A3
Flippen 26 C5
Flora Hammock 57 B6
Florence Creek 30 A2
Flovilla 27 E8
Flowery Branch 21 B7
Floyd 20 E1
Floyd Creek 37 B9; 65 E7; 72 C4
Floyds Island 71 A9
Floyds Island Prairie 71 A9
Fodder Creek 15 B9
Fodderstack 16 A4
Folkston 72 A2
Folsom Creek 52 A2,3
Footlog Bay 63 C6
Forbes Lake 42 C3
Fords Creek 29 E9; 37 E8
Foreman Bay 62 E4
Foreman Mill Branch 49 A7
Forest Park 26 B3
Forester Spring 12 C2
Fork Creek 23 C7;D6
Fork Ridge 15 A10
Forky Creek 62 A2
Forsyth 35 B7
Fort Benning 40 C2
Fort Camp Branch 64 C1
Fort Creek 29 E6; 30 E2; 37 A6
Fort Gaines 49 E6
Fort Mountain 13 B9
Fort Mountain 15 B7
Fort Oglethorpe 12 A4
Fort Pt 56 D3
Fort Stewart 56 B1
Fort Stewart 56 B1
Fort Valley 42 B2
Fortson 40 A2
Fortsonia 23 D9
Foster Bend 18 B3
Fouche Gap 18 A3
Four Acre Creek 54 A5
Fourmile Branch 28 C2
Fourmile Creek 20 A3; 67 A6
Fourmile Island 56 E4
Fourmile Pt 56 E4
Fowl Roost Island 71 D10
Fowler Mountain 14 B2
Fowlstown 67 A6
Fowltown Creek 50 C3;D4
Fox Creek 50 B5; 65 A8
Fox Hill 21 B7
Fox Mountain 12 C1; 14 C4
Frady Mountain 15 B7
Franklin 25 E6
Franklin Springs 22 B5
Franks Creek 61 E8; 69 A8
Frazer Creek 22 E1
Free Bend 14 B4
Free Home 20 B4
Free Lake 42 C3
Freecastle Swamp 56 E1
Freeman Creek 28 A2
Freeman Spring 13 C6
Friars Bay 62 E1
Friendship 41 E7
Frosty Mountain 14 D4
Frozen Knob 14 B2;C5
Frozentop 15 B8
Fry Mountain 16 C2
Fuller Mountain 13 E10
Fullwood Creek 63 B6
Fulsome Creek 29 D8;E8
Funston 60 C3
Furniture City 26 A1

G

Gab Creek 14 E5
Gabbettville 32 C5
Gaddis Mountain 15 C7
Gadny Bay 47 E8
Gainesville 21 B8
Gainey Island 63 E6
Galey Creek 41 E9
Gamble Spring 12 E3
Game Creek 36 E2
Gap Creek 28 D1
Garbage Stink Cave 12 C1
Garden City 47 E10
Gardi 55 E9
Gardi Creek 55 E9
Gardi Swamp 55 E9
Garfield 46 A1
Garland Mountain 14 B4; 20 A1
Garrison Creek 22 A2
Gatling Branch 68 A3
Gator Branch 61 B6
Gator Creek 54 A2
Gator Head 55 D10
Gator Slide 52 B4
Gator Wallow 63 D8
Gay 34 B1
Gayton Gulf 12 D3
Generals Island 65 B7
Geneva 41 A6
Gentry Gap 13 D6
George Mountain 14 D4
Georgetown 49 B6
Georgetown 56 A4
Georgia Southern 46 C4
German Mountain 33 E7
Germany Creek 30 C2
Gerrell Mountain 15 D10
Gibbs Mountain 16 A5
Gibson 38 A1
Gibson Island 34 D2
Gibson Island 64 B5
Giddens Mill Creek 61 C7
Gilbert Creek 40 C2
Gill Bay 55 D10
Gill Island 55 D10
Gillespie Hollow 13 E9
Gillsville 21 A10
Gilreath Creek 12 D2
Gin Creek 23 C8; 41 C7; 42 B1
Ginger Cake Creek 26 C2
Girard 39 B9
Glade Creek 16 D2
Glade Shoals 15 E9
Gladesville Creek 35 A9
Glady Creek 28 D2; 36 A1
Glass Mine Top 15 C7
Glassy Knob 15 B9
Glassy Mountain 16 B2
Glawson Creek 35 C10
Glen Haven 26 A5
Glencoe Swamp 64 D4
Glenn 32 A5
Glennville 55 B7
Gloster 21 E6
Goat I 64 D5
Goat Mountain 16 D4; 34 D2
Gobblers Knob 15 A6
Godfrey 28 D1
Godwinsville 43 E10
Gola Creek 34 B4
Golden Creek 25 E8; 37 D10
Goldens Creek 29 D10
Gooch Mountain 15 C6
Good Hope 28 A1
Gooding Bay 63 D7
Goose Creek 55 D6,8
Goose House Gap 71 C9
Goose Run Creek 55 D10
Goosepond Creek 23 D7
Gordon 36 D3
Gordon Spring 12 C5
Gordy 60 A3
Goshen Mountain 15 B10; 16 B1
Goshen Swamp 56 B1
Goss Creek 36 C3
Gothards Creek 25 A9
Gough 38 B4
Gould Mountain 14 C4
Goulding Creek 22 E4
Gow Hill 40 C4
Gowrie Island 64 D5
Grace Branch 54 A4
Gracewood 31 D6
Graham 54 C2
Grand Bay 61 E10
Grand Bay Creek 62 E1; 69 B10; 70 A1
Grandview Lake 14 E2
Grangerville 64 A4
Granite Hill 29 E7
Granny Knob 15 A8
Granny Marr Mountain 14 A2
Granny Mountain 14 B1
Granny Top 15 C7
Grant G Hill 14 B4
Grantville 33 A8
Grapevine Cove 15 B9
Grass Creek 40 E2
Grassy Flat 59 B7
Grassy Gap 15 C6
Grassy Island 63 E8; 72 A5
Grassy Knob 15 A10
Grassy Mountain 13 B10; 16 C1
Grassy Pond Island 72 A5
Gravelly Gap 14 A3
Graves Mountain 30 A1
Graves Spring 51 D6
Gray 36 C1
Grays Creek 30 A2
Grayson 21 E7
Graysville 12 A5
Greasy Branch 63 D6,7
Greasy Branch Island 63 E8
Greasy Mountain 15 C6
Green Bay 47 B8; 70 A4;B3
Green Gap 16 B3
Green Hill 34 C2; 40 C3
Green Island 57 B6
Green Island Sound 57 B6
Green Mountain 14 B4
Green Swamp 63 D10; 65 B6
Greenbrier Creek 28 A3;B3; 30 C3,C4
Greene Creek 24 A4
Greens Cut 39 A7
Greensboro 28 C5
Greenville 33 B10
Greenville 72 A3
Gregeory Creek 53 B6
Gregory Gap 15 B6
Gresham Park 26 B4
Gresston 43 D9
Griers Cave 49 B9
Griffin 34 A4
Griffin Creek 52 B5
Griffin Lake 47 C7
Griffin Mountain 27 B7
Grimes Nose 15 C10
Griswold Hill 40 C3
Griswoldville 36 D1
Grogan Mountain 14 D4
Grovania 42 C5
Grove Creek 21 A10; 22 A1;B1,2;E5; 23 D6
Grove River 56 B5
Groveland 46 E4
Grover Island 72i D4
Grovetown 30 D5
Gulf Creek 12 C2
Gulf Mountain 12 D2; 34 D2
Gulley Branch 52 E1
Gully Creek 51 B8
Gum Branch 35 E9
Gum Creek 24 D5; 27 A8;B8; 34 E2; 51 A8;D8; 61 A7,9;B6;C6
Gum Log Branch 23 B8
Gum Log Creek 16 E5
Gum Swamp 63 D8
Gum Swamp Branch 43 A8
Gum Swamp Creek 43 A8;B9;C10;E10
Gumlog 17 E6
Gumlog 17 E6
Gumlog Lead 15 A7
Gumm Creek 37 C6
Gunn Hill 29 C7
Gunn Spring 12 B2
Guyton 47 C8

H

Habersham 16 D1
Hacklebarney Creek 63 C9
Hackney Spring 13 A7
Haddock 36 B2
Hadley Creek 67 B9
Hagan 46 E2
Hagen Creek 15 E10
Hahira 61 E8
Hair Spring 12 E2
Hale Gap 12 A2
Hale Ridge 16 A4
Halfmoon Bluff 65 E7
Halfmoon Bluff 72i C5
Halfmoon Landing 56 D4
Halfmoon River 57 A7
Halloca Creek 40 C4
Halloway Gap 14 B2
Halls 19 B7
Halls Creek 53 D6
Halls Pond 59 A8
Halls Swamp 72 D3
Hamburg Millpond 37 A9
Hamilton 33 E8
Hamilton Creek 18 C3
Hamilton Mountain 13 B7
Hammock Springs 58 E2
Hammocks Branch 36 D2
Hammond Gap 12 D4
Hammonds Slough 68 B2
Hampton 26 D4
Hampton River 65 B8;C8
Hanging Mountain 19 B10
Hanley Branch 43 D8
Hanna Creek 22 B5
Hannah Branch 38 A2;B3
Hannahatchee Creek 40 E2,4,5
Hanner Island 55 D9
Hanson Mountain 15 B10
Hapeville 26 B3
Haralson 34 A1
Hard Labor Creek 27 A10; 28 B1,3
Hardee Swamp 65 D6
Harden Creek 29 B9;C8
Hardin Canal 47 E9; 56 A4
Hardin Creek 34 B4
Hardslate Gap 14 C4
Hardwick 36 B4
Hardy Mill Creek 61 B8
Hardys Creek 27 D9
Harlem 30 D3
Harp Branch 39 B6
Harp Ridge 12 C2
Harper Creek 14 B2
Harper Slough 55 E9
Harpers Hammock 71 B7
Harris Creek 14 D1; 24 A4; 25 E6; 28 B4; 72 C1
Harris Gap 13 B7
Harris Mountain 15 A9
Harris Neck 56 E4
Harrisburg Gap 12 D3
Harrison 37 D9
Harrison Lake A 30 C2
Harrison Lake B 30 C2
Harry Hammock 57 C6
Hart Creek 29 C10; 30 C1
Hartford 43 D7
Hartsfield 60 C2
Hartwell 23 A7
Hartwell Lake 23 A8
Harvest Mountain 16 D1
Harvey Creek 56 B5
Harveys Island 56 B5
Hat Creek 52 D1;E1,2
Hatley 52 B1
Hatley Gap 14 B2
Haw Pond Creek 52 B3
Hawk Cliff 12 A3
Hawk Mountain 14 C5
Hawkins Branch 51 C6
Hawkinsville 43 D6
Hawks Creek 22 D5
Hayes Creek 36 C5
Haylow 70 A3
Hayne Swamp 64 D5
Haynes Swamp 56 C2
Hayneville 42 C5
Hazel Creek 16 D1,2
Hazlehurst 54 B1
Heads Creek 26 E3
Heads Creek Reservoir 26 E3
Headstall Creek 30 E3
Heard Creek 52 E1
Heards Lake 68 A3
Heath Creek 18 A4
Heath Mountain 18 B3
Helen 15 C9
Helena 53 A7
Hellgate Swamp 59 A8
Hellhole Mountain 15 B10
Hells Hollow 14 A2
Helm Gap 34 E1
Hemp Top 14 A2
Hemptown Gap 15 B6
Hen Coop Branch 39 E9
Henderson 42 C4
Henderson Mountain 19 B8; 20 A1
Hendley Pond 46 A1
Hendricks Creek 25 B6
Hendrix Bay 63 D6
Hendrix Mountain 14 E3
Henricks Gap 18 A3
Hephzibah 31 E6
Herds Creek 27 E8
Herds Pond 37 D8
Herman Hill 40 C3
Hermitage Island 65 C6
Herod 50 D2
Herod Creek 50 D2
Hess Hill 40 D3
Hewett Spring 34 C2
Hiawassee 15 A9
Hichitee Creek 40 D3,4
Hickey Knob 14 B4
Hickman Island 34 D3
Hickory Creek 14 A1
Hickory Hammock 63 E8
Hickory Knob 15 B6;B10
Hickory Level Creek 22 A1
Hickory Log Creek 20 A2
Hickory Mountain 18 C5
Hickory Ridge 14 A1
Hickoryland Mountain 14 B4
Hickorynut Mountain 14 B2; 15 C9
Hickox 64 C2
Hicks Ridge 15 B6
High Falls 14 C5
High Falls Lake 35 A6
High Gap 14 E4
High Head 39 B9
High House 14 C4
High Knob 16 C1
High Point 12 B3; 18 A3; 6 E4
High Rock 12 E2; 13 B9; 14 A2,5;C4; 15 A7; B6; 52 A1
Highland Mills 26 E4
Hightop 13 C10
Hightower Falls 18 E5
Hightower Gap 14 C5
Hightower Lake 34 C3
Hightower Mountain 18 E5
Hightower Shoals 34 D3
Hillabahatchee Creek 24 D4;E5
Hillard Island 63 E8
Hillhouse Hill 36 C5
Hilliard Island 56 A1
Hilliards Pond 62 A2
Hills Creek 19 D7
Hillsboro 35 A10
Hilltonia 39 D10
Hilltop 34 B2
Hilokee Creek 50 B4
Hinesville 56 C1
Hinton Creek 18 A3; 33 E10
Hinton Shoals 27 B9
Hiram 19 E9
Hird Island 65 A8
Hise Gulf 12 C2
Hiwassee Ridge 15 B9
Hoboken 63 C10
Hobson Creek 14 E2
Hodchodkee Creek 49 A8,9;B7
Hodge Mountain 19 C8
Hog Bay 62 C4
Hog Branch 50 A2
Hog Creek 15 A9; 36 B1; 49 C8;D7,8; 53 D10;E10; 60 D4; 61 A9 62 C2; 63 A6;B6
Hog Creek Bay 62 B2
Hog Fork 29 A9
Hog Gallus Island 63 E7
Hog Island 63 E7; 71 B9
Hog Mountain 15 E9; 16 B3; 34 B5
Hogan Branch 43 B8
Hogans Spring 52 B3
Hogansville 33 A7
Hogback Mountain 15 D6
Hogcrawl Creek 42 C3;D2;E1
Hogg Mountain 33 C6
Hogjowl Creek 12 D2
Holanna Creek 49 C7,8
Holcomb Creek 16 A4
Holden Creek 14 C4
Hole-in Swamp 31 E8
Hollis Creek 40 C5
Hollman Creek 40 E3
Holly Creek 13 B9,10;C8; 13 C9; 23 C6
Holly Creek Gap 14 B1
Holly Springs 20 C2
Hollywood 16 D2
Homeland 72 A1
Homer 22 A2
Homerville 62 E4
Hominy Creek 25 B7
Honey Bluff 64 C3
Honey Creek 27 B6; 65 D6
Honey Island 55 E10; 71 B8
Honey Island Prairie 71 B8
Honey Scrub Island 71 B8
Honey Swamp 64 E5
Hood Branch 23 E8
Hoods Creek 16 A4
Hopeful Branch 38 A5
Hopkins Branch 13 C6
Horn Mountain 16 D3;E6
Horns 35 E7
Horse Creek 35 D6; 39 D9;E8; 41 B10; 42 B1; 43 A6; 53 A6;B7,8; 55 B10; 60 A3,4;E1
Horse Gap 15 C6
Horse Hammock 57 C6
Horse Island 71 B10
Horse Knob 15 C6
Horse Pen Bay 46 A5
Horse Pen Swamp 47 E8
Horse Range Mountain 15 D8
Horse Ridgea 14 B2
Horsehead Creek 42 C2
Horsehead Creek Lake 42 C2
Horseleg Mountain 18 B4
Horsepen Bluff 65 F7
Horsepen Mountain 14 C4
Horseshoe Bend 14 A1; 59 C8
Horseshoe Island 63 D6
Horseshoe Ridge 15 D6
Horseshoe Shoals 65 E7
Horseshoe Swamp 71 B6
Horsetrough Mountain 15 B9
Hortense 64 B2
Horton Bend 19 A6
Hoschton 21 C9
House Creek 33 D6; 52 B3,4
House Lake 71 A10
Houston Lake 42 B5
Houston Valley 13 B6
Howard 41 A8
Howard Mountain 16 A2
Howards Mill Creek 58 C2
Howell 70 A1
Howell Mountain 14 D4
Howell Sinks 68 B3
Huber 36 E1
Huckleberry Bay 63 D8
Huckleberry Pinnacle 34 C1
Huckleberry Point 12 D2
Hudson Gap 14 B2
Hudson Mill Rapids 33 E7
Hudson River 16 E1; 21 A10; 22 A1,2;B4
Hughes Gap 15 C6
Hughes Mountain 14 A4
Hughes Prong 45 A8,9
Hull 22 D4
Hull Island 64 D5
Hullander Cove 15 A8
Hunnicut Creek 27 C10
Hunnon Branch 29 D7
Hunter Knob 15 A8
Hunters 47 A6
Hunters Creek 16 E3; 53 D6
Hurricane Branch 38 D1
Hurricane Creek 14 D5; 35 B10; 53 C9,10;E10; 54 C1;D1;E2; 63 A8
Hurricane Knob 14 A5
Hurricane Mountain 13 C6
Hurricane Ridge 15 B6
Hutchcraft Hill 40 D3
Hutchings 22 E5
Hutchinson Mill Creek 61 D8
Hutchinson Pond 61 D8

I

Ichawaynochaway Creek 50 B1;C1;E1; 59 A6;B7;C7
Ideal 41 C10
Ila 22 C4
Indian Bay 70 B4
Indian Branch 39 D10
Indian Creek 21 C9; 22 A3; 23 E6; 24 B4;C4;D5; 26 E5; 27 E6; 28 A1; 42 A3; 60 B4;C5; 61 D6
Indian Grave Knob 14 B1
Indian Grave Mountain 34 C3
Indian Island 71 A10
Indian Lake 60 C4
Indian Mound Island 71 C7
Indian Swamp 64 C1; 71 A6
Inman 26 D3
Inman Branch 37 C10
Inman Creek 54 A4
Intracoastal Waterway 65 B8
Iric Branch 47 D6
Iron City 58 E3
Iron Mine Bluff 54 B5
Iron Mountain 13 A10 ; 19 A8
Irondale 26 D3
Irwin Mountain 15 C10
Irwinton 36 D5
Irwinville 52 D3
Isiac Bay 62 D4
Island Creek 36 A5
Island Shoals Creek 27 D6
Israel Creek 34 D5
Ivey Branch 38 B1
Ivy Creek 21 C7;D7
Ivy Island 34 D2
Ivy Knob 15 A9
Ivy Mountain 15 A9
Ivylog Creek 15 A6,7
Ivylog Mountain 15 A7

J

J Strom Thurmond Lake 30 A4
Jack Creek 52 E3
Jack Hall Branch 68 A1
Jack sland 71 B8
Jackie Camp Swamp 56 E2
Jacks Branch 47 C8
Jacks Creek 13 E8; 27 A10; 28 A1,2; 33 C10; 45 C9
Jacks Creek Mountain 27 A10
Jacks Knob 15 B9
Jacks River 14 A1
Jackson 27 E7
Jackson Bay 71 A9
Jackson Branch 32 D2; 46 A5
Jackson Spring 12 A3
Jackson Springs 27 E10
Jacksonville 15 A8
Jacksonville 53 C7
Jacobs Knob 15 C7
Jake Mountain 14 D5
Jakin 58 D2
James 36 C2
James Creek 20 C5
James Pond 50 D5
Jameson Mountain 16 B2
Jardine Bay 64 C2
Jarrell Pond 46 A5
Jasper 14 E2
Jasper Gap 15 C9
Jeff Mountain 14 C4
Jefferson 22 C1
Jeffersonville 36 E3
Jekyll Island 65 D7
Jekyll Point 65 E7
Jekyll Sound 65 D7
Jenkins Gap 12 E3; 15 A7
Jenkinsburg 27 E6
Jerico River 56 C3
Jerry Reeves Creek 34 D3
Jersey 27 A9
Jerusalem 64 E3
Jess Gap 15 A10
Jesup 55 E8
Jeter Creek 51 D9
Jewell Mountain 15 A10
Jewells Mill 29 E9
Jim Mountain 15 B8
Jims Creek 46 C2
Jobs Creek 13 C7
Joe Creek 51 D8
Joe Mountain 16 B2
Joel Mountain 14 C4
Joes Creek 29 E10; 38 A1
Joes Island 64 B5
John Gunn Mountain 19 A7
John Jones Mountain 15 D6
Johns Bay 64 A5
Johns Creek 13 D6;E6; 60 A5
Johns Mountain 12 E5
Johnson Bay 70 A2
Johnson Corner 54 A3
Johnson Creek 29 D7; 53 B6; 56 D5
Johnson Mountain 19 A10
Jointer Creek 65 D7
Jointer Island 65 D7
Jonas Mountain 15 B8
Jones Bay 56 A1
Jones Bend 18 A5
Jones Branch 19 C7
Jones Creek 14 D5; 51 C8,9; 55 C8;D9; 56 C2,3; 62 E4; 70 A4,5
Jones Creek Swamp 71 A6
Jones Gap 12 D3
Jones Gap 15 B9
Jones Hammock Creek 56 C5
Jones I 59 A7
Jones Island 57 A7
Jones Knob 15 B8
Jones Mountain 15 B9
Jonesboro 26 C3
Jonica Gap 14 A5
Jordan Bay 62 E5
Jordan Branch 38 A3
Jordan Creek 43 C7
Jordan Hill 40 C3
Journey Hill 40 C3
Jove Creek 65 C7
Judy Mountain 18 B3
Julienton River 56 E4
Juliette 35 B8
Jumping In Creek 24 B4
Junction City 41 A7
Juniper 41 B6
Juniper Creek 35 E9; 41 B6
Juniper Lake 41 B6
Justus Mountain 15 C6
JW Smith Reservoir 26 D3

K

Kaiser Bay 70 B4
Kanady Creek 18 C2
Kaney Head Creek 58 C3
Kathleen 43 B6
Katy Knob 16 A4
Keel Creek 59 A7
Keene Bay Branch 55 C6
Keener Mountain 16 A2
Keg Creek 25 E10; 26 E1; 30 B3; 37 A8;B8;C7
Kegles Creek 23 D7
Keithsburg 20 B2
Keller 56 C4
Kelley Mountain 16 E2
Kells Creek 14 C2; 37 D9; 59 D9
Kelly Ridge 15 A10
Kemp Creek 30 B1
Ken Mountain 14 A1
Kendal Creek 33 C10
Kendall Branch 34 D5
Kendall Creek 40 A5;B5
Kendrick Creek 29 C9
Kennedy Hill 61 E6
Kennedy Mountain 21 B9
Kennesaw 20 D1
Kenyon Creek 13 A7
Keown Falls 13 D6
Kettle Creek 29 A7;B8; 63 C8
Keysville 38 A4
Kildare 47 B7
Kilkenny Creek 56 C5
Kimbro Creek 28 D5
Kimbrough Creek 34 E2
Kimmons Mountain 14 D3
Kincaid Mountain 18 A3
Kinchafoonee Creek 41 D6;E6; 50 A1;B3,4;D5
Kinderlou 69 A8
King Swamp 65 A7
Kings Bay 64 D3; 72 D4
Kings Bay Base 72i E3
Kings Creek 18 B2
Kings Mountain 34 C3
Kings Pond 40 C4
Kingsland 72 B4
Kingston 19 B7
Kinnard Creek 27 E9
Kiokee Creek 30 B4;C3; 50 D3;E3; 59 A8
Kirkis Gulf 12 C2
Kirkland 62 B3
Kirkland Creek 58 D2
Kitchen Gap 18 A3
Kite 38 E2
Kittrell Creek 37 B9
Kneeknocker Swamp 64 C1
Knight Spring 12 A3
Knights Creek 69 A9
Knights Swamp 64 C4
Knox Spring 12 D2
Knoxville 35 E7
Kolomoki Creek 49 E6
Kyle Hollow 14 A3

L

La Vista 26 A3
LaFayette 12 C4
Lafayette City Reservoir 12 C4
LaGrange 33 B6
Lake Alligator Creek 54 A2
Lake Amicalola Creek 14 D4
Lake Arrowhead 20 A1
Lake Back River 47 D10
Lake Battleground Creek 38 E1
Lake Blackshear 51 A7
Lake Bluff 55 D9
Lake Brier Creek 30 E1
Lake Buck Creek 34 A5
Lake Burton 16 B1
Lake Cedar Creek 18 C3;D3;E5
Lake Cedar Creek 23 A8,9
Lake Chickamauga Creek 12 B5;C5
Lake City 26 C3
Lake Coldwater Creek 23 B8
Lake Collins 41 E9; 46 B2
Lake Creek 18 D5
Lake Creek 52 D1
Lake Cypress 52 A4
Lake Cypress Creek 59 B6
Lake Dow 27 D6
Lake Dry Creek 18 A4
Lake Ebenezer Creek 47 C9
Lake Erma 26 D4
Lake Goose Creek 55 D7
Lake Gum Swamp Creek 43 C10
Lake Haynes Creek 27 A7
Lake Hearst Branch 47 E9
Lake Hurricane Creek 54 D1
Lake Ichawaynochaway Creek 50 C1
Lake Jackson 27 E8
Lake Joy 42 B5
Lake Juliette 35 B9
Lake Kolomoki Creek 58 A2
Lake Limestone Creek 43 C8

Continued on page 4

Lake Lindsay Grace 55 E6
Lake Lotts Creek 46 C4
Lake Marvin 13 D6
Lake Mayers 54 C2
Lake Meriwether 34 C1
Lake Nichols 60 E5
Lake Oconee 28 B4;D5
Lake Ogeechee River 47 E8
Lake Ohoopee River 38 D1
Lake Olympia 24 A5
Lake Park 69 C10
Lake Pennahatchee Creek 42 E3
Lake Petit 14 E4
Lake Philema 50 A5
Lake Potato Creek 34 B4
Lake Red Bluff Creek 62 C4
Lake River 27 B10
Lake Russell 16 E2
Lake Rutledge 28 B1
Lake Sandy Creek 27 A10
Lake Seminole 66 B3; 67 A6
Lake Shoal Creek 17 E7
Lake Sidney Lanier 15 E7; 21 B6
Lake Sinclair 28 E4; 36 A4
Lake Spivey 26 C4
Lake Stocking Head Creek 46 C1
Lake Swamp Creek 13 C7
Lake Swift Creek 34 D4
Lake Tamarack 14 E3
Lake Tchukolaho 36 D4
Lake Tenmile Creek 54 B4
Lake Tennessee River 16 A2
Lake Tobesofkee 35 D9
Lake Twelve Oaks 26 D3
Lake Verne 70 A3
Lake Wildwood 35 D9
Lake Woodruff 14 A5
Lake Zwerner 15 D7
Lakeland 62 E1
Lakemont 16 B3
Lakeview 12 A4
Lamar Creek 22 B4
Lamar Mounds 36 D1
Lamars Creek 37 C8
Lambert Branch 38 B5
Lampkin Branch 53 C7
Lanahassee Creek 41 D6;E7; 50 A2
Lance Mountain 14 A5
Lane Creek 22 E1
Lanes Creek 47 C6
Lanett 32 D5
Laney 60 C1
Langdale Lake 69 B8
Lanier Island 65 C7
Laurel Grove Creek 64 C5
Laurel Springs 33 D8
Laurel View River 56 C4
Lavender Creek 18 A4
Lavender Mountain 18 A4
Lavonia 17 E6
Lawrenceville 21 D7
Lawson Mountain 12 A2
Layway Swamp 64 A5
Lazer Creek 33 D10;34 D1;E1,2
Leading Ridge 14 C2
Leadpole Mountain 15 D9
Leary 59 A6
Leathersville 30 B2
Leatherwood Creek 16 E3
Leatherwood Mountain 14 B2
Lebanon 20 C2
Ledford Mountain 15 B8; 16 A2
Lee Creek 35 A8
Lee Mountain 16 D3
Lee Pope 42 A2
Lees Bay 62 E4; 70 A4;B4
Lees Creek 68 B1
Leesburg 50 D5
Leland 26 A1
Lenox 61 B7
Leslie 51 B6
Levelland Mountain 15 C8
Lewis Creek 65 A6
Lewis Island 65 B6
Lexington 23 E6
Liberty Creek 16 C2
Lick Creek 13 D7;E9,10
Lick Log Creek 19 E9
Licklog Creek 14 D3
Licklog Mountain 14 B5
Light Bay 62 D3;E4
Lightsey Bay 62 E3
Lightsey Hammock 61 E10
Lightwood Log Creek 23 A6
Lilburn 20 E5
Lilly 42 E3
Lilly Branch 42 E3
Lime Branch 58 B3
Lime Creek 51 A6;B10;C10
Lime Rock 64 D2
Limestone Creek 37 C8; 38 D1; 42 C5; 43 C8;D8; 45 E6; 51 A8
Lincoln Park 34 D3
Lincolnton 30 A2
Line Creek 25 D10; 26 C1;E1; 34 A2
Linesville Branch 23 E8
Lingerfelt Island 63 C7
Linton 37 B7
Lion Mountain 16 B4
Liss Gap 15 C6
Lithia Springs 25 A10
Lithonia 27 B6
Little Abrams Creek 51 D8
Little Alligator Creek 53 B6; 63 D6
Little Andy Mountain 15 C9
Little Armuchee Creek 12 E5
Little Attapulgus Creek 67 B6
Little Bald 15 C7
Little Bald Cove 15 A8
Little Bald Knob 16 A1
Little Bald Mountain 14 C3
Little Bear Creek 25 B9;C10; 49 A10
Little Beaverdam Creek 23 B6,7; 29 A9
Little Bee Mountain 14 C3
Little Black Creek 36 C5
Little Branch 33 E7
Little Brier Creek 30 E2
Little Broughton Island 65 B8
Little Brushy Creek 38 A4; 52 E4
Little Buckhead Creek 39 D7
Little Buffalo Creek 37 A7; 64 B5;E1
Little Buffalo Swamp 64 B4
Little Bull Creek 46 E3
Little Buzzard Mountain 15 C8
Little Camp Creek 36 C4
Little Canoochee Creek 45 B10
Little Cedar Creek 36 B2
Little Cedar Creek 37 D10
Little Cedar Mountain 15 C6
Little Clouds Creek 22 E5
Little Coldwater Creek 23 B7
Little Commissioner Creek 36 D4
Little Creek 13 C7; 18 E3; 24 A3; 25 D10; 28 C5;E3; 30 A3; 33 B10; 36 C2; 41 C6; 42 D3;D4;E3; 49 B9; 50 E1; 51 E10; 52 E3; 54 D1; 60 A5;C1,3;D1;D3,5;E5; 61 A7,8;E6; 62 A1; 64 A4; 69 A6
Little Crumbly Knob 15 C9
Little Cumberland Island 65 E7
Little Curry Creek 22 C2
Little Deer Creek 35 C8
Little Doctor Creek 55 C9
Little Don Island 57 B6
Little Dove Creek 23 C7
Little Duncan Ridge 15 B7
Little Eastanollee Creek 16 D4
Little Echeconnee Creek 35 D7
Little Falling Creek 35 A9
Little Fiddlers Island 71 C7
Little Fishing Creek 36 B3
Little Flat Creek 27 A8
Little Germany Creek 30 C2
Little Glady Creek 28 D2
Little Grassy Knob 15 B7
Little Greenbrier Creek 28 A3
Little Haynes Creek 27 A8
Little Hichitee Creek 40 D4
Little Hickorynut Mountain 15 C9
Little Hog Creek 36 B1
Little Horse Creek 39 E9; 53 B8
Little Hurricane Creek 53 D10; 54 E1; 63 A7,8
Little Ichawaynochaway Creek 49 B10;C10
Little Indian Creek 23 E6; 28 C2
Little Island 63 D8
Little Island 71 B10;C6
Little Island Creek 36 A5
Little Keg Creek 37 B8
Little Kettle Creek 29 A8
Little Kiokee Creek 30 C4
Little Lightwood Log Creek 23 A7
Little Lime Creek 50 A5
Little Long Creek 38 E5
Little McElory Mountain 14 E4
Little Mountain 14 E5; 15 A10
Little Mountain Ridge 12 E5
Little Muckalochee Creek 50 A3
Little Mud Creek 15 E10
Little Mud River 65 B8
Little Mulberry River 21 D8
Little Nell Knob 15 A10
Little Ochlocknee River 60 B1;D2;E1
Little Ocmulgee River 53 A8,10
Little Ogeechee River 29 E8; 37 A8; 56 A4
Little Ohoopee River 37 D10; 38 E1,2; 45 A7;B7
Little Okefenokee Swamp 64 A4;E1
Little Pachitla Creek 49 E9
Little Patsiliga Creek 34 E4
Little Penholoway Creek 64 A2
Little Pine Island 63 D8
Little Pine Knot Creek 40 C5
Little Pine Log Creek 19 A9
Little Pine Log Mountain 19 B9
Little Pumpkin Creek 49 B9
Little Pumpkinvine Creek 19 E7
Little Reedy Creek 45 C8
Little River 18 E5; 20 C1-3; 25 A6; 27 C10; 28 C1;D1;E2; 29 B8-10; 30 B1; 36 A3; 51 D9,10;E10; 52 E1; 61 A6;B7;C6;D6;E7; 69 A7,8
Little Rock Sink 59 D8
Little Rocky Creek 43 A9
Little Saint Simons Island 65 C9
Little Sal Mountain 14 D5
Little Sand Creek 52 D1
Little Sand Mountain 12 E5
Little Sandy Creek 22 C3; 28 A1;B1 36 C2; 37 E7
Little Sandy Hill Creek 37 D8
Little Sapelo Island 65 A9
Little Satilla Creek 54 C4; 55 D6;E7; 64 A1
Little Satilla River 64 A1;B2;D5; 65 D6
Little Satilla River Swamp 64 C4
Little Scarecorn Creek 14 E1
Little Shoal Creek 21 E10
Little Shoulderbone Creek 29 D6
Little Slaughter Creek 40 E5
Little Spirit Creek 31 E6
Little Sturgeon Creek 53 D6
Little Sugar Creek 28 C3
Little Suwannee Creek 63 D6
Little Swannee Creek 71 C6
Little Sweetwater Creek 32 B1
Little Swift Creek 34 C4
Little Tallapoosa Lake 25 B7
Little Tallapoosa River 25 A7;B6
Little Texas Valley 18 A5
Little Tired Creek 59 E10; 67 A10
Little Tobesofkee Creek 35 C6,7
Little Towaliga River 35 B6
Little Tybee Creek 57 B8
Little Tybee Island 57 A8
Little Wassaw Island 57 B6
Little Wehadkee Creek 32 A4
Little White Oak Creek 34 A1
Little Whitewater Creek 41 A8
Little Wildcat Mountain 15 C8
Liz Hill 65 B6
Lizella 35 D9
Lloyd Creek 30 A1;B4
Lloyd Island 71 B10
Locust Grove 27 E6
Locust Mountain 14 D4
Log Dam Creek 28 E5
Loganville 21 E8
Lollis Creek 21 C8
Lolly Creek 60 A4;B4
London Hill 72i D3
Long Branch 12 B3;D1; 15 E7; 26 E5; 33 A9; 37 E6; 38 A2; 39 E8; 55 A9; 58 B5;C4; 60 E3; 64 B3; 70 B5; 72 B1
Long Cane Creek 32 C5; 33 B7;C6
Long Cove 12 B4
Long Creek 23 D9;E7; 28 A5; 29 A6;D9;E9; 45 C7
Long Gap 14 B2
Long Island 57 A7
Long Island 71 A8
Long Island 72i D3
Long Island Creek 20 E2
Long Mountain 15 D9
Long Pond 50 D3; 59 B7; 69 B10
Long Ridge 15 A9
Long Swamp Creek 14 E3; 20 A3
Lookout Creek 12 A3;B1;C1
Lookout Mountain 12 A3
Lookout Valley 12 A2
Looks Branch 39 C8
Lost Creek 60 C1; 60 D1
Lost Swamp 56 A4
Lott Creek 21 C9
Lotts Creek 45 E6; 46 A2;B2;C3;D4
Louise 33 B7
Louisville 38 C2
Louvale 40 E3
Lovejoy 26 D4
Lovejoy Creek 12 E5
Loveless Mountain 18 E3
Lovett 69 C6
Lovett Branch 39 C9
Low Gap 14 E4
Low Gap 15 D6
Low Gap 16 C1
Lower Black Creek 46 D5; 47 D6
Lower Roundabout 38 D3
Lowry Branch 27 E10
Ludowici 55 D9
Luella 26 E5
Luke 58 B2
Luke Swamp 46 D5;E4
Lula 21 A10
Lula Falls 12 A3
Lumber City 53 B9
Lumpkin 49 A8
Lumpkin Ridge 15 D6
Lundy Creek 29 D6
Luthersville 33 A9
Lynch Mountain 15 C10
Lynn Creek 13 E8
Lynn Knob 15 A7
Lyons 45 D9

M

Mableton 26 A1
Macedonia Slough 19 C6
Mack Mountain 15 C10
Mack White Gap 12 E4
Mackay River 65 C7
Mackey Creek 27 D7
Macks Creek 23 E7,8
Macks Mountain 15 C10
Macland 19 E10
Macon 35 D10
Maddox Gap 12 C5
Madison 28 C2
Madras 25 D9
Magnolia Bluff 64 E3
Magnolia Spring 50 A3
Magnolia Swamp 42 A1
Magruda Creek 38 E2
Magtail Branch 38 A1
Maiden Creek 36 E5; 65 D6
Malden Branch 56 A2
Manassas 46 E2
Manchester 33 D10
Manchester 34 D1
Manhead Sound 65 C8
Mann Creek 18 E3; 24 A4
Manor 63 D6
Mansfield 27 C9
Manson Branch 38 C3
Manson Spring 38 C3
Marble Spring 12 E3
Marbury Creek 21 E10
Mare Branch 43 B10
Marietta 20 D1
Marion Clayton Mountain 14 D4
Market Branch 50 E2
Marlow 47 D8
Marsh Island 56 C4
Marshall Creek 33 E10; 34 E1
Marshallville 42 B2
Martin 16 E5
Martinez 31 C6
Mary Gap 15 A6
Mason Hill 40 C3
Mason Ridge 15 B6
Mason Spring 37 E9
Masons Mill Creek 22 B5
Masse Branch 68 A3
Mathews 38 A3
Mathews Creek 35 E6
Mathias Branch 49 A7
Mattox Creek 30 D1
Mauk 41 B7
Maul Hammock Lake 63 E9
Maul Hammock Prairie 63 E9
Maxeys 28 A5
Maxwell Creek 67 B9
May Hall Island 65 B8
Mayapple Knob 15 A10
Mayfield 29 E9
Mays Bay 64 A5
Maysville 22 B1
McBean 39 A7
McBean Creek 30 E5; 31 E8; 39 A6
McCanless Creek 20 B1
McCaysville 14 A3
McClain Bay 70 A3
McClendon Creek 19 E7; 65 A6
McClendon Swamp 65 A6
McClure Creek 14 B2
McCory Creek 20 A1
McCoys Branch 34 D3
McCullough Creek 45 B9
McCurry Creek 18 E4
McDaniel Creek 32 B1
McDonald Island 71 A10
McDonough 26 D5
McGar Pond 38 E5
McGarrity Bay 70 B5
McGrady Bend 18 A5
McGraw Mountain 34 C2
McIntosh Creek 39 B7
McIntyre 36 D5
McKeever Slough 68 B3
McKenny Gap 14 B2
McKinney 34 C4
McKinnon 64 A2
McNutt Creek 22 E1
McQuaddy Branch 38 B2
McQueen Hammock 56 D5
McQueens Island 57 A7
McRae 53 A7
McWhorter Creek 28 B5
Meadow Creek 41 B9;C10; 42 C1
Means Creek 27 B10
Meansville 34 B3
Meat Island 63 E8
Mechanicsville 20 E4
Medicine Sink 59 D9
Medway River 56 C5
Meeting House Bay 62 B1
Meetinghouse Branch 69 A10
Meigs 60 D1
Meinhard 47 E9
Meldrim 47 E8
Melvin Swamp 56 C1
Menlo 12 E2
Meridian 65 A8
Merrett Creek 49 D10; 50 E1
Merrillville 60 E3
Mershon 63 A9
Mesena 30 D1
Metcalf 68 B2
Mett Bay 71 C6
Metter 46 C1
Middle Bald 15 B7
Middle Creek 29 A9;D10; 30 C1; 50 C3
Middle Fork Broad River 16 E2; 22 A3
Middle Fork Little River 12 D2
Middle Fork Suwannee River 63 E9; 71 A8
Middle Ground 56 D5
Middle Marsh Island 56 B5
Middle Mountain 13 C6
Middle Oconee River 21 C10; 22 D1
Middle Prong Indian Creek 60 B4
Middle Ridge 15 B10
Middle Strange Island 71 B8
Midland 40 A3
Midville 38 D4
Midway 12 A4
Midway 55 C2
Milan 53 A6
Milford 59 B6
Mill Branch 39 E7; 46 A4;D4; 53 B7; 62 C5;E5; 63 A7; 71 A6; 72 E1
Mill Creek 13 A10;B7;B9,10;C6; 19 E9; 20 B3;C2; 22 D5; 31 B8; 33 B10; 34 E2; 37 A6; 38 C5;D2; 39 C7;E6; 42 D1; 45 C8; 46 B3,4;C5; 47 B6;C10;D7;E6,7; 50 A5; 51 D7;E8; 52 B2;E1,3; 53 B6;C7; 55 B10; 58 A5; 59 A6; 60 E2; 61 A9;C6; 62 A2;D1; 63 C9; 64 C3
Mill Creek Mountain 13 C6
Mill Dam Creek 35 A8
Mill Mountain 13 D6
Mill Ridge 15 A9
Mill Shoal Creek 23 B6
Milledgeville 36 B4
Millen 39 D7
Miller Gap 12 B3
Miller Gap 15 A7;C7
Miller Sprs 59 A10
Miller Top 15 C7
Millhaven 39 C10
Milligan Creek 25 D6; 45 E6; 54 A1,2
Millpond Branch 64 C1
Millrace Creek 69 A7
Mills Creek 12 E2; 13 A7
Millsap Mountain 14 A2
Millstone Creek 23 D7
Millwood 62 C5
Milner 34 B5
Mims Creek 72 D1
Mims Island 71 C9
Mincle Mountain 15 E8
Mine Branch 30 A1
Mineral Bluff 14 A4
Mineral Spring 14 B4; 20 A1
Mineral Spring Branch 39 A8
Mining Gap 15 A8
Minnies Island 71 A8
Miona Springs 42 C1
Mitchell 37 A10
Mitchell Gap 34 D1
Mitchell Island 71 C9
Mitchell Pond 68 B2
Mixons Hammock 71 A8
Mizell Creek 52 B5
Mizell Prairie 71 B10
Moates Knob 16 C1
Mobley Bay 46 A5
Mobley Creek 25 B8
Mobley Swamp 32 B1
Moccasin Creek 16 B1
Mock Spring 43 D6
Modoc 45 A9
Mole Mountain 14 E3
Molena 34 C2
Mollclark River 56 D5
Moniac 71 D9
Monkey Island 64 E4
Monroe 27 A10
Montezuma 42 D1
Montgomery 56 B5
Monticello 27 E10
Montrose 43 A10
Moody Creek 55 B6
Moon Change Swamp 32 D2
Moore Creek 36 B3
Moore Gap 12 B3
Mora 62 A2
Moreland 25 E9
Moreland Gap 15 A10
Morgan 50 E1
Morgan Bay 46 A5
Morgan Bend 15 A6
Morgan Falls Reservoir 20 D3
Morgan Valley 19 D6
Morganton 14 B4
Morganville 12 A2
Morning Creek 26 B2;C2
Morris 49 C7
Morris Creek 23 E10; 31 B8
Morris Pond 61 C9
Morrison Creek 61 D7
Morrow 26 C3
Morton Bend 18 B2
Morven 61 E7
Mose Mountain 16 A5; 34 D2
Moseley Springs 18 A2
Mosely Bay 55 E7
Mosquito Creek 43 D9;E8
Moss Creek 13 A3; 22 E4
Moss Island 56 D5
Mossy Creek 15 D9;E10; 42 A3,4; 43 B6
Mossy Lake 42 B5
Mosteller Spring 19 A8
Moultrie 60 C4
Mount Airy 16 E2
Mount Carmel 12 C4
Mount Hope Creek 18 B3; 56 B2,3
Mount Vernon 21 E10
Mount Vernon 45 E6
Mount Zion 24 B5
Mountain City 16 A3
Mountain Creek 16 E1; 21 C9; 24 D4; 25 E7,8; 27 A9; 33 D6,8; 34 C2; 42 E1
Mountain Creek Lake 33 D8
Mountain Oak Creek 33 E6
Mountain Park 20 C3;E5
Mountain View 26 B3
Mountaintown Creek 14 C1
Moxley 38 C3
Mt Oglethorpe 14 E3
Muck Creek 12 E5
Muckalee Creek 41 D7;E8,9; 50 A4;B5; 51 D6
Muckaloochee Creek 50 A3,4;B5
Mud Creek 12 C2; 15 E10; 16 A3;E1; 18 C2; 19 B8;E10; 25 A7,8; 33 C7; 34 D1; 50 A1
Mud River 56 E4; 65 A9
Mud Swamp 64 B1; 69 B8-10
Muddy Slash Ridge 34 C2
Mulberry Creek 21 C8; 33 E6,8,10; 40 A1
Mulberry River 21 C8,9;D10
Mulberry Rock 25 A7
Mule Creek 42 A4; 60 E4,5
Mule Top 14 A2
Mulepen Creek 45 A6
Muley Mountain 16 B1
Mullinax Mountain 19 C6
Mullis Bay 62 C2
Munnerlyn 39 C7
Murder Creek Lake 27 D9,10; 28 E1; 36 A2
Murphy Hollow Creek 12 A1
Murphy Spr 12 A2
Murphy Top 14 E1
Murray Branch 42 E1
Murrayville 15 E7
Murry Creek 31 B9
Musella 35 D6
Mushmelon Creek 55 B7
Musket Bay 63 C7
Mystic 52 D3

N

Nacoochee Indian Mound 15 C10
Nahunta 64 C2
Nails Creek 22 A3;B4; 38 D2
Naked Creek 45 D7
Nance Ridge 15 C8
Nancy Creek 20 E2
Nancy Spring 58 A5
Nancy Town Creek 16 E2
Nash Creek 26 D2
Nashville 61 C9
Nasty Pond 69 C9
Nathan Creek 45 A10
Naylor 70 A1
Neal Gulf 12 D2
Nealey Creek 38 D1
Neals Creek 49 E9,10
Needmore 70 C5
Neel Creek 29 D7
Neels Creek 38 E1; 45 A6
Nell Knob 15 B10
Nelson 20 A3
Nelsons Bluff 65 A10
New Hope 19 D9
New Hope Branch 31 E6
New Hope Swamp 72 A5
New River 25 E9; 33 A7; 61 A7;B7;C8
New Rsland 71 B8
New Savannah Bluff 31 D7
Newberry Creek 39 A8
Newborn 27 C10
Newell Branch 51 C10
Newford Creek 23 E10
Newford Creek 31 B7
Newington 47 A7
Newnan 25 D9
Newsom Gap 12 B2
Newton 59 B8
Newton County Reservoir 27 B9
Newtown 20 D4
Nicholls 53 E10
Nichols Gap 16 A2
Nicholson 22 C2
Nickajack Gap 12 B5
Nimblewill Creek 14 D5; 15 D6
Ninemile Creek 53 D8
Ninetynine Branch 13 E10
No 1 Island 71 C10
No Business Creek 27 A6
Noblet Creek 13 D9
Noel Island 34 D3
Noonday 20 D1
Noonday Creek 20 C1;D1
Noontootla Falls 14 C5
Norcross 20 E4
Norman Park 60 B5
Normantown 45 D8
Norris Lake 27 A6
Norristown 45 B7
Nort Fork Double Branch 22 C4
North Branch Swift Creek 51 B9
North Decatur 26 A4
North Druid Hills 26 A4
North Field 57 C6
North Fork Broad River 16 D3;E3,5; 22 A5
North Fork Little River 28 A5; 29 B6,7
North Fork Ogeechee River 29 B6;C7
North Fork Sun Hill Creek 37 C9
North Fork Wolf Creek 27 E10; 28 E1
North Glory Hole 49 A7
North High Shoals 28 A2
North Metro 20 D5
North Mosquito Creek 66 B4
North Newport River 56 C3;D3-5
North Oconee River 21 A9,10; 22 B1; 22 D2
North Prong Canoochee Creek 38 E3
North Prong Kolomoki Creek 49 E7
North Prong Saint Marys River 71 E10
North Prong Sumac Creek 13 A9
North Prong Williams Creek 29 C9
North River 65 A8
North Strange Island 71 B7
North Sugar Creek 28 C3
NorthAtlanta 20 E3
Northeast Point 56 E5
Norton Gap 15 A8
Norton Hill 16 E2
Norwat Hill 40 D2
Norwood 29 D10
Noses Creek 19 E10
Nottely Lake 15 A6
Nottely River 15 A6;B8
Nunez 45 B8

O

Oak Grove Island 65 C6
Oak Island Swamp 65 A6
Oak Mountain 33 E9
Oak Mountain Spring 33 E10
Oak Park 45 C9
Oak Ridge 15 C8
Oakdale 26 A2
Oakey Mountain 16 A2,3;B2;C1; 20 A1
Oakey Top 16 A5
Oakfield 51 C7
Oakland Heights 19 B9
Oakman 13 D10
Oakwood 21 B8
Oaky Woods Creek 60 D1
Oatland Island 57 A7
O'Bryan Gap 18 A4
Ocean Pond 69 C10
Ocee 20 D4
Ochillee Creek 40 C4
Ochlocknee 60 E1
Ochlockonee River 60 A3;C3;D3;E2; 67 A10;B9; 68 A1
Ocilla 52 E4
Ocmulgee River 27 D8;E8; 35 A8;B9;D10; 36 E1; 43 A6;B6;C7;D7;E8; 52 A4;B4;C5; 53 B9;C6,7; 54 B1
Oconee 37 D7
Oconee Creek 45 E7
Oconee River 28 A4;B4; 36 B5; 37 C6;D7;E7; 45 E6 54 A1
Odingsell River 57 B7
Odom Creek 58 A1
Odum 55 D6
Offerman 64 A1
Ogeechee Creek 39 D9;E10; 47 A6;B6
Ogeechee River 29 C8;D8;E9; 37 A9;B10; 38 C2,3;D5; 39 D7;E8; 46 A4,5; 47 B6;C7;E8; 56 A3;B4,5; 57 B6
Ogeechee Run 47 D8
Oglesby 23 C7
Oglesby Pond 46 A2
Oglethorpe 42 D1
Oglethorpe Bluff 55 D7
Ohoopee River 37 D9;E9; 45 A6;B6,8;C9;E10; 54 A5;B5
Okapilco Creek 60 B3;C4;D4,5; 61 E6; 69 A6;B7
Okeetuck Creek 42 C5
Okefenokee Swamp 63 E8; 71 B8
Old Bill Knob 15 B8
Old Mill Branch 39 B10
Old Nell Knob 15 A10
Old Ninety Bay 62 C3
Old Rocky Knob 15 A9
Old Teakettle Creek 65 A8
Oldnor Basin 56 E5
Oldnor Island 56 E5
Olive Creek 68 B3
Oliver 47 B6
Oliver Mountain 18 C3
Oliver Swamp 32 B1
Olley Creek 20 E1
Olmstead Pasture 56 D3
Omaha 40 B2
Omega 61 B6
Onslow Island 47 E10
Oochee Creek 37 E6; 41 C7
Oostanaula River 18 A5
Oothkalooga Creek 19 A7
Open Creek 39 E6; 45 B8; 54 A3
Open Pond 59 E7
Opossum Creek 53 B9
Oquina Creek 68 A2
Orchard Hill 34 A5
Oscar Swamp 56 E2
Osceechee Spring 52 B5
Osierfield 53 D6
Ossabaw Island WMA 57 C6
Ossabaw Sound 57 B6
Ossahatchie Creek 33 E8; 40 A4
Oswichee Creek 40 D3
Otter Bay 62 D5
Otter Creek 52 C4,5; 53 E9; 63 B10; 64 B1; 69 A10
Otter Hole Branch 46 E5
Owen Mountain 16 A2
Owenby Cove 15 A10
Owens Creek 41 D8
Owens Island 34 D2
Owl Bay 62 E2
Owl Creek Gap 15 B9
Owl Gap 16 A4
Owl Mountain 16 B2
Owltown Creek 14 C3
Owltown Mountain 14 C2
Oxford 27 B8
Oyster Shell 65 A6

P

Pachitla Creek 49 C9;D10;E10
Pack Mountain 13 E10
Pack Mountain 14 A2
Padgett Bay 55 B6
Padgett Falls 14 E2
Page Mountain 16 A4
Paint Bank Gap 13 A10
Painter Gap 14 B1
Palm Creek 21 E8
Palmer Branch 30 E4
Palmer Creek 15 E6; 21 A6
Palmer Spring 38 B4
Palmetto 25 C10
Palmetto Creek 33 D8;E8
Palmetto I 64 A4
Palmyra Springs 50 D5
Panola Mountain 26 B5
Panther Bluff 14 A1
Panther Creek 16 C3; 27 E8; 33 C7
Pantherville 26 B4
Pappy Jack Spring 43 E7
Pappys Creek 34 C1
Paramore Hill 39 E8
Paris Mountain 14 A4 ; 19 E6
Parkers Bluff 62 C1
Parkers Mill Creek 41 B6;E9; 67 A9
Parks Creek 22 C1; 33 B9
Parks Ridge 14 B1
Parrott 50 B2
Pasley Shoals 34 D2
Pataula Creek 49 A10;B8,9;C7;D6
Pates Creek 26 C4
Patrick Bay 47 E6
Patrick Gap 34 D1
Patsiliga Creek 41 A7,9,10; 42 A1
Patterson 63 A10
Patterson Creek 14 A2
Patterson Knob 14 A5
Patterson Swamp 55 D8
Patton Top 15 B6
Paul Creek 37 B8; 53 C7;D8
Pavo 60 E4
Payne Creek 16 E3; 56 C1;D2,3
Payne Gap 12 B2; 14 B5
Payne Mountain 14 A2
Pea Creek 25 B10
Peachtree City 26 D1
Peacock Creek 56 B1;C1,2
Peaky Top 13 A10
Pearson 62 B3
Pearson Creek 27 E9
Peavine Creek 12 A5;B4
Peavine Ridge 12 B5
Pee Dee Bay 62 C3
Peeksville Creek 27 D6
Pelham 59 D10
Pelican Point 57 C6
Pelican Spit 65 C9;E8
Pembroke 46 E5
Pendergrass 21 C10
Pendleton Creek 45 B6;C7,8;E9;D9
Penholoway Bay 64 A3
Penholoway Creek 55 E8; 64 A3
Penholoway Swamp 55 D9
Penitentiary Cove 14 D5
Pennahatchee Creek 42 E3
Pennant Hill 65 B6
Penson Knob 16 A2
Pepper Hammock 64 B5
Perch Creek 62 C5
Perch Lake 63 E10; 71 A10
Perennial Springs 12 E2
Perkins 39 C7
Perry 42 B4
Perry Creek 58 A4
Perry Mountain 19 C6
Persimmon Creek 16 A2
Persimmon Gap 14 C3; 5 D6
Persimmon Hill 14 B4
Persons Creek 27 E9
Pessell Creek 50 A3
Peter Knob 14 C4; 16 A1
Peter Young Mountain 15 B6
Peters Bay 62 E1
Petit Gauke Hammock I 57 B6
Pettit Creek 19 B9
Pettyjohn's Cave 12 C3
Pharm Spring 15 B6
Phelps 13 C7
Phelps Bluff 52 A4
Phillips Gap 15 A9
Phillps Pond 49 B7
Philomath 29 A7
Phinazee Creek 35 B6
Phinizy Swamp 31 D7
Phoeba Bay 62 C1
Pickens Creek 23 B9
Picketts Knob 15 B7
Picklesimer Mountain 14 B5
Piedmont 34 B4
Pierce Creek 29 D6
Pigeon Bay 62 E3; 70 A3
Pigeon Creek 14 E5; 34 D1
Pigeon Island 57 B6
Pigeon Mountain 12 C3; 16 B2;C2
Pike Pond 69 C9
Pike Swamp 63 D8
Pikes Bluff 65 C8
Pilcher Hill 65 A6
Pilot Mountain 15 C6
Pine Barren Swamp 72 D3
Pine Creek 60 E1; 68 B1,2
Pine Gap 16 A3
Pine Head Creek 50 B1
Pine Hill Swamp 56 E2
Pine Island 57 B6; 59 A8; 63 D8; 64 E5; 71 A7
Pine Islands 56 C5; 62 E1
Pine Knot Creek 40 B4; 41 C6
Pine Lake 26 A5
Pine Lake 33 D6
Pine Log 19 A9
Pine Log Creek 13 E9; 19 A10; 52 E2
Pine Log Mountain 19 A10
Pine Mountain 33 D8
Pine Mountain 14 B5;C3;D1; 16 A5; 19 D8; 27 B6; 33 D8; 34 B4;C2
Pine Mountain Valley 33 D8
Pine Ridge 15 B8; 16 B3
Pineflat Gap 15 B7
Pinehurst 42 E4
Pineview 43 E7
Piney Bay 62 D5; 64 A3; 70 B3
Piney Island 64 E5
Piney Island Creek 64 E5
Piney Mountain 14 A4; 15 C8;E8
Piney Top 15 A7
Piney Woods Branch 59 A8
Piney Woods Creek 33 A10; 51 E6,7
Pinhook Creek 13 B8
Pink Mountain 15 D9
Pinkston Creek 29 E7
Pinnacle Knob 16 A3
Piscola Creek 60 E4; 68 A4;B5; 69 B6
Pistol Creek 23 E10; 31 B8
Pittman 20 D5
Pittman Bay 63 C6;E7
Pittman Branch 27 D10
Pittman Creek 27 D9
Pitts 52 B1
Plainfield 43 D10
Plains 50 A3
Plainville 19 A6
Player Creek 52 C3
Pleasant Gap 13 A10
Pleasant Valley 34 C2
Plumorchard Creek 16 A1
Po Joe Branch 51 A6
Pocket Gap 13 D6
Poe Knob 15 C9
Pole Branch 47 D6
Polecat Creek 13 D8; 33 C8
Polecat Mountain 20 B1
Polly Creek 47 D9
Polly Pt 57 C6
Pollywah Knob 16 A4
Pompey Island 65 E7
Pond Fork 21 B9,10
Pond Spring 18 A3
Pool Mountain 21 D8
Pooler 47 E9
Pooles Creek 23 A6
Poor Mountain 15 C8
Poor Robin Spring 52 A3
Pope Island 63 D8
Popes Branch 27 E10
Poplar Cove Mountain 16 A1
Poplar Spring 12 A5;C1
Poplar Swamp 56 B4
Port Wentworth 47 E10
Portal 46 B2
Porter Creek 36 E3-5 ;56 C2
Porter Mountain 14 B2
Porter Springs Cedar Mountain 15 D7
Porterdale 27 C8
Porters Creek 22 E3
Possum Creek 19 D9; 61 D9
Pot Gap Ridge 16 A1
Potato Creek 33 A7
Potato Creek 34 A4;B4;C4;D3; 36 A3;B2
Potato Hill 16 A2; 18 D3
Potlikker Hill 32i B1
Potosi Island 65 B7
Potter 70 C2
Potters Creek 34 E3; 41 A8
Potterville 42 B1
Potts Mountain 14 E4
Poulan 51 E9
Powder Creek 34 B3
Powder Springs 19 E10
Powder Springs Creek 19 E9
Powell Creek 29 D7
Powell Dairy Farm Lake 50 A5
Powell Mountain 15 A10
Powell Spring 13 A7
Powelton 29 D8
Pratts Creek 35 C10
PrAuitt Creek 50 D1
Prentis Branch 18 C5
Preston 50 A1
Price Creek 14 D2
Price Mountain 21 C9
Pride Branch 69 B6
Pridgen 53 D7
Primrose 33 A9
Prince Mountain 14 B3
Providence Hill 35 C8
Pruitt Creek 23 A6
Puckett Creek 20 B2
Pudding Creek 62 B1,3
Pudding Ridge 12 B1
Pulaski 46 C2
Pump Gulf 12 B4
Pumpkin Creek 49 B9
Pumpkin Swamp 64 B5
Pumpkinvine Creek 19 C9;E8
Puncheon Gap 14 C5
Putney 60 A1
Pyles Swamp 64 D5

Q

Queen Bess Island 56 C5
Queens Mountain 15 B6
Quitman 69 B6

R

Rabbit Island 64 E1; 65 B8
Rabun Bald 16 A4
Rabun Gap 16 A3
Raccoon Branch 56 B2
Raccoon Creek 12 E3; 19 C8;D7; 60 B1,2
Raccoon Flat 55 C8
Raccoon Key 57 B6
Ragsdale Creek 22 A2
Raiden Creek 29 A6
Rainy Mountain 16 B3
Rall Mountain 14 C4
Rambulette Creek 41 B8,9
Ramey Mountain 15 A9
Ramhurst 13 C9
Ramp Gap 14 C3
Rand Knob 14 C4
Rand Mountain 16 A5
Randy Poynter Lake 27 A7
Range Gap 12 A2
Range Point 12 A1
Ranger 13 E10
Raoul 16 E1
Rape Gap 12 D3
Raper Creek 16 C1
Raper Knob 14 A5
Raper Mountain 16 B1
Rattlesnake Knob 15 B10 ;C6
Rattlesnake Ridge 51 C9
Raulerson Swamp 64 C1
Raven Cliff Falls 15 C8
Raven Knob 16 A3
Raven Rock 16 A3
Ravencliff Knob 15 A8
Rawlings Branch 27 B10
Rawls Pond 50 E4
Ray City 61 D10
Ray Hill 40 C4
Rayle 29 A8
Raymond 25 E10
Rayonair Pond 38 E1
Rayonier Lake 55 D9
Rays Swamp 36 E1
Rebecca 52 C2
Rector Knob 15 B6
Red Bluff 52 C5; 59 A10;E6
Red Bluff Creek 62 B5;C3
Red Hill Branch 37 E10
Red Lick Creek 29 D8
Red Mountain 19 B10
Red Oak 26 B2
Red Oak Creek 33 A10;B10; 34 B1
Red Oak Hammock 64 B5
Red Oak Island 64 A5
Redan 26 A5
Redbird Creek 56 B5
Redbird Prairie 71 A10
Redbud Creek 13 E9; 25 E6
Redcap Swamp 64 D4
Redding Branch 42 B5
Redis Mountain 14 A2
Redmond Gap 18 A4
Redoak Creek 51 B10
Redwood Hill 40 C2
Reece Creek 15 A6
Reed Bingham Park Lake 61 C6
Reed Branch 46 D4
Reed Creek 16 A5; 17 E7; 31 C6
Reeds Mountain 24 B5
Reedy Branch 42 E2; 46 D4; 51 B10; 53 D8

Reedy Creek 29 C9; 30 E2,3; 35 C8; 36 C5; 38 A4; 43 B9;E7; 45 A10;B10;C7,9;D9; 50 C4; 52 D3;E3,4; 53 E7; 54 D5; 55 E6; 60 C5;E4; 61 C9 62 A2;B2; 64 A1; 70 A2
Reese Mountain 14 D3
Reeves 13 E7
Reeves Creek 26 C4; 34 D2
Reeves Shoals 34 E5
Register 46 C3
Reidsville 54 A5
Renfroe 40 D4
Resaca 13 D7
Rest Haven 21 C7
Rex 26 C4
Reynolds 42 A1
Reynolds Bend 19 B6
Reynolds Creek 52 B2
Reynolds Swamp 59 A8
Reynoldsville 66 A4
Rhetts Island 65 B8
Rhine 52 A5
Rhodes Cut 47 E10
Rhodes Mound 31 E8
Rhodes Mountain 14 B5
Rice Creek 22 A5
Riceboro 56 C2
Riceboro Creek 56 C1,2
Rich Knob 14 B1
Rich Mountain 14 E1 ; 15 C6
Rich Ridge 15 C7
Richards Knob 14 B5
Richardson Creek 39 E6,7
Richardson Flat 59 B7
Richland 40 E5
Richland Creek 19 C8; 28 C4,5; 34 E3; 41 A7; 43 A8
Richmond Hill 56 B4
Richmond Hollow 12 A2
Richwood 51 A9
Ricketson Bay 62 B4
Ridley Hill 13 C9
Riggins Branch 71 A6
Riley Creek 72 A3
Riley Mountain 14 C4
Rincon 47 D9
Ringgold 13 A6
Ripshin 14 C5
Rising Fawn 12 C1
River Hill 58 A1
River Styx 71 D10
River Swamp 55 D9
Riverdale 26 C2
Roaring Branch 49 E6
Roaring Creek 54 B4
Roasting Ear Island 71 C10
Robbins Branch 32 E1
Robbins Creek 13 E7
Roberta 35 E6
Roberts Bay 71 B10
Robin Bay 60 E2
Robins Creek 45 A6
Robinson Creek 27 D9; 28 A2; 37 E8
Rochelle 52 B2
Rock Branch 23 B8; 35 B7
Rock Chapel Mountain 27 A6
Rock Creek 12 B2; 13 C9,10; 14 E2; 16 D4; 19 A9; 20 A2; 21 D8; 26 B5; 36 C1
Rock Eagle Lake 28 D3
Rock Falls 53 D8
Rock Hole Creek 50 D4
Rock Island 65 A8
Rock Mountain 16 A3
Rock Ridge 16 A4
Rock Spring 12 B4
Rock Spring Top 15 C7
Rockdedundy Island 65 B8
Rockfish Creek 56 B4
Rockhouse Mountain 34 D2
Rockmart 19 D6
Rocky Branch 38 A3
Rocky Branch 43 D6
Rocky Comfort Creek 29 D9;E10; 38 A1;B2
Rocky Creek 21 D9; 27 B10;D9; 29 B10; 30 B1; 31 D7; 32 B1; 35 A7;B6;D9;E10; 37 A7; 38 B5;D3;E3; 39 B6,8;C6; 43 A9;B10; 45 E8; 53 C8; 54 A4; 60 B5
Rocky Face 13 B6
Rocky Face 14 B1
Rocky Face Mountain 13 B6
Rocky Ford 39 E8
Rocky Ford 46 A3
Rocky Knob 14 B4; 16 A3; 15 A8,10;B8 16 A1
Rocky Mountain 14 B3;C5 15 B8,9;C6; 16 C3
Rocky Shoals Creek 22 C5
Rodgers Spring 19 B8
Rogers Branch 42 D3
Rogers Knob 15 A7
Roland Ridge 12 C2
Rolston Creek 14 C3
Romerly Marsh Creek 57 B6
Romerly Marshes 57 B6
Roopville 24 D5
Rooty Creek 28 D3;E3
Roper 53 C10
Rose Creek 28 A3; 34 C4; 72 A4
Rose Dhu Island 56 B5
Rose Hill 53 D7
Rosemary Creek 39 C7
Roses Creek 53 D7;E8
Rosier 38 C4
Ross Gap 15 A7
Ross Ridge 15 A7
Rosston Creek 43 A6
Rossville 12 A4
Roswell 20 D3
Rough Creek 14 A1
Rough Island 71 C7
Rough Ridge 14 A1
Round Mountain 14 B2;C4
Round Oak 36 B1
Round Timber Island 63 E8
Round Top 12 B3; 15 B10
Roundabout Swamp 62 B2; 63 E7
Roundtop 15 A6
Roundtop Mountain 14 A4; 15 A8
Rousseau Creek 30 B2
Rowells Island 71 A6
Royston 23 B6
Ruddy Bay 70 A2
Ruff Creek 12 D5
Rum Creek 35 B7
Running Ridge 40 C2
Runs Branch 47 A7;B8,9
Rupert 41 B9
Rush Creek 28 E4; 33 E10
Russell Branch 34 E1
Russell Swamp 56 C2
Rutledge 28 B1
Ryans Hill 40 C3
Rydal 19 A10

S

Saddle Ridge 14 B1
Sagegrass Creek 52 A3
Saint Andrew Sound 65 E7
Saint Augustine Creek 47 E9
Saint Catherines Island 56 D5
Saint Catherines Sound 56 D5
Saint Clair 38 A4
Saint George 72 D1
Saint Marys 72i E4
Saint Marys Entrance 72 E5
Saint Marys River 71 E10; 72 A3;B2,4;C1,4;E1
Saint Paul Branch 42 C2
Saint Simons Island 65 D8
Saint Simons Island 65 C8
Saint Simons Sound 65 D7
Sal Mountain 15 C10
Salacoa Creek 13 E9; 19 A10; 19 A9
Sale City 60 C1
Salem 34 E5
Sally Ann Mountain 14 A2
Sally Branch 40 B4
Sally Free Ridge 15 D6
Salt Creek 56 A5
Salt Log Knob 16 A5
Salt Pond Shoal 57 B7
Salter Branch 38 D1
Salter Mountain 34 C2
Saltpeter Cave 19 B8
Saltpeter Mountain 14 B3
Sam Hole Bay 47 B9
Sampson Creek 27 C7
Sams Creek 46 A1;B1
Sand Branch 40 D3
Sand Creek 33 D6; 36 C1; 41 C9; 52 D1,2
Sand Hill Bay 70 B2
Sand Hill Branch 39 E6
Sand Hill Lake 45 B6
Sand Mountain 13 A6
Sand Mountain 12 A1
Sanderlin Mountain 14 E3
Sandersville 37 C9
Sands Pond 46 E4
Sandy Branch 39 B8
Sandy Creek 22 C3; 25 E8; 26 D1; 27 A7; 28 A4; 33 B9; 49 D6
Sandy Flats 62 D5
Sandy Hammock 43 E8
Sandy Hill Creek 37 D7,8
Sandy Mount Creek 42 E3
Sandy Plains 20 D2
Sandy Run 36 A5
Sandy Run Creek 30 D4;E4; 37 A7; 42 A5 43 A6
Sandy Springs 20 E3
Sansavilla Bluff 64 A5
Santa Claus 45 E8
Sapelo Island 65 A9
Sapelo Island 65 A9
Sapelo River 56 E3,4
Sapelo Sound 56 E4
Sapling Gap 14 C5
Sapling Prairie 63 E9
Sapp Creek 59 E9
Sapp Prairie 71 C8
Sarahs Creek 16 A4
Sardis 39 C9
Sardis Creek 38 E2
Sargent 25 D8
Sassafras Mountain 15 D6
Sassafras Mountain 14 E3
Sasser 50 D3
Satilla Bluff 64 E3
Satilla Creek 52 D5; 53 E6
Satilla River 62 A1,2;B4,5; 63 B6,8;C9; 64 B2,3;C3;D2;E3,5; 65 E6,7; 72 A3
Satilla Swamp 64 C3
Satolah 16 A5
Sautee 15 C10
Sautee Creek 16 C1
Savage Creek 43 A7; 47 E6; 56 A2
Savannah 57 A6
Savannah Bay 70 B4
Savannah Beach 57 A8
Savannah River 23 A9; 30 B5; 31 B9;C6;D7;E8; 32 B1,2;C2;E3; 39 A8;B10 47 A8;C10;E10
Sawhatchee Creek 58 B2;C1
Sawmill Ridge 16 B2
Sawnee Gap 20 B5
Sawnee Mountain 20 B5
Scaly Knob 16 A2
Scarecorn Creek 14 E1
Schaffer Creek 38 B3
Schoolhouse Gap 15 A10
Scoggin Bay 71 B6
Sconti Gap 14 E4
Scotland 53 A8
Scott Bay 53 C8
Scott Creek 16 B2; 46 D3
Scottdale 26 A4
Screven 64 A2
Scroggin Knob 14 B3
Scroggins Branch 40 A5
Scrub Island 63 E6
Scruggs Top 15 B8
Scuffle Creek 43 A7
Scull Shoal Creek 22 C5
Sculls Creek 39 E7 46 A2
Sea Island 65 C8
Sea Island 65 C8
Seals Bay 64 C3
Seals Creek 38 D4
Seals Knob 16 B2
Seals Ridge 16 B2
Self Mountain 15 B8
Selman Lakes 18 A4
Senoia 26 E1
Settingdown Creek 20 B5; 21 B6
Seven Creek 53 D8
Seven Islands 34 D2
Seventeen Mile River 53 D7;E8,9; 62 A4;B5
Seville 52 B1
Shady Dale 28 D1
Shankle Ridge 12 C2
Shannon 19 A6
Sharon 29 C9
Sharp Hill 15 A8
Sharp Mountain 14 E2
Sharp Mountain Creek 14 E2; 20 A3
Sharp Top 14 C5
Sharp Top Mountain 19 B9
Sharpsburg 25 E10
Sharptop 15 A6
Sharptop Mountain 14 E3
Shaver Branch 41 D7
Shaw Creek 67 B8
Shaw Gap 12 C5
Shaw Mountain 19 A7
Shawnee 47 B8
Sheep Knob 14 B2; 15 A8;B8;C6;C10; 16 A4
Sheep Rock Top 15 B8
Sheep Wallow Mountain 14 D5
Sheffield Island 72i D3
Sheffield Mill Creek 58 C2
Shellman 50 C1
Shellstone Creek 43 B7,8
Shelly Island 34 D3
Sheppard Creek 27 D9
Sheriff Knob 15 B7
Sherrills Creek 29 B6
Sherwood Creek 21 C8
Shiloh 33 D10
Shiloh Creek 22 B5
Shiloh Fork 30 C3
Shinbone Ridge 12 C3;D3
Shine Mountain 15 D9
Shingle Mill Gap 15 C8
Shingler 51 E9
Shirley Bluff 64 E2
Shiver Branch 42 D5
Shoal Creek 15 E9; 16 C1; 17 E6
Shoal Creek 20 A1;A5;B1; 21 E9,10; 22 E4; 24 D4; 25 D10; 26 E3; 27 C10; 33 B7,8; 36 B1; 41 B7
Shoals Creek 34 A1
Shope Gap 15 B6
Shope Knob 15 B6
Short Creek 29 E9; 49 C8
Shorty Mountain 18 D3
Shoulderbone Creek 29 E6
Shrimp Creek 47 C7
Shriver Creek 30 A3
Sids Mountain 14 C5
Signal Mountain 19 D7
Signal Mountain 19 C9
Sigsbee 60 B3
Sikes Creek 29 E6
Silco 72 A3
Silk Hope 56 A5
Sills Branch 30 C2
Sillycook Mountain 16 C1
Siloam 29 C6
Silver City 21 A6
Silver Creek 18 C5
Silver Lake 66 A4
Simmons Bay 70 B2
Simmons Branch 46 A5
Simmons Point 55 A10
Simms Mountain 18 A3
Simon Creek 45 A10
Simpson Creek 19 D6
Sims Spr 12 A2
Singers Hill 34 C1
Singers Pond 49 A9
Sirmans 62 D2
Sister Island 57 B7
Six Weeks Bay 71 C7
Sixty Foot Branch 64 B1
Skeenah Creek 14 B5
Skeenah Gap 14 A5
Skidaway Island 57 B6
Skidaway River 57 A6
Skinner Bay 62 E3
Skinners Bay 47 D9
Skipperton 35 E10
Skitt Mountain 15 E9
Skut Knob 15 A10
Sla Island 47 E10
Slash Creek 36 C2
Slaughter Creek 40 D5;E5; 54 B5 61 E6,7
Slaughter Gap 15 C7
Slaughter Mountain 15 C7
Slow Run Creek 42 C3
Slygo Ridge 12 A2
Smarr 35 C8
Smith Creek 38 D1
Smith Gap 12 C5
Smith Mountain 15 C10
Smithee Jack Creek 49 B7
Smithville 50 B4
Smithwick Creek 20 A3;B3
Smokehouse Jam 63 E7
Smokehouse Knob 16 A2
Smyrna 20 E1
Snake Creek 13 D6; 25 C7,8
Snake Creek Gap 13 C6
Snake Nation Mountain 14 B3
Snapfinger 26 B5
Snapping Shoals Creek 27 C7
Snellville 21 E7
Snipes Grave Rock 34 D3
Snipes Shoals 34 E3
Snow Springs Mountain 19 A7
Snuff Box Canal 56 E1
Snuff Box Swamp 56 E1; 65 A7
Soap Creek 20 A2; 30 A1; 31 C9
Soapstone Creek 49 A7;B6
Social Circle 27 B10
Sofkee Creek 67 A8
Soldiers Camp Island 71 C9
Sooky Gap 15 B9
Sope Creek 20 D2
Soperton 45 C6
Soquee River 16 C1;D1
South Channel Savannah River 57 A7
South Fork Broad River 22 C4; 23 D6
South Fork Little River 29 B6,7
South Fork Ogeechee Creek 39 E9; 45 A5
South Fork Ogeechee River 29 C6,7
South Fork Upatoi Creek 41 A6
South Fork Wolf Creek 27 E10; 28 E1
South Glory Hole 49 A7
South Hampton Creek 56 D3
South Newport Cut 56 D4
South Newport River 56 D1,2,3;E5
South Prong Big Creek 63 C10
South Prong Buck Creek 32 D1
South Prong Canoochee Creek 38 E3
South Prong Creek 30 D5; 42 D4
South Prong Elko Creek 42 C4
South Prong House Creek 52 C3,4
South River 26 B3,4; 27 B6;C7;D8; 65 B8
South Sandy Creek 37 E6
South Shellstone Creek 43 C7
South Sugar Creek 28 C2
Sow Bay 62 C2
Sow Branch 58 D3
Spaniard Mountain 15 B9
Spaniards Knob 15 B9
Spanish Creek 72 A1
Spanish Hammock 57 A8
Sparkman Creek 65 E6; 71 E10
Sparks 61 C7
Sparks Creek 33 D9;E9
Sparks Gap 14 A5
Sparta 29 E7
Spence Mill Creek 59 D10
Spencer Ridge 15 B6
Spewrell Bluff 34 D2
Spider Ridge 57 C6
Spirit Creek 30 D5; 31 E7
Spooner Springs 58 E3
Spring Branch 12 D4; 71 B6
Spring Creek 13 E8; 18 D3; 19 C6; 37 B6; 38 C4; 40 B5; 42 D1; 46 B5; 49 E8; 50 E2; 58 A-E4; 59 A7 66 A4
Spring Hill Creek 42 C2
Spring Lake 37 C6
Springing Mountain 34 C2
Springer Mountain 14 D5
Springfield 47 C9
Springvale 49 C8
Sproull Mountain 19 C8
Spur Island 72 A5
St Augustine Creek 47 E8
St Peters Bluff 47 C7
Stafford Island 72 D4
Stalking Head Creek 35 A9
Stallard Bay 63 D6
Stalsby Creek 63 C6
Stalvey Bay 70 A4
Stamp Creek 19 B10
Standing Boy Creek 40 A1,3
Stanley Creek 14 C3
Stanley Gap 14 B4
Stapleton 38 A2
Star Creek 14 B5
Starrs Mill 26 E2
Starrsville 27 C8
Statenville 70 B1
Statesboro 46 B4
Statham 22 D1
Steadman Island 56 B5
Steamboat Eddy 55 E9
Steedley Bay 71 B6
Steedly Mountain 15 B9
Steel Creek 37 C10
Steele Knob 16 A2
Stekoa Creek 16 B2,3
Stekoa Falls 16 B3
Stella Lake 68 B5
Stephens 28 A5
Stephens Creek 16 E4; 22 A4; 29 C7; 37 B9
Stephenson Gap 34 D1
Sterling 65 B6
Sterling Creek 56 B4
Steve Bay 62 D1
Stevens Bay 63 E7
Stevens Pottery 36 C4
Stevenson Hill 40 D3
Stewart 27 D8
Stewart Homes 56 B1
Stewart Knob 14 A3
Stewart Mountain 14 A4
Stewarts Creek 28 D5
Stiles Creek 19 B8
Still Bay 53 C8; 62 C2
Still Branch 34 B1 39 B10
Stillhouse Knob 15 B10
Stillmore 45 B10
Stillwell 47 C9
Stink Creek 15 B8
Stockbridge 26 C4
Stocking Head Creek 46 B1
Stockton 62 E2
Stockton Creek 22 B1
Stone Creek 36 D2;E1; 52 C3
Stone Mill Mountain 24 E5
Stone Mountain 26 A5
Stone Mountain 26 A5
Stone Pile Gap 14 C2
Stone Springs Gap 15 D7
Stonewall 26 C1
Stonewall Creek 16 B2
Stonewall Knob 16 B2
Stoney Mountain 16 A5
Stony Knob 15 C9
Stony Mountain 16 C2
Storey Mill Creek 12 E4
Storm Branch 30 E1
Stovall 33 C8
Stover Creek 14 C4
Stover Knob 14 B4
Stover Mountain 14 C3
Strange Island 71 C7
Straw Mountain 16 A1
Strawberry Mountain 12 D5
Strawberry Top 15 C8
Strickland Bluff 64 B3
Strickland Island 64 A4
Stripling Mountain 14 E1
Stroud Mountain 16 B3
Strouds Creek 27 B9
Stump Creek 52 D4;E4
Sturgeon Creek 52 D5; 53 C6
Suches 15 C6
Suches Creek 15 C6
Sugar Creek 13 A6;A8;C10; 14 A3;B3; 28 C3; 43 D9;E10; 50 C4; 53 A7-9
Sugar Hill 21 C6
Sugar Hill 19 A10; 42 D5
Sugar Hill Creek 19 A10
Sugar Valley 13 D7
Sullivan Creek 34 C4
Sulphur Creek 33 C8
Sulphur Spring 40 C3
Sulphur Spring Branch 22 D4
Sumac 13 A9
Sumac Creek 13 A10;B8
Sumlin Swamp 64 B5
Summertown 38 E4
Summerville 12 E3
Sumner 51 E9
Sumter 50 B4
Sun Hill Creek 37 C9,10
Sunny Side 26 E4
Sunnyside 63 C8
Surrency 54 D4
Surveyors Creek 62 E5; 63 E6
Sutherland Bluff 56 E3
Sutton Mill Creek 16 C1
Suwanee 21 D6
Suwanee Creek 21 C7;D6
Suwannee Canal 71 B9
Suwannee Creek 62 D5; 63 D7
Suwannee River 70 C5; 71 A8;B7;C6
Suwannoochee Creek 62 D2;E3; 70 A3;B4; 71 B6
Swainsboro 45 A8
Swallow Creek 15 A10
Swamp Creek 13 C6,7; 67 A8;B8
Swan Creek 35 B6
Swan Lake 26 C5
Sweat Mountain 20 C2
Sweet Gum Island 64 E1
Sweetgum Bay 62 C3
Sweetwater Creek 19 B10; 25 A7,8;A10; 30 D2; 35 E8; 39 B10; 41 E9; 42 E1; 54 D4;E4; 62 E3
Sweigoffer Creek 47 D9
Swift Creek 27 A6; 34 D4;E4; 37 A6; 45 D8,9; 51 C8,9
Swinney Branch 19 E6
Swords 28 C4
Sycamore 51 D10
Syls Fork 29 A6;B6
Sylvania 39 E10
Sylvester 51 E8

T

Tails Creek 13 C10; 14 C1
Talahi Island 57 A7
Talbotton 34 E1
Talent Knob 15 B8
Talipahoga Rum Creek 40 E1
Talking Rock 14 E2
Talking Rock Creek 13 D10; 14 E1; 14 E2
Tallahassee Creek 50 E3
Tallapoosa 24 A3
Tallapoosa River 18 E5; 19 E6
Tallulah Falls 16 C2
Tallulah Mountain 16 C2
Tallulah River 16 A1
Tally Mountain 14 E1 ; 24 B4
Talmo 21 B9
Talmo 63 B6
Talona Creek 14 D2
Talona Mountain 14 D2
Tan Trough Creek 63 A9
Tan Yard Branch 18 D4
Tanyard Creek 35 D6
Tarboro 64 E3
Tarkiln Knob 15 A7
Tarrytown 45 C6
Tarver 70 B2
Tate 14 E3
Tate Spring 12 D5
Tatum Creek 62 E4; 70 A5; 71 A6;B6
Tatum Gulf 12 C2
Tatum Mountain 12 A2; 13 B10; 15 D10
Taylor Mill Lake 41 B10
Taylor Ridge 12 B5;D4;E4; 15 B9
Taylors Creek 55 A8;B9,10
Taylors Swamp 19 C7
Taylorsville 19 C7
Telfair Bay 32 B1
Telfair Pond 39 B9
Tell 26 B1
Teloga Creek 12 D3
Temple 25 A10
Temple Creek 58 A2
Ten Acre Rock 34 E3
Tenmile Bay 61 B10
Tenmile Creek 34 C3; 42 E5; 43 E6; 46 C2; 54 B5;C4;E3; 61 B10;C10; 63 A8
Tenmile Swamp 64 B4
Tennessee Valley Divide 12 C3
Tennga 13 A9
Tennille 37 C8
Terrapin Creek 18 E3
Tesnatee Creek 15 D8,9
Thalmann 64 B5
The Bay 51 B7; 52 D2; 64 A3
The Bay Branch 51 B6
The Canal 38 C5
The Cove 34 C1
The Flat 59 C10
The Gorge 15 A9
The Hammocks 58 E2
The Level 59 E8
The Mountain 32 D5
The Narrows 18 B3
The Pocket 71 B8
The Rock 34 C4
The Rocks 62 E1
The Sinks 68 B4
The Top 34 C2
Thick Creek 45 B10;
Thomas Creek 25 D7; 46 E1; 55 A6
Thomason Creek 13 C7
Thomasson Creek 19 E6
Thomaston 34 D3
Thomasville 68 A1
Thompson Creek 19 D6; 26 D4
Thompson Mill Creek 43 B6
Thomson 30 D1
Thomson Ford Branch 30 E2
Thornhill Bay 61 C8
Thornton Creek 38 B4
Three Men Swamp 47 D9
Three Sisters Mountain 15 D7
Threemile Creek 34 B3
Thunderbolt 57 A6
Thundering Spring 34 C2
Tickanetley Bald 14 C3
Tide Rips 56 E4
Tifton 61 A7
Tiger 16 B2
Tiger Bay 61 B10; 64 D1
Tiger Creek 16 B2; 37 B7; 45 C6;D7,8; 53 E9; 69 B8
Tiger Leap Bluff 47 A7
Tiger Mountain 16 B2
Tiger Swamp 64 D4
Tignall 23 E9
Tilton 13 C7
Timmons River 56 D4
Timms Creek 41 A9
Timpson Creek 16 B2
Timpson Mountain 16 B2
Tip Top 33 D8
Tipton Gap 14 B3
Tipton Mountain 14 B5
Tired Creek 67 A9;B9
Tired Creek Lake 59 E9
Tivoli River 56 C4
Tob Hammock 64 A5
Tobannee Creek 49 B6
Tobesofkee Creek 35 B6;C8;D9; 36 E1
Tobler Creek 34 B5;C5;D4; 35 C9; 36 B4
Toblers Creek 39 B9
Toccoa 16 D3
Toccoa Creek 16 D3,4
Toccoa River 14 A3;C5; 15 C6
Todd Creek 35 C7; 65 E6
Toland Mountain 14 B3
Tom Brown Spring 34 D1
Tom Thumb Bay 63 D7
Toms Creek 16 E4; 19 B7; 55 C7; 70 B3;C3,4
Toomsboro 37 D6
Tooni Gap 14 C5
Toonowi Mountain 14 C5
Toonigh Creek 20 C2
Topeka Junction 34 C4
Toteover Creek 41 B10;D9; 42 B1
Towaliga River 26 D4;E5; 27 E6; 35 A6;B8
Tower Bay 62 E5
Tower Mountain 15 A10
Tower Swamp 64 E4
Town Branch 13 C8; 49 C9
Town Creek 12 C4; 14 D1; 15 C8;D8; 24 E4; 28 B4,5;C5; 35 B7;C10; 37 A6;B6; 42 C1; 51 E8 53 D9
Towns 53 A9
Towns Mountain 15 B10
Townsend 56 E1
Toy Hill 40 C4
Trammel Mountain 14 B3
Treasure Lake 25 B7
Treat Mountain 18 E3
Trenton 12 B2
Tribble Gap 20 B5
Trion 12 D3
Triple Creek 41 D10
Tripp Gap 15 B10
Troublesome Creek 23 E6; 26 E4
Troup Creek 65 C7
Trout Lake Prairie 71 C10
Truelove Knob 15 A7
Tubbs Hill 40 D3
Tuckaluge Creek 16 A3
Tucker 20 E5
Tudor Branch 30 C5
Tugaloo River 16 D4,5
Tuggle Creek 29 B6
Tumbling Creek 14 A2
Tumbling Lead 14 A2
Tunnel Hill 13 B6
Turin 25 E10
Turkey Branch 47 C8; 71 A6
Turkey Creek 14 D3; 22 A5;E1; 24 B5; 28 D1; 34 C2; 36 C3;E3; 42 D3;E2; 43 A8,10; 50 B1; 51 A7; 67 A9
Turkey Creek Mountain 27 A10
Turkey Gap 16 A1
Turkey Hill 15 E7
Turkey Island 62 E4; 64 E2
Turkey Knob 14 C3
Turkey Knob 34 D1
Turkey Mountain 18 A5
Turkey Mountain 14 B1; 16 A1; 18 A5
Turkey Nest Head 71 C7
Turkey Pond 38 C4
Turkey Swamp 64 C4
Turkeypen Mountain 15 B9
Turkeypen Ridge 14 A2
Turkeytoter Spr 19 A10
Turner Bend 18 B3
Turner Branch 38 B4
Turner Creek 15 D9; 49 A7
Turner Gap 14 A5
Turnerville 16 C2
Turnip Mountain 18 B3
Turniptown Creek 14 C3
Turniptown Mountain 14 C3
Turnpike Creek 34 A4; 53 A6,7;B7
Turntime Branch 33 E8
Turtle Island 57 A8
Turtle River 64 C5; 65 C6;D6
Turtle River Swamp 64 C4
Turvin Creek 43 A8
Tussahaw Creek 27 D6,7
Twenty Mile Creek 53 E7
Twentynine Mile Creek 62 A4
Twin City 45 A10
Twin Creek 61 E8
Twin Lakes 67 A6
Two Run Creek 19 B7,8
Twomile Creek 21 B7; 29 E7
Twomile Gap 15 C6
Ty Ty 60 A5
Ty Ty Creek 50 A3; 51 E9,10; 60 A5;B5; 61 B6
Tybee Creek 57 A8
Tybee Cut 57 B7
Tybee Island 57 A8
Tyrone 26 D1

U

Uchee Creek 30 C5;D4
Ugly Creek 36 E3
Ulcohatchee Creek 34 E5; 35 E6
Umbrella Creek 65 E7
Unadilla 42 D4
Unawatti Creek 22 A5
Union City 26 C1
Union Point 13 C7
Union Point 29 B6
Unionville 61 A7
Upatoi 40 B4
Upatoi Creek 40 B4,5;C3; 41 B6
Upper Black Creek 46 C5; 47 D6
Upper Roundabout 38 D3
Upton Creek 29 B10; 30 B1
Useless Bay 62 D3
Utoy Creek 26 A1
Uvalda 54 A2

V

Valdosta 69 A9
Valley 32 D5
Valona 65 A8
Van Creek 23 C9
Vandyke Creek 56 D4
Vanns Creek 13 D8
Varnell 13 A7
Veal 24 D4
Vernon River 57 B6
Vesta 23 D7
Vidalia 45 D8
Vidette 38 B4
Vienna 42 E3
Villa Rica 25 A7
Village Creek 65 C8
Vinings 20 E2
Vinson Mountain 19 E6
Vinzant Swamp 55 C8
Visavis Island 65 C6

W

Waco 24 B5
Wade Lake No 1 32 C1
Wadley 38 D3
Wadsworth Hill 40 C3
Wahachee Creek 23 C9
Wahoo Creek 15 E8; 25 D8,9
Wahoo Island 56 E4
Wahoo River 56 E4
Walburg Creek 56 D5
Walburg Island 56 D5
Walden Branch 47 B6
Waleska 20 A1
Walker Creek 24 B4; 55 E7
Walker Mountain 18 B4 ; 19 B8
Walk-Ikey Creek 50 C1
Wallace Mountain 14 C4
Wallalah Mountain 14 B5
Wallys Leg 65 B7
Walnut Branch 39 B6
Walnut Creek 21 C10; 26 D4; 27 C6; 33 B9,10; 34 B1; 35 D7; 36 C1
Walnut Fork 16 A4
Walnut Gap 15 C8
Walnut Knob 15 A7
Walnut Mountain 14 C2
Walter F George Reservoir 49 D6
Walthourville 55 C10
Walton Creek 16 D4; 43 C9;D10
Walton Spring 59 B10
Wamble Creek 58 B3
War Hill 29 B8
Ward Creek 15 D7; 19 C9; 20 E1
Ward Gap 15 D6
Ward Mountain 19 A6
Wards Creek 16 D4; 68 B2
Waresboro 63 C7
Waring 13 B7
Warm Springs 33 D10
Warm Springs 33 D10
Warm Springs Branch 33 C10
Warner Robins 43 A6
Warren Creek 12 A1
Warren Island 64 E2
Warrenton 29 D10
Warrenton City Pond 29 D10
Warrior Creek 51 E8; 60 A4;B4,5; 61 C6
Warsaw 20 D5
Warthen 37 B9
Warwick 51 C8
Warwoman Creek 16 A4
Washington 29 A9
Wasp Creek 34 A4
Wassaw Breaker 57 B7
Wassaw Creek 57 B7
Wassaw Sound 57 B7
Wastewater Treatment Pond No 5 31 E7
Water Fork 36 E5
Water Oak Creek 63 E7
Waterhole Branch 39 D10
Watering Hole Branch 46 B3
Watermelon Creek 55 B7
Watery Branch 60 C2
Watkinsville 22 E3
Watson Creek 36 B3; 45 E9; 54 A5
Watson Gap 14 A1
Watson Hill 40 C3
Watson Mountain 14 A4
Watson Pond 45 A10
Wauka Mountain 15 E9
Waukeefriskee Creek 49 D7
Waverly 64 D4
Waverly Creek 64 D4,5
Waverly Hall 33 E9
Waverly Swamp 64 D4
Wax Lake 19 C6
Waycross 63 C8
Waynesboro 39 B6
Waynesville 64 C4
Wayside 36 B1
Weaver Creek 58 C1
Webb 20 C4
Webb Creek 18 C4
Weber 61 C10
Weed Island 65 A6
Weeks Mountain 14 B4
Well Island 63 D8
Wells Creek 30 A3
Wells Mill Creek 61 D7
Wenona 51 B9
Wesley 45 B8
West Armuchee Creek 12 D5
West Armuchee Valley 12 D4
West Branch Barnetts Creek 59 E10
West Chickamauga Creek 12 A4;C3
West Fork Deep Creek 51 C10
West Fork Ichawaynochaway Creek 49 A10
West Fork Lanahassee Creek 41 D6
West Fork Little River 12 C1; 15 E8
West Fork Pumpkinvine Creek 19 D8
West Fork Trail Creek 22 D3
West Green 53 E9
West Hill 24 A4
West Point 32 D5
West Point Lake 32 C5
Westoak 20 D1
Weston 50 A1
Wet Mountain 14 E4
Wethington Slough 59 B10
Wheeler Knob 16 A1
Whetstone Creek 29 D9
Whiddons Mill Creek 52 E1
Whigham 67 A8
Whim Hill 15 E6
Whiskey Island 70 C3
Whissenhunt Mountain 15 D6
White 19 B9
White Arm Bay 71 C7
White Arm Swamp 71 C7
White Creek 15 D10; 29 B7; 35 B6
White Cut 13 A7
White Oak 64 E4
White Oak Branch 30 C3; 50 C5
White Oak Creek 25 E10; 27 E10; 33 A10; 34 A1; 64 D3,5
White Oak Hammock 16 A2
White Oak Mountain 13 A6
White Oak Mountain 15 C8
White Oak Swamp 64 D4
White Plains 29 D6
White River Cave 19 D7
White Sulphur Creek 33 C8;D9
White Swamp 56 E3
Whitecut Ridge 13 A7
Whitehall 22 E3
Whitehead Bay 70 B3
Whitehead Creek 53 C10;D9
Whitehouse Hill 16 E2
Whitemarsh Island 57 A7
Whiten Creek 16 E4
Whiteoak Gap 12 B1
Whites Creek 30 D2
Whites Flat Bay 71 D10
Whites Mound 31 E8
Whitesburg 25 C8
Whitesville 13 D6
Whitewater Club Lake 69 C9
Whitewater Creek 26 C1;D2;E2; 32 A5; 35 E8; 41 B8,9;C10; 42 C1
Whitewater Pond 42 C1
Whittakers Lake 66 A4
Whitten Creek 29 D6,7
Wide Gap 15 C8
Wiggins Creek 53 D6;E6
Wike Gap 15 B10
Wike Knob 15 A9
Wildcat Creek 16 B1; 27 C7; 28 A3; 33 D6; 42 E5; 49 C7
Wildcat Island 63 D9; 71 C6
Wildcat Mountain 15 C8
Wildcat Spring 59 B9
Wildwood 12 A3
Wildwood Lake 45 C7
Wiley 16 B3
Wiley Creek 20 A1
Wilkey Creek 49 A6
Will Field Gap 15 C8
Willacoochee 62 B1
Willacoochee Creek 52 D4,5; 67 B6
Willacoochee River 52 E5
Willbanks Branch 13 D10
Willeo Creek 20 D3
Williams Creek 24 B4; 29 C9; 49 E9; 54 A3
Williams Gap 14 C5
Williams Mountain 33 E6
Williamson 34 A3
Williamson Creek 21 D9
Williamson Island 57 B8
Williamson Lake 27 A9
Williamson Swamp Creek 37 A8;B9,10; 38 C1,2;D3
Willingham Spring 34 C3
Willis Creek 52 C2
Willis Knob 16 A5
Wilmington Island 57 A7
Wilmington Island 57 A7
Wilmington River 57 A7
Wilscot Mountain 14 B5
Wilson Blue Spring 59 A10
Wilson Branch 46 B4
Wilson Cove 15 A9
Wilson Creek 13 A7
Wilson Falls 16 B1
Wilson Hammock 64 E1
Wilson Mountain 15 B7
Wilson Mountain 14 C4
Winder 21 D10
Winding Branch 64 E1
Windmill Pond 59 A8
Windy Gap 12 A2
Windy Gap 16 A3
Winky Branch 34 A1
Winokur 64 E2
Winslow Creek 33 B9
Winstead Hill 40 C4
Winston 25 A8
Winterville 22 D4
Wise Creek 27 E9
Wisnaint Mountain 14 C1
Withers 70 A3
Withlacoochee River 61 B-E9; 69 A7,9;B7
Wolf Bay 62 C2; 70 B4
Wolf Branch 22 C3; 61 B8;C8
Wolf Cave Mountain 19 A7
Wolf Creek 25 C8; 27 E6,7; 28 A3; 34 D4; 36 C2;D2; 40 B3; 43 E7; 50 A3;C1; 67 A9
Wolf Island 65 B8
Wolf Knob 16 A2
Wolf Pit Branch 60 C3
Wolfe Creek 46 C1
Wolfpen Gap 14 B1,5; 15 A6;C9; 19 B10
Wolfpen Mountain 14 C3
Wolfpen Ridge 15 A8;B10
Wolvins Springs 52 A4
Womble Creek 34 D2
Wood Creek 35 C6
Woodbine 64 E4
Woodbury 34 C1
Woodcock Branch 46 C4
Woodland 34 E1
Woodring Gap 15 A9
Woodstock 20 C2
Woodville 29 B6
Woodward Creek 19 A6
Woody Mountain 14 C5
Woodyard Creek 62 D4
Woolsey Creek 26 D2
Wray 53 D6
Wrens 38 A3
Wright River 57 A7
Wrights Creek 27 C8
Wrights Island 65 B7
Wrightsville 37 E10
Wyatts Branch 46 A3
Wynn Creek 29 A10

XYZ

Yahoola Creek 15 D7
Yam Grandy Creek 45 A8;B8
Yankee Reach 55 C8
Yates Spring 12 B5; 58 E4
Yatesville 34 C5
Yellow Bluff 53 C6
Yellow Bluff 56 D4
Yellow Creek 20 A4;B4; 35 C7
Yellow Jacket Mountain 19 B6
Yellow Jacket Shoals 34 D3
Yellow Mountain 16 C1
Yellow River 21 D7; 27 A6;B7;C8;D8
Yellow Water Creek 27 E6,8
Yellowback Mountain 16 C4
Yellowbank Mountain 16 C1
Yellowdirt Creek 25 D6
Yellowjacket Creek 33 A8
Yonah Mountain 15 D9
Yorkville 19 E7
Young Creek 52 C2
Young Harris 15 A8
Young Stone Creek 14 A4
Youngs Mill Creek 61 C8
Zachry Creek 25 E6; 33 A6
Zebina 38 A3
Zebulon 34 B3
Zeiterower Branch 46 C4
Zellner Island 35 B9
Zero Bay 64 A1
Zuta Branch 65 B6

Introduction

Georgia, one of the original 13 colonies, was the last to be established in 1733. The state is named for George II, king of Great Britain at the time of settlement. Bordered by Tennessee and North Carolina to the north, Florida to the south, South Carolina and the Atlantic Ocean to the east and Alabama to the west. Much of the borders follow popular riverways including the Chattahoochee, Tugaloo, Savannah and Chattooga rivers. The Chattooga River is a National Wild & Scenic River, a delight for paddlers.

Three geographic regions define the state. The Blue Ridge Mountains cover most of the north. The Piedmont, a plateau region, sits between the mountainous region and the Coastal Plain, the latter being the third and largest region. The Coastal Plain is situated between the Atlantic Ocean and the Fall Line, the ancient Atlantic Ocean shoreline. Georgia's recreational opportunities are as diverse as the states physical geography.

Many parks hold battleground re-enactments at historic forts where much of America's history unfolded. Fort King George State Historic Site in Darien was the southernmost fort of the British Empire in America.

Opportunities to camp, hike, fish, hunt and view wildlife abound in the state. Providence Canyon State Park is a popular destination where the absence of foliage and vegetation create breathtaking views of the often referred to "Little Grand Canyon". Georgia has a variety of water activities from paddling along the St Mary's River, to fishing at one of many public piers or in Walter F George Reservoir, a bass-lover's dream.

Several museums and art centers are found within the state including the 39th President Jimmy Carters' Presidential Library & Museum and Martin Luther King Jr's boyhood home in Atlanta.

Modern festivals celebrate the unique foods of Georgia including the Annual Rock Shrimp Festival in St Mary's and the Jekyll Island Shrimp & Grits Festival.

The Peach State's diverse history and geography has made it a popular location for film production including *Gone with the Wind*, *Fried Green Tomatos*, *The Blind Side* and *Remember the Titans*.

As a starting point, this Gazetteer features a selection of activities for all ages and skill levels. For a more comprehensive list of destinations contact the agencies listed below.

RECREATION

The Georgia Department of Natural Resources' Division of State Parks & Historic Sites manages over 60 properties ranging from mountains and canyons to battlefields, historic homes and Native American sites. Tallulah Gorge State Park is a breathtaking canyon where visitors hike and traverse a suspension bridge that offers 1,000-foot high overlooks.

13 designated state historic sites highlight Georgia's rich history. Wormsloe in Savannah features an avenue sheltered by live oak trees leading to the ruins of Wormsloe, a colonial estate and the oldest standing structure in Savannah. Along the marsh, trails lead visitors to the Colonial Life Area which hosts events and exhibits of Georgia's colonial era.

Georgia Department of Natural Resources
State Parks & Historic Sites
www.gastateparks.org
(800) 864-7275

Georgia Tourism & Travel
www.exploregeorgia.org
(800) 847-4842

The Georgia Power Company operates several parks on large lakes making them the biggest non-government entity to offer recreational facilities in the state. The North Georgia section alone has 6 lakes providing a variety of outdoor activites and camping.

Georgia Power
www.georgiapowerlakes.com/

The US Forest Service manages the Chattahoochee and Oconee National Forests. These forests make up more than 867,000 acres of land and includes the southern terminus of the 2,180 mile long Appalachian National Scenic Trail at Spring Mountain.

Outdoor enthusiasts enjoy everything from OHV riding, hiking, and bicycling to camping, hunting and boating.

USDA Forest Service
www.fs.usda.gov/conf
(770) 297-3000

The National Park Service administers several properties in Georgia. Cumberland Island National Seashore is a 17 mile long land mass and is one of the largest of Georgia's Golden Isles. A major attraction for hiking around the coastline and has a wide variety of flora and fauna for the wildlife enthusiasts.

National Park Service
www.nps.gov/state/ga/index.htm
(404) 507-5600

The US Fish & Wildlife Service protects diverse flora and fauna throughout the state. The Okefenokee National Wildlife Refuge trails offer visitors a chance for spectacular wildlife viewing.

National Wildlife Refuges, US Fish & Wildlife Service
www.fws.gov/refuges
(800) 344 WILD (9453)

CAMPGROUNDS

Campgrounds with a variety of different facilities are located on state, federal and private lands. The public campground symbol, as shown in the legend (see inside front cover), identifies campgrounds within and surrounding national and state forests and parks. For information on fees, services and reservations at public campgrounds, contact one of the agencies listed above.

The Gazetteer also lists information on a selection of privately owned and operated campgrounds. To locate the gazetteer selections, look on the appropriate map for the purple campground symbol and corresponding four-digit number.

TRAVEL

The Georgia Department Transportation (GDOT) supplies information for all forms of travel within the State. The GDOT website links residents and travelers to current road conditions due to traffic, weather and construction. Commute Options are available as well as information for optional toll lanes, known as Georgia Express Lanes, for those seeking faster alternative ways to drive through the most congested corridors around metro Atlanta. Links and maps for those looking to bike and walk can also be found at the link below.

Georgia Department of Transportation
www.dot.ga.gov/
(404) 631-1990

Driving Conditions
511ga.org/

STATE FACTS

Admitted to Union: January 2nd, 1788; 4th state
Capital: Atlanta
Size: 59,425 square miles
Population: 11,029,227 (2023 Estimate)
Nickname: Peach State
Motto: *Wisdom, Justice and Moderation*
Song: "Georgia on My Mind"
Bird: Brown Thrasher
Animal: White-tailed deer
Bird: Peach
Butterfly: Eastern Tiger Swallowtail
Insect: Honeybee
Marine Mammal: Right Whale
Flower: Cherokee Rose
Tree: Live Oak
Gemstone: Quartz
Reptile: Gopher tortoise
Fossil: Shark Tooth
Dance: Square Dance
Name for Residents: Georgian
Major Industries: Agriculture, Energy, Automotive.

Highest Point:
Brasstown Bald..............................4,784 feet
Lowest Point:
Atlantic Coast ....Sea level
Major Cities (with population):
Atlanta 499,127
Savannah 148,004
Athens 128,561
Sandy Springs 107,763
Roswell 92,950
Major Rivers:
Chattahoochee River..................430 miles
Ogeechee River ....294 miles
Coosa River..................................280 miles
Tallapoosa River..........................265 miles
Major Lakes:
J Storm Thurmond Lake..........71,100 acres
Lake Hartwell ....56,000 acres
Walter F. George Lake.............45,000 acres
Lake Lanier ....38,000 acres
Richard B. Russell Lake...........26,650 acres

FISHING AND HUNTING

Georgia has an abundance of fishing and hunting opportunities throughout the state. The Gazetteer features a selection of freshwater fishing locations. To locate the gazetteer selections, look on the appropriate map for the purple fishing symbol and corresponding four-digit number. It is important to be familiar with local rules, regulations and restrictions before fishing and hunting in any area.

The Georgia Department of Natural Resources provides information on all regulations and licensing requirements.

Georgia Department of Natural Resources
www.georgiawildlife.com/
(706) 557-3333

Recreation Areas

NAME, LOCATION	PAGE & GRID	ACREAGE	AGENCY	VISITOR CENTER	CAMPING	CABINS/YURTS	SWIMMING	BOATING	HUNTING	FISHING	PICNICKING	HIKING	BIKING	HORSEBACK RIDING	DISC GOLF
Allatoona Lake Project, Cartersville	19 C9	12,010	USACE	•	•		•	•	•	•	•	•			
Amicalola Falls State Park & Lodge, Dawsonville	14 D4	829	GDNR	•	•	•					•	•			
Banks Lake National Wildlife Refuge, Lakeland	62 D1	3,559	USFWS					•	•						
Black Rock Mountain State Park, Mountain City	16 A3	1,743	GDNR	•	•	•					•	•			
Blackbeard Island National Wildlife Refuge, Sapelo Island	65 A10	5,618	USFWS						•	•		•			
Brasstown Wilderness, Chattahoochee National Forest	15 A9	12,853	USFS									•			
Carters Lake Project, Chatsworth	13 D10	8,900	USACE	•	•		•	•	•	•	•	•	•		
Chattahoochee Bend State Park, Newnan	25 D7	2,910	GDNR		•			•		•	•	•	•		
Chattahoochee National Forest, Blairsville	15 B7	751,070	USFS	•	•	•	•	•	•	•	•	•	•	•	
Chattahoochee River National Recreation Area, Atlanta	20 D3	48 miles	NPS	•				•		•	•	•	•	•	
Chattooga National Wild & Scenic River, Chattahoochee National Forest	16 B4	50	USFS					•		•		•			
Chehaw Park, Albany	50 D5	700	CPA	•	•						•	•	•		
Cloudland Canyon State Park, Rising Fawn	12 B2	3,538	GDNR	•	•	•					•	•	•		
Cohutta Wilderness, Chattahoochee National Forest	13 B10	37,033	USFS						•			•			
Crooked River State Park, St Mary's	72 D3	500	GDNR		•	•					•	•	•		
Cumberland Island National Seashore, St Mary's	72 E4	36,415	NPS	•	•						•	•			
Don Carter State Park, Gainesville	21 A9	1,316	GDNR		•	•	•	•		•	•	•	•		
Elijah Clark State Park, Lincolnton	31 B10	447	GDNR		•	•	•	•		•	•	•			
Ellicott Rock Wilderness, Chattahoochee National Forest	16 A5	8,300	USFS									•			
FD Roosevelt State Park, Pine Mountain	33 D9	9,049	GDNR	•	•	•	•	•		•	•	•	•	•	
Florence Marina State Park, Omaha	40 E1	173	GDNR		•	•		•		•	•	•			
Fort Mountain State Park, Chatsworth	13 C10	3,712	GDNR		•	•	•	•		•	•	•	•	•	
Fort Yargo State Park, Winder	21 D9	1,816	GDNR		•	•	•	•		•	•	•	•		•
General Coffee State Park, Douglas	53 E9	1,511	GDNR		•	•					•	•	•	•	
George L Smith State Park, Twin City	45 B10	1,634	GDNR		•	•		•		•	•	•	•		
George T Bagby State Park & Lodge, Fort Gaines	49 D6	700	GDNR		•	•	•	•		•	•	•			
Georgia Veterans State Park, Cordele	51 B8	1,308	GDNR	•	•	•	•	•		•	•	•	•		
Goat Rock Lake, Columbus	40 A1	940	GPC					•		•	•				
Gordonia–Alatamaha State Park, Reidsville	45 E10	662	GDNR		•	•		•		•	•	•			
Gray's Reef National Marine Sanctuary, Meridian	65 B10	14,080	NOAA					•		•					
Hamburg State Park, Mitchell	37 A9	741	GDNR		•			•		•	•	•			
Hard Labor Creek State Park, Rutledge	28 B1	5,804	GDNR		•	•	•	•		•	•	•	•	•	
Harris Neck National Wildlife Refuge, Townsend	56 D4	2,762	USFWS	•						•		•			
Hart State Park, Hartwell	23 A8	147	GDNR		•		•	•		•	•	•			
Hartwell Lake Project, Hartwell	23 A8	76,450	USACE	•	•		•	•	•	•	•	•			
High Falls State Park, Jackson	35 A6	1,050	GDNR		•	•	•	•		•	•	•			
Indian Springs State Park, Flovilla	35 A7	528	GDNR	•	•	•	•	•		•	•	•			
J Strom Thurmond Lake Project, Appling	30 B5	150,000	USACE	•	•		•	•	•	•	•	•			
James H "Sloppy" Floyd State Park, Summerville	12 E3	561	GDNR		•			•		•	•	•			
Lake Burton, Clayton	16 B1	2,775	GPC		•			•		•	•				
Lake Harding, Antioch	40 A1	5,850	GPC		•			•		•					
Lake Jackson, Monticello	27 E8	4,750	GPC					•		•	•	•			
Lake Juliette, Juliette	35 B9	3,600	GPC					•		•	•	•			
Lake Oconee, Sparta	28 E5	19,071	GPC		•		•	•		•	•	•			
Lake Rabun, Tallulah Falls	16 C2	835	GPC		•		•	•		•	•				
Lake Seed, Tallulah Falls	16 C2	240	GPC					•		•					
Lake Sidney Lanier Project, Buford	21 C6	57,211	USACE	•	•		•	•	•	•	•	•			
Lake Sinclair, Milledgeville	36 A5	15,330	GPC		•		•	•		•	•	•			
Lake Tugalo, Tallulah Falls	16 C3	597	GPC					•		•					
Lake Yonah, Tallulah Falls	16 C3	325	GPC					•		•					
Laura S Walker State Park, Waycross	63 D10	626	GDNR		•		•	•		•	•	•			•
Little Ocmulgee State Park & Lodge, Helena	44 E3	1,360	GDNR		•	•	•	•		•	•	•			
Magnolia Springs State Park, Perkins	39 D7	1,070	GDNR		•	•	•	•		•	•	•			
Mistletoe State Park, Appling	30 B3	1,920	GDNR		•	•	•	•		•	•	•	•		
Moccasin Creek State Park, Clarkesville	16 B1	32	GDNR		•			•		•	•	•			
Oconee National Forest, Eatonton	28 D3	116,156	USFS		•		•	•	•	•	•	•	•	•	
Okefenokee National Wildlife Refuge, Folkston	71 B10	353,981	USFWS	•				•		•	•	•			
Panola Mountain State Park, Stockbridge	26 B5	1,635	GDNR	•							•	•	•		•
Piedmont National Wildlife Refuge, Hillsboro	35 B10	35,000	USFWS	•					•	•		•			
Providence Canyon State Park, Lumpkin	49 A8	1,003	GDNR	•	•						•	•			
Raven Cliffs Wilderness, Chattahoochee National Forest	15 C8	9,240	USFS									•			
Red Top Mountain State Park, Acworth	19 C9	1,776	GDNR		•	•	•	•		•	•	•	•		
Reed Bingham State Park, Adel	61 C6	1,613	GDNR		•		•	•		•	•	•			
Rich Mountain Wilderness, Chattahoochee National Forest	14 C3	10,790	USFS									•	•		
Richard B Russell Lake Project, Elberton	31 B8	53,672	USACE	•	•		•	•	•	•	•	•			
Richard B Russell State Park Elberton	23 C9	2,508	GDNR		•	•	•	•		•	•	•	•		•
Sapelo Island National Estuarine Research Reserve, Sapelo Island	65 A9	7,500	NOAA	•						•		•			
Savannah National Wildlife Refuge, Savannah	47 E10	29,175	USFWS	•				•	•	•		•			
Seminole Lake Project, Bainbridge	66 B3	37,500	USACE	•	•		•	•	•	•	•	•			
Seminole State Park, Donalsonville	66 A3	604	GDNR		•	•	•	•		•	•	•	•		
Skidaway Island State Park, Savannah	57 B6	588	GDNR		•						•	•	•		
Smithgall Woods State Park, Helen	15 C9	5,664	GDNR	•		•			•	•	•	•	•	•	
Southern Nantahala Wilderness, Chattahoochee National Forest	16 A1	23,365	USFS									•			
Stephen C Foster State Park, Edith	71 A8	80	GDNR		•	•		•		•	•	•			
Sweetwater Creek State Park, Lithia Springs	25 A10	2,549	GDNR	•				•		•	•	•			•
Tallulah Falls Lake, Tallulah Falls	16 C3	63	GPC					•		•					
Tallulah Gorge State Park, Tallulah Falls	16 C3	2,739	GDNR	•	•		•	•		•	•	•	•		
Tray Mountain Wilderness, Chattahoochee National Forest	15 B10	10,343	USFS						•			•	•		
Tugaloo State Park, Lavonia	17 E6	393	GDNR		•	•	•	•		•	•	•			
Unicoi State Park & Lodge, Helen	15 C9	1,050	GDNR		•	•	•	•		•	•	•	•		
Victoria Bryant State Park, Royston	22 B5	502	GDNR		•		•				•	•			
Vogel State Park, Blairsville	15 C7	233	GDNR		•	•	•	•		•	•	•			
Walter F George Lake Project, Fort Gaines	49 D6	45,181	USACE	•	•		•	•	•	•	•	•			
Wassaw National Wildlife Refuge, Savannah	57 B7	10,050	USFWS	•											
Watson Mill Bridge State Park, Comer	23 D6	1,118	GDNR		•						•	•	•	•	
West Point Lake Project, LaGrange	32 C5	25,900	USACE	•	•		•	•	•	•	•	•			

Unique Natural Features

ANNA RUBY FALLS – Chattahoochee National Forest – 15 C10 Waterfalls from Curtis and York creeks converge to create dramatic twin falls through scenic gorge. Curtis Creek falls, higher of the two, drops 154 feet.

BIG HAMMOCK NATURAL AREA – Big Hammock WMA – 55 B6 Varied ecosystem features broadleaf evergreen hammock forest on the site of Pleistocene-epoch sand ridge. Many endangered plant and animal species thrive here, including Georgia plume, a threatened flowering shrub.

BRASSTOWN BALD – Chattahoochee National Forest – 15 B9 Highest peak in state at 4,784 feet. 360-degree observation deck at summit visitor center. Cloud cover keeps forested mountain climate moist and able to support hardwood pine usually found far north of area. Picnic areas and history museum.

CUMBERLAND ISLAND NATIONAL SEASHORE – Cumberland Island National Seashore – 72 D4 Georgia's largest and southernmost barrier island comprised of saltwater marshes, maritime forest and beaches. Settlement ruins from late 1700s and Plum Orchard Mansion. Foot traffic only.

DESOTO FALLS – Chattahoochee National Forest – 15 C7 Series of clear streams and cascades add to the picturesque beauty of Blood Mountain, highest peak on Georgia section of Appalachian National Scenic Trail.

LEWIS ISLAND TRACT – Altamaha WMA – 65 A6 Series of island swamps interspersed with winding creeks border the north bank of Altamaha River. Part of extensive bottomland hardwood swamp. Contains some of the largest remaining virgin bald cypress in state.

OKEFENOKEE SWAMP – Okefenokee National Wildlife Refuge – 71 B9 One of the largest and most primitive swamps remaining in the country. Extremely diverse ecosystem supports endangered plant, mammal and reptile species, including American alligator and native flora and fauna.

PANOLA MOUNTAIN 946 FT – Panola Mountain State Park – 26 B5 One of the least disturbed monadnocks of exposed granite rock in Piedmont region of southeastern US. Rises 220 feet above surroundings. Mixed forest, granite outcrops and soil-filled depressions.

PIGEON MOUNTAIN 2,330 FT – Crockford–Pigeon Mountain WMA – 12 C3 Mountain characterized by bright blue springs, unusual sand formations and hardwood forest. Base of mountain features entrance to one of the deepest caves in world at 1,062 feet deep.

RADIUM SPRINGS – Albany – 50 E5 Largest natural spring in state remains 68 degrees Fahrenheit year-round with water flow of 70,000 gallons per minute.

TALLULAH GORGE – Chattahoochee National Forest – 16 C3 2-mile-long, 1,000-foot-deep quartzite rock gorge carved by Tallulah River. Longest of three falls drops 700 feet to canyon floor. State park features hikes into gorge and scenic overlooks.

TOCCOA FALLS – Chattahoochee National Forest – 16 D3 Spectacular scenery characterizes 186-foot-high waterfall. 19 feet higher than Niagara Falls. Located on campus of Toccoa Falls College.

WASSAW ISLAND – Wassaw National Wildlife Refuge – 57 B7 Excellent example of untouched sea island ecosystem, where natural processes of progression, erosion and deposition remain primitive. Forest, sand dunes and salt marsh. Bird-watching.

Family Outings

AH STEPHENS STATE PARK – Crawfordville – 29 C8 Memorial to former Confederate vice president, US congressman and Georgia governor. Fully renovated and period furnished 1875 Liberty Hall. Confederate Museum houses collection of Civil War artifacts.

ALTAHAMA SCENIC BYWAY – Darien – 65 B7 Driving tour on SR 99 features Fort King George, Hofwyl-Broadfield Plantation, tabby warehouse ruins in Darien and St Cyprian's Episcopal Church, built in 1876 by former slaves. 17 miles.

ANDERSONVILLE CIVIL WAR VILLAGE – Andersonville – 41 E10 Restored Civil War village once point of disembarkation for prisoners on their way to Confederate prison.

ANDERSONVILLE NATIONAL HISTORIC SITE – Andersonville – 41 E10 Civil War's largest prisoner of war camp is the only site to memorialize all American prisoners of war. Civil War Museum and National POW Museum. Driving tour. Adjacent Andersonville National Cemetery.

ARCHIBALD SMITH PLANTATION HOME – Roswell – 20 D3 Life on mid-19th-century cotton plantation interpreted by costumed guides. Plantation home, barn, spring house, carriage house, greenhouse and slave cabin contain some original furnishings and artifacts.

ATLANTA HISTORY CENTER – Atlanta – 20 E3 Grounds encompass gardens, woodlands, 19th-century farmhouse and slave cabin, and museum. Cyclorama features *The Battle of Atlanta*, the world's largest painting. Steam engine *Texas*. Exhibits include extensive Civil War, African-American and Southern folklife artifacts. Traces history of Atlanta.

ATLANTA MOTOR SPEEDWAY – Hampton – 26 D4 Quad-oval track hosts NASCAR Cup races, Friday night drag races and more.

AUGUSTA CANAL NATIONAL HERITAGE AREA – Augusta – 31 D7 Interpretive Center features exhibits that relate history of the city of Augusta, the Savannah River and the Augusta Canal. Guided boat tours, Kayaking, Canoeing, Hiking and biking.

BABYLAND GENERAL HOSPITAL – Cleveland – 15 D9 Birthplace of Xavier Roberts' Cabbage Patch Kids doll phenomenon. Uniformed "doctors" and "nurses" work delivery room, day care center and cabbage patch, where hundreds of dolls await adoption.

BLUE & GRAY MUSEUM – Fitzgerald – 52 D4 Extensive collection of Civil War memorabilia includes Union and Confederate uniforms, newspaper articles and other artifacts. Chronicles town's rich Civil War history.

CALLAWAY PLANTATION – Washington – 29 A9 Working plantation features dwellings dating to 1785. Plantation life illustrated at Grand Brick Manor. Complex includes Federal-style house, one-room schoolhouse, barn and smokehouse.

CENTER PARC STADIUM – Atlanta – 26 A3 Baseball stadium built for 1996 Olympic Games served as home field of the Atlanta Braves of the National League, now home to the Georgia State Panthers football team.

CHICKAMAUGA & CHATTANOOGA NATIONAL MILITARY PARK – Ringgold –12 A4 Oldest and largest military park in US commemorates 1863 battles for control of Chattanooga. Chickamauga marks last major Confederate victory in the War Between the States. Weeks later, a northern victory at Chattanooga opened the Union's route to the deep south. Museum features Fuller gun collection. Over 1,400 monuments and historical markers on battlefields.

CHIEF VANN HOUSE STATE HISTORIC SITE – Chatsworth – 13 C8 Federal-style brick mansion, known as the "Showplace of Cherokee Nation," built in 1804 by Chief James Vann. Features cantilevered staircase and Cherokee hand carvings. Site of educational meetings between Cherokee and Moravian missionaries. Guided tours.

CHIEFTAINS MUSEUM/MAJOR RIDGE HOME – Rome – 18 B5 Late-18th-century home of Cherokee leader Major Ridge, best known for signing treaty that led to removal of his people from Georgia. Museum contains dioramas, photographs and tribal artifacts.

DAHLONEGA GOLD MUSEUM STATE HISTORIC SITE – Dahlonega – 15 E7 Town is site of the first US gold rush in 1828. Features exhibits on mining history, gold coins and nuggets, and audiovisual displays. Housed in one of Georgia's oldest standing courthouses built in 1836.

ETOWAH INDIAN MOUNDS STATE HISTORIC SITE – Cartersville – 19 C9 Ceremonial earthen burial mounds of Mississippian culture corn farmers, AD 1000–1500. Largest mound stands 63 feet tall. Museum features artifacts, ceremonial objects and exhibits.

FERNBANK MUSEUM OF NATURAL HISTORY – Atlanta – 26 A3 Interactive exhibits include "A Walk Though Time in Georgia," which uses the state as a microcosm of Earth from 15 billion years ago into the future. IMAX theater.

FIRST AFRICAN BAPTIST CHURCH – Savannah – 57 A6 Oldest African American church in North America founded in 1773. Also site of first African American Sunday School, organized in 1826, and 1940s birthplace of regional Civil Rights Movement. Guided tours. Museum.

FLINT RIVERQUARIUM – Albany – 50 E5 Aquarium focuses on rivers and estuaries of Georgia. Aquarium centers on Blue Hole Spring, a natural spring.

FORT FREDERICA NATIONAL MONUMENT – Saint Simons Island – 65 C8 Most expensive fort in British-ruled colonies built by Georgia founder James Oglethorpe in 1736 to protect against the Spanish. Town burned in 1758. Tabby ruins. Museum features artifacts and video presentation.

FORT KING GEORGE STATE HISTORIC SITE – Darien – 65 B8 Reconstructed four-story cypress blockhouse, barracks and earthen fort originally built in 1721 as the southernmost outpost of the British empire in North America. Also includes ruins and museum with audiovisual presentation.

FORT MCALLISTER STATE PARK – Richmond Hill – 56 B5 Best-preserved earthwork fortification of the Confederacy. Fort rebuffed several attacks from ironclads before falling in 1864 during General William T. Sherman's March to Sea. Museum with Civil War artifacts.

FORT MORRIS STATE HISTORIC SITE – Midway – 56 C4 Earthwork fort built by 200 patriots as protection against the British during the Revolutionary War. Known as Fort Defiance during the War of 1812. Museum features interpretive and military exhibits.

FORT PULASKI NATIONAL MONUMENT– Tybee Island – 57 A7 Built out of 25 million bricks in 1847 to protect Savannah and other ports from sea attack. Taken by cannon attack April 11, 1862, ending the era of masonry fortifications. Guided tours of fortifications. Indoor exhibits on history of the fort.

FORT SCREVEN – Tybee Island – 57 A8 Ruins of 1875 fort guarding the entrance to Savannah River. Battery houses a museum exploring Tybee Island's 400-year history. Island alternatively held by British, Spanish, French, American, Confederate and pirate forces.

GEORGIA AQUARIUM – Atlanta – 26 A3 Aquarium hosts over 100 species of aquatic animals. Features whale sharks, hammerhead sharks and belugas. Polar region exhibit.

GEORGIA MUSEUM OF AGRICULTURE & HISTORIC VILLAGE – Tifton – 61 A6 Living history museum features over 35 restored buildings, including gristmill, drugstore, print shop and farmsteads. Working Steam Locomotive. Costumed interpreters depict life in late-19th-century town.

GEORGIA STATE RAILROAD MUSEUM – Savannah – 57 A6 Former railroad station serves as a museum exploring Georgia's railways. Collection of engines and railcars. Restored operating turntable.

HOFWYL–BROADFIELD PLANTATION STATE HISTORIC SITE – Brunswick – 65 B7 1807 rice plantation was worked by over 350 slaves who continued to work at the same jobs for pay after emancipation. Features dwellings, servant quarters, museum with artifacts and photo exhibits. Audiovisual presentation.

JARRELL PLANTATION STATE HISTORIC SITE – Juliette – 35 B9 Family owned for over 140 years, John Fitz Jarrell built first of 20 buildings in the 1840s. Later additional structures include three-story barn, 1895 dwelling and cotton gin. Original furnishings. Self-guided tours.

JEFFERSON DAVIS MEMORIAL STATE HISTORIC SITE – Fitzgerald – 52 D3 Monument marks spot where Confederate President Jefferson Davis was captured on May 4, 1865, en route to unite rebel troops. Civil War museum.

JIMMY CARTER NATIONAL HISTORIC SITE – Plains – 50 A3 Site encompasses most of tiny Plains, Georgia, birthplace of 39th US president. Boyhood home and former campaign headquarters in Plains Depot. High school attended by Jimmy and Rosalynn Carter is now a museum and visitor center. Guided tours.

JIMMY CARTER PRESIDENTIAL LIBRARY & MUSEUM – Atlanta – 26 A3 Life and administration of 39th US president portrayed through films, videos, interactive exhibits and memorabilia. Replica of White House Oval Office.

KENNESAW MOUNTAIN NATIONAL BATTLEFIELD PARK – Marietta – 20 D1 Site of the Battle of Kennesaw Mountain, which paved the way for the Union siege and burning of Atlanta. Earthworks preserved. Visitor center with video presentation. Guided tours.

KING–TISDELL COTTAGE – Savannah – 57 A6 Restored 1896 Victorian-style home serves as museum of African American culture of Savannah and Sea Islands. Period furnishings. Heritage trail leading from museum features 17 historic sites.

KOLOMOKI MOUNDS STATE PARK – Blakely – 58 A2 Seven burial and ceremonial mounds built by Swift Creek and Weeden Island Kolomoki between 350 and 750AD. Interior of small burial mound visible. Museum interprets life from 5000 B.C. to end of Kolomoki period.

LAPHAM–PATTERSON HOUSE STATE HISTORIC SITE – Thomasville – 68 A2 Built 1884–1885 by shoe merchant C.W. Lapham. Superior craftsmanship features Oriental-style porch, double-flue chimney, walk-through stairway and fish-scale shingles.

LECONTE–WOODMANSTON PLANTATION & BOTANICAL GARDENS – Riceboro – 56 D2 One of state's earliest inland rice plantations, once owned by Dr. Louis LeConte, is now a natural preserve. Once-famous botanical garden re-created with antique plants.

LUCY CRAFT LANEY MUSEUM OF BLACK HISTORY – Augusta – 31 D7 Former home of teacher who founded a school for black children in 1883. Exhibits on life and times of Laney. Period garden.

MARTIN LUTHER KING JR NATIONAL HISTORIC SITE – Atlanta – 26 A3 Site encompasses birthplace and grave site of Civil Rights leader. Ebenezer Baptist Church, where King served as co-pastor from 1960–1968, and King Center for Nonviolent Social Change. Visitor center.

MICHAEL C CARLOS MUSEUM – Atlanta – 26 A3 Art museum hosts diverse art collection, including art from antiquity to the present. Asian, Egyptian, Near Eastern, American and African collections.

MOSAIC, JEKYLL ISLAND MUSEUM – Jekyll Island – 65 D7 Former stable holds exhibits on the island's natural and cultural history. Guided tours of historic district. Jekyll Island served as winter retreat from 1886–1942 for America's wealthiest families. Federal Reserve Act of 1912 drafted at Jekyll Island Club.

MUSEUM OF ARTS & SCIENCES – Macon – 35 D10 Features changing art and science exhibits including Discovery House, a hands-on children's exhibit hall. Planetarium, indoor animal habitat and nature trails on grounds.

MUSEUM OF AVIATION – Warner Robins – 43 A6 51-acre site with four buildings displays aviation memorabilia and over 85 historical aircraft and missiles. Includes Georgia Aviation Hall of Fame. Audiovisual presentation.

MUSEUM OF COASTAL HISTORY – Saint Simons Island – 65 D8 1872 lighthouse keeper's home houses changing exhibits chronicling coastal and island history. Displays include period furnishings and shipbuilding tools. Adjacent lighthouse offers scenic views.

NEW ECHOTA STATE HISTORIC SITE – Calhoun – 13 D8 1825–1838 capital of Cherokee Nation. Treaty signed here in 1835 led to forced expulsion to Indian Territory on the "Trail of Tears." 12 original and reconstructed buildings include Vann's Tavern, home of *Cherokee Phoenix*, the only Native American language newspaper ever printed in US. Museum.

OAK HILL & THE MARTHA BERRY MUSEUM – Rome – 18 B5 Restored white-columned mansion was home to Martha Berry, educator and founder of Berry College. Adjacent to sprawling campus. Chronicles Berry's life through video and artifacts. Gardens.

OCMULGEE MOUNDS NATIONAL HISTORICAL PARK – Macon – 36 D1 Museum traces 12,000-year history of area's Native American heritage, from Ice Age hunters to the Creek. Temple mounds remain from village built A.D. 900–1150 near Ocmulgee River. Wetlands boardwalk.

OLD FORT JACKSON – Savannah – 57 A6 Built in 1808 over 1776 fort by Savannah residents to protect the city during the American Revolution. One of eight pre-1812 forts still standing in the country. History demonstrations.

OWENS–THOMAS HOUSE & SLAVE QUARTERS – Savannah – 57 A6 Regency home built 1816–1819 for wealthy cotton merchant and banker. Fashioned after English villa. Rare antiques and artwork. Formal garden connects to carriage house containing original slave quarters.

PEACH BLOSSOM TRAIL – Jonesboro – 26 C3 Trail begins in Jonesboro, the setting for Margaret Mitchell's classic *Gone with the Wind*. 100-mile route follows US 41 and US 341 south past many pick-your-own peach orchards.

PICKETT'S MILL BATTLEFIELD STATE HISTORIC SITE – Dallas – 19 D9 One of the best preserved Civil War battlefields in the country. Site of May 27, 1864 Confederate victory, one of the most successful in the War Between the States. Earthworks, museum and visitor center. Audiovisual presentation.

RIDGE & VALLEY SCENIC BYWAY – Summerville – 12 E4 51-mile loop tours national forest land, passing Keown Falls Scenic Area, featuring waterfalls and abundant wildlife.

ROAD TO TARA MUSEUM – Jonesboro – 26 C3 One of the country's largest collections of *Gone with the Wind* memorabilia. Exhibits include doll collection, original sketches and costume reproductions. Documentary of film's production.

ROBERT TOOMBS HOUSE STATE HISTORIC SITE – Washington – 29 A9 Restored and furnished home built in 1794 by Confederate secretary of state, who later refused political pardon and lived the remainder of his life here. Audiovisual presentation.

ROOSEVELT'S LITTLE WHITE HOUSE STATE HISTORIC SITE – Warm Springs – 33 D10 Built in 1932 by future US President Franklin Delano Roosevelt as home and retreat for polio treatment. Preserved exactly as it was on April 12, 1945, when Roosevelt died here of stroke. Adjacent museum with personal belongings.

RUSSELL–BRASSTOWN SCENIC BYWAY – Helen – 15 C9 Driving tour highlights spectacular views of Brasstown Bald, Georgia's highest mountain, and Dukes Creek Falls. 40-mile loop through the hills and valleys of the southern Appalachians.

SAVANNAH HISTORIC DISTRICT – Savannah – 57 A6 More than 1,400 restored structures include 1886 Cotton Exchange, 1852 US Customs House and Beach Institute, established circa 1865 by Freedman's Bureau to educate newly freed African-Americans.

SAVANNAH HISTORY MUSEUM – Savannah – 57 A6 Restored train shed on site of 1779 Siege of Savannah. Audiovisual presentation and exhibits trace Savannah's history from 1733 founding to present.

SAVANNAH RIVERBOAT CRUISES – Savannah – 57 A6 Narrated sight-seeing cruises along the Savannah River. Brunch, dinner and moonlight cruises feature live entertainment.

SIX FLAGS OVER GEORGIA – Austell – 26 A1 Popular theme park with more than 40 rides, attractions and shows. Features 12 roller coasters. Hurricane Harbor water park.

STATE BOTANICAL GARDENS OF GEORGIA – Athens – 22 E3 313-acre site comprised of formal and themed gardens and natural settings. Nature trails. Tropical conservatory.

STATE FARM ARENA – Atlanta – 26 A3 Indoor arena provides a home for the Atlanta Hawks of the NBA. Built in 1999.

STONE MOUNTAIN PARK – Stone Mountain – 26 A5 3,200-acre park contains one of world's largest relief sculptures. Discovering Stone Mountain museum. Historic Square and 1872 town. Scenic railroad. Skyride. Laser light show.

TRAVELERS REST STATE HISTORIC SITE – Toccoa – 16 D4 Plantation home built in 1815 by James R. Wyly, later sold to Devereaux Jarrett, also served as stagecoach inn. Highlights include 90-foot-long porch and hand-numbered rafters. Original furnishings. Guided tours.

TUBMAN MUSEUM – Macon – 35 D10 Museum dedicated to the achievements of African-American, African and Caribbean artisans. Art and culture featured in eight galleries. Research library and museum shop.

WILD ADVENTURES – Valdosta – 69 B8 Combination theme park, water park and zoo. Seven roller coasters, amusement rides and kiddie rides. Open and enclosed water slides. Up-close animal encounters.

WILD ANIMAL SAFARI – Pine Mountain – 33 C7 Drive through park with free-roaming animals. Rhinos, zebras and giraffes from Africa and American bison. Walk-about features traditional exhibits.

WORLD OF COCA-COLA – Atlanta – 26 A3 Museum chronicles history of the popular soft drink from its first appearance in an Atlanta drugstore in 1886 to the present-day worldwide phenomenon. Expansive collection of memorabilia includes 1930s soda fountain. Working bottling line. Product testing. 4D theater.

WORMSLOE STATE HISTORIC SITE – Savannah – 57 A6 Live oak-lined avenue leads to estate built by Nobel Jones, one of Georgia's original settlers. Museum exhibits local artifacts. Living history demonstrations.

WRENS NEST – Atlanta – 26 A2 Victorian-era home of author Joel Chandler Harris (1848–1908), known for writing popular *Uncle Remus* stories around the turn-of-the-20th-century. Period furnishings. Library.

ZOO ATLANTA – Atlanta – 26 A3 Zoological gardens home to over 1,000 animals across 250 species. Features a large collection of Western Lowland Gorillas and a pair of giant pandas.

Fishing

NUMBER, NAME	PAGE & GRID	LARGEMOUTH	SPOTTED	HYBRID STRIPED	STRIPED	WHITE BASS	BLUEGILL	BREAM	CHANNEL CATFISH	CATFISH	CRAPPIE	PERCH	PICKEREL	SUNFISH	TROUT	WALLEYE
2004 Allatoona Lake	19 C10	●	●	●	●		●	●		●	●	●			●	
2008 Altamaha River	55 D8						●	●	●	●	●			●		
2012 Averys Millpond	61 C10	●					●	●			●	●				
2016 Banks Lake	62 E1	●					●	●		●	●	●				
2020 Bartletts Ferry Lake	40 A1	●	●	●		●	●			●	●					
2028 Blalock Reservoir	26 C4	●								●					●	
2032 Blue Ridge Lake	14 B4	●	●				●			●	●				●	●
2036 Boggs Creek	15 C8														●	
2040 Boston Creek	19 B10														●	
2044 Cartecay River	14 C3	●	●												●	
2048 Carters Lake	13 D10	●	●	●	●		●			●	●				●	●
2052 Cedar Grove Lake	25 C10						●			●		●				
2056 Chapman Lake	22 D3						●			●					●	
2060 Charlie Elliot Wildlife Center	27 D9						●			●						
2064 Chattahoochee River	15 C9														●	
2068 Chattahoochee River Tailwaters	21 D6														●	
2072 Chattooga River	16 B4														●	
2076 Chatuge Lake	15 A9	●		●			●			●	●				●	●
2080 Coleman River	16 A1														●	
2084 Conasauga River	14 A1														●	
2088 Cooper Creek	14 C5														●	
2092 Cornish Creek – Newton County Reservoir	27 B9	●			●	●		●	●		●	●				
2096 Dicks Creek	15 C7														●	
2100 Dougherty Creek	12 D2														●	
2104 Eufaula National Wildlife Refuge	49 A6	●		●	●		●			●						
2108 Fightingtown Creek	14 A2														●	
2112 Fort Stewart Ponds	55 B10	●					●			●	●	●				
2116 Fort Yargo State Park	21 D9	●					●			●	●					
2120 Furnace Creek	13 D6														●	
2124 George L Smith State Park	46 A1	●					●	●		●	●					
2128 George W Andrews Lake	58 A1	●		●			●	●		●	●					
2132 Griffin Lake	47 C7						●	●			●					
2136 Hamburg State Park	37 A9	●					●			●	●					
2140 Hard Labor Creek State Park Lakes	28 B1	●					●			●	●					
2144 Hartwell Lake	17 E7	●	●	●	●		●			●	●					
2148 Heads Creek Reservoir	26 E3	●				●				●	●					
2152 High Falls State Park	35 A6	●					●	●		●	●					
2156 Holly Creek	13 B10														●	
2160 Hoods Creek	16 A4														●	
2164 J Strom Thurmond Lake	30 B3	●	●	●	●		●			●	●					
2168 Jacks River	14 A1														●	
2172 Johns Creek	13 E6														●	
2176 Jones Creek	14 D5														●	
2180 JW Smith Reservoir	26 D3						●	●			●					
2184 Keas Old Millpond	45 B6						●									
2188 Lake Blackshear	51 B7	●		●			●	●		●	●					
2192 Lake Burton	16 B1	●	●			●	●				●				●	●
2196 Lake Carroll	25 C6						●			●						
2200 Lake Chehaw	50 E5	●					●	●		●	●					
2204 Lake Jackson	27 E8	●	●	●			●	●		●	●					
2208 Lake Juliette	35 B9	●	●				●				●	●				
2212 Lake Lindsay Grace	55 E6	●					●	●			●					
2216 Lake Mayers	54 C2	●					●			●	●					
2220 Lake Meriwether	34 C1	●					●			●	●					
2224 Lake Oconee	28 D5	●	●	●			●	●		●	●					
2228 Lake Oliver	40 B2	●	●	●			●			●	●					
2232 Lake Olympia	24 A5						●			●						
2236 Lake Rabun	16 C2	●					●				●				●	
2240 Lake Seed	16 C2	●					●				●				●	
2244 Lake Seminole	66 B3	●	●	●	●		●	●		●	●					
2248 Lake Sidney Lanier	21 B7	●	●	●	●		●			●	●	●			●	●
2252 Lake Sinclair	36 A5	●	●	●			●	●		●	●					
2256 Lake Tobesofkee	35 D9	●		●			●	●		●	●					
2260 Lake Twelve Oaks	26 D3						●			●						
2264 Lake Val-Do-Mar	25 A8	●					●			●						
2268 Lake Weiss	18 C3	●		●		●				●	●					
2272 Laura S Walker State Park Lake	63 D9	●					●			●		●				
2276 Lewis Lake	38 D1	●														
2280 Little Cedar Creek	18 C3															●
2284 Little Chickamauga Creek	12 B5															●
2288 Little Ocmulgee Lake	44 E3	●					●	●		●	●					
2292 Long Swamp Creek	20 A3														●	
2296 Middle Fork Broad River	16 E2	●					●								●	●
2300 Mill Creek	13 B10														●	
2304 Moccasin Creek	16 B1														●	
2308 Mountaintown Creek	14 C1														●	
2312 Nimblewill Creek	14 D5														●	
2316 Noontootla Creek	14 C4														●	
2320 Nottely Lake	15 A6	●	●	●	●		●			●	●	●			●	●
2324 Nottely River	15 B7	●	●				●				●				●	
2328 Ocmulgee River	35 C9	●	●	●			●	●		●	●					
2332 Owltown Creek	14 C2														●	
2336 Panther Creek	16 C2														●	
2340 Paradise Public Fishing Area	61 A8	●					●			●	●					
2344 Piedmont National Wildlife Refuge	35 A9	●					●			●	●					
2348 Pumpkin Pile Creek	18 D4															●
2352 Pumpkinvine Creek	19 E8						●			●						
2356 Queen City Lake	12 C4	●					●									
2360 Raccoon Creek	19 D8															●
2364 Rays Millpond	61 D10	●					●				●	●				
2368 Reed Bingham State Park	61 C6	●					●			●	●	●				
2372 Richard B Russell Lake	23 B9	●	●	●	●		●			●	●	●	●			
2376 Rock Creek	12 A3														●	
2380 Rock Creek	13 B9														●	
2384 Rock Creek	14 B3														●	
2388 Rock Creek	14 C5														●	
2392 Rock Eagle Lake	28 D3	●					●			●	●					
2396 Salacoa Creek Park	13 E9	●					●			●	●					
2400 Sand Hill Lake	45 B6	●														
2404 Sarahs Creek	16 A4														●	
2408 Satilla River	64 C3	●					●			●	●	●				
2412 Smith Creek	15 C9														●	
2416 Soapstone Creek	15 B9														●	
2420 Soquee River	16 C1														●	
2424 Stamp Creek	19 B10									●	●					
2428 Stanley Creek	14 B4														●	
2432 Stone Mountain Park Lakes	26 A5	●					●			●	●					
2436 Suwannee Canal	71 B10						●			●		●				
2440 Suwannee River	71 A8						●			●		●				
2444 Sweetwater Creek	25 A10	●	●				●				●					
2448 Taliaferro Creek	18 A3															●
2452 Tallulah River	16 A1	●					●				●				●	
2456 Tiger Creek	13 A7														●	
2460 Toccoa River	14 B4	●	●							●					●	
2464 Tribble Mill Park	21 E8						●			●	●					
2468 Tugalo Lake	16 C3	●			●		●	●			●				●	
2470 Turniptown Creek	14 C3														●	
2472 Walter F George Lake	49 D6	●		●		●	●	●		●	●					
2476 Warwoman Creek	16 A4														●	
2480 Water Mill Creek	19 E6														●	
2484 Waters Creek	15 C7														●	
2488 West Armuchee Creek	12 D5									●	●					
2492 West Fork Chattanooga River	16 A5														●	
2496 West Point Lake	32 C5	●	●	●		●	●	●		●	●					
2500 Whittakers Lake	66 A3															●
2504 Wildcat Creek	16 B1														●	
2508 Yonah Lake	16 C3	●														

Outdoor Adventures

BIKING

BULL MOUNTAIN TRAIL – *Chattahoochee National Forest – 14 D5* Singletrack loop features numerous elevation changes, climbing and descending rapidly throughout 4.9-mile length. Forest roads provide further mountain biking opportunities.

IRON MOUNTAIN TRAIL – *Chattahoochee National Forest – 13 A10* Moderately difficult singletrack traverses a variety of terrain. 12 mile trail fords the Conasauga River, continues past grassy areas and finishes with a forested ascent. Views of the Cohutta Mountains.

JEKYLL ISLAND TRAILS – *Jekyll Island – 65 D7* 25-mile network of paved and dirt trails tours marshes, beaches and forest of resort island. Picturesque barrier island was developed in the late 1800s by a group of millionaires. Extremely flat.

HIKING

AH STEPHENS STATE PARK TRAILS – *AH Stephens State Park – 29 C8* Diverse ecosystem of bogs, lakes and hardwood forest. 21 miles of equestrian trails also open to hiking; 4 miles of hiking trails. Easy

APPALACHIAN NATIONAL SCENIC TRAIL – *Chattahoochee National Forest – 14 D5* Southern terminus of 2,190-mile wilderness trek. Georgia portion traverses Chattahoochee National Forest in Great Smoky Mountains. Elevation ranges from 2,500–4,500 feet. 76 miles in Georgia.

APPROACH TRAIL – *Chattahoochee National Forest – 14 D4* Rugged trail to Springer Mountain, southern terminus of the Appalachian Trail. Waterfall en route, named Amicalola (tumbling waters) by the Cherokee. 8.1 miles.

ARKAQUAH TRAIL – *Chattahoochee National Forest – 15 B9* Many rhododendron and laurel line path of moderately difficult hike to the ridge crest of Chimneytop Mountain. Remainder of trail to Track Rock Gap quickly drops over 2,000 feet. 5.5 miles. Trailhead at Brasstown Bald parking area.

ASKA TRAILS – *Chattahoochee National Forest–14 B4* 17-mile network of trails in an area of hardwoods, laurel and rhododendron. Steep climbs and descents, with some ascents reaching 3,200 feet. Mountain ridge vistas. Stream crossings. Hiking.

BARTRAM TRAIL – *Chattahoochee National Forest – 16 A4* Follows multi-state route of naturalist/explorer William Bartram. Crosses summit of Rabun Bald, state's second-highest peak; Georgia section ends at Chattooga River. 37 miles in Georgia.

BEAR HAIR GAP TRAIL – *Chattahoochee National Forest – 15 C7* Moderately difficult climb to the top of 3,100-foot-high ridge. Descends to trailhead in a 4-mile loop. Optional side trail to overlook, where a clearing offers view of Lake Trahylta.

BENTON MACKAYE TRAIL – *Chattahoochee National Forest – 14 D5* Moderately difficult trail follows western crest of the Appalachian Mountains from Springer Mountain to Tennessee border. 82-mile route traverses ridgetops and footbridges and country roads.

BCANYON LOOP TRAIL – *Providence Canyon State Park – 49 A8* 2.5-mile trail loops around several scenic canyons, offering vistas of impressive rock faces, dry riverbeds and drop-offs. Additional trails descend into the canyons. Colorful views including rare plumleaf azalea.

DUKES CREEK FALLS TRAIL – *Chattahoochee National Forest – 15 C9* Steep but well-maintained trail leads down three switchbacks to 150-foot-high waterfall. Paved, barrier-free access to midway observation deck. Rest of trail is gravel. 2 mile roundtrip.

GAHUTI TRAIL – *Chattahoochee National Forest – 13 B10* Backcountry trail around crest of Fort Mountain, named for ancient, 855-foot-long stone wall at top. Difficult trail features 8 miles of steep climbs and rapid descents. Sweeping views of Cohutta Wilderness.

HARD LABOR CREEK STATE PARK TRAILS – *Hard Labor Creek State Park – 27 B10* Wooded park offers more than 24 miles of hiking and equestrian riding trails, with portions bordering Lakes Brantley and Rutledge. Easy-Moderate.

HARRIS NECK NATIONAL WILDLIFE REFUGE TRAILS – *Harris Neck National Wildlife Refuge – 56 D4* Trails through woods and on resurfaced roads of WWII airfield runway system. Saltwater marsh and grassland is nesting refuge of herons, egrets and ducks. Easy-Moderate.

KEOWN FALLS TRAIL – *Chattahoochee National Forest – 13 D6* Short trail follows creek to observation deck overlooking seasonal, 50-foot-high Keown Falls. Deck is trailhead for 3.5-mile-long ridge-top hike, Johns Mountain Trail.

LADYSLIPPER TRAIL – *Chattahoochee National Forest – 16 E2* 6.2-mile loop winds up and down rolling hills and through wooded areas. Abundant wildflowers in spring and summer. Several panoramic vistas along trail. Moderate difficulty.

OCMULGEE RIVER TRAIL – *Oconee National Forest – 35 A8* Easy trail follows river through pine forest over 3.8 miles of relatively flat terrain in Oconee National Forest.

OKEFENOKEE NATIONAL WILDLIFE REFUGE TRAILS – *Okefenokee National Wildlife Refuge – 71 B10* Seven short trails of varying lengths and terrain. Highlights varied forest and swamp ecosystems of the refuge. Old Chesser Family Homestead, observation tower views and boardwalk directly over swamp. Abundant wildlife.

PINE MOUNTAIN TRAIL – *FD Roosevelt State Park – 33 D8* 23-mile trail follows long ridge of Pine Mountain past waterfalls, beaver dams, rock outcrops and azaleas. Moderately difficult route features primitive camping and several side trails.

RED COCKADED WOODPECKER TRAIL – *Piedmont National Wildlife Refuge – 35 B10* Trail highlight is nesting site of Red Cockaded Woodpeckers in stand of loblolly pines. Best viewed May-June. Portion of trail follows Allison Creek. Easy.

SANDPIPER NATURE TRAIL – *Skidaway Island State Park – 57 B6* Interpretive hike in park on coastal barrier island surrounded by both salt and fresh water. Marsh habitat. Trail passes Confederate earthwork fortification. Easy.

SMITH CREEK TRAIL – *Chattahoochee National Forest – 15 C9* 5-mile hike of moderate difficulty parallels Smith Creek through a hardwood forest. Ascends and descends Hickorynut Ridge to reach Anna Ruby Falls, twin falls formed by the convergence of Curtis and York creeks. Trailhead at visitor center.

STONEPLACE TRAIL – *Chattahoochee National Forest – 16 C3* 10-mile mountain biking trail on rock and hard dirt surfaces. Additional 5-mile loop possible. Moderately difficult for bikers, hiking also allowed.

TENNESSEE ROCK TRAIL – *Chattahoochee National Forest – 16 A3* Marked trail climbs to the top of Blackrock Mountain at 3,640 feet. 2.2-mile loop encounters wildflowers and lush forests. Relatively easy.

WEST RIM LOOP TRAIL – *Cloudland Canyon State Park – 12 B2* Trail loops around canyon rim in dramatic setting on western edge of Lookout Mountain. Deep gorge carved by Sitton Gulch Creek. Sandstone boulders and waterfalls. 5 miles.

WILLIS KNOB HORSE TRAIL – *Chattahoochee National Forest – 16 A4* Scenic trail in southern Blue Ridge Mountains. Deep ridges end in Chattooga River. 15-mile loop can be broken into smaller segments by using forest roads.

PADDLING

ST MARY'S RIVER – *Saint George – 71 E10* Easy, beginner-level paddle along Florida-Georgia border features the cypress trees common south of Okefenokee Swamp. Put-in at SR 121 bridge. Take-out 60 miles downstream at Scotts Landing, near Boulogne. Several access points. Abundant wildlife.

WITHLACOOCHEE RIVER – *Valdosta – 69 C9* Gentle, slow-moving river for beginning paddlers traverses hardwood forests. Put-in at SR 145 bridge on the Georgia border. Take-out 28 miles downstream at Suwannee River State Park. Several access points.

Campgrounds

NUMBER, NAME, LOCATION	PAGE & GRID	RV SITES	TENTING
4000 3 Creeks Campground, LaGrange	32 B5	43	•
4010 Albany RV Resort, Albany	51 E6	93	
4020 Americus KOA, Americus	51 A6	59	•
4030 Atlanta South RV Resort, McDonough	26 D4	140	
4040 AtlantayMarietta RV Resort, Marietta	20 E2	60	
4050 Battlefield Campground & RV Park, Ringgold	12 A5	145	
4060 Beaver Run RV Park, Metter	46 C2	78	•
4070 Biltmore RV Park, Savannah	56 A5	30	
4095 Cedar Break RV Park & Campground, Calhoun	13 E8	85	
4100 Cedar Creek RV & Outdoor Center, Cave Spring	18 C4	62	•
4105 Commerce Station RV Resort, Commerce	22 B2	70	•
4110 Cordele KOA, Cordele	51 B9	53	•
4120 Country Boys RV Park, Madison	28 C2	109	
4130 CreekFire RV Resort, Savannah	56 A4	206	
4140 Crossroads Travel Park, Perry	42 B4	73	
4150 Devencrest Travel Park, Albany	59 A10	110	
4160 Eagle's Roost RV Resort, Lake Park	69 C10	115	
4170 Fair Harbor RV Park & Campground, Perry	42 B4	280	
4180 Forsyth KOA, Forsyth	35 B7	131	•
4200 Golden Isles RV Park, Brunswick	64 C4	136	•
4210 Holiday Travel Park of Chattanooga, Rossville	12 A5	170	
4220 Jacksonville North/St Marys KOA, Kingsland	72 B5	103	
4230 Jenny's Creek Campground, Cleveland	15 D8	33	
4240 Jones RV Park, Norcross	20 E5	144	
4250 Lake Harmony RV Park, Townsend	56 E2	49	
4260 Lake Oconee/Greensboro KOA, Greensboro	28 C4	144	•
4265 Lake Pines RV Park, Columbus	40 B3	110	
4270 Lakepoint Campground, Acworth	19 D10	100	
4280 Leisure Acres Campground, Cleveland	15 D9	140	
4290 Lookout Mountain/Chattanooga West KOA, Trenton	12 A2	52	•
4300 McIntosh Lake Campground, Townsend	56 E2	37	
4310 Mountain View Campground, Hiawassee	15 A10	28	
4320 Perry Ponderosa Park, Fort Valley	42 B4	60	
4330 Pine Lake RV Campground, Bishop	28 A2	81	
4340 Pine Mountain RV Resort, Pine Mountain	33 D8	168	•
4360 Ramsey RV Park, Warm Springs	33 C10	30	
4370 Red Gate Campground & RV Resort, Savannah	56 A5	24	
4380 River Falls at the Gorge, Lakemont	16 C3	141	•
4390 River's End Campground & RV Park, Tybee Island	57 A8	86	•
4400 Riverside Estates RV Park, Covington	27 B8	172	
4410 Robins Travel Park, Byron	42 A4	30	
4420 Savannah Oaks RV Resort, Savannah	56 A3	113	
4430 Savannah South KOA, Richmond Hill	56 B3	110	•
4440 Scenic Mountain RV Park & Campground, Milledgeville	36 B4	73	
4450 Southern Gates RV Park & Campground, Arabi	51 C9	44	
4460 Southern Trails RV Resort, Unadilla	42 D5	191	
4465 Southern Retreat RV Park, Brunswick	65 D6	166	
4470 Stone Mountain Park Campground, Stone Mountain	26 A5	410	
4480 Sugar Mill RV Park, Ochlocknee	60 E1	121	
4500 Tifton RV Park I-75, Tifton	61 A6	55	
4510 Trackrock Campground & Cabins, Blairsville	15 B8	95	
4520 Turner Campsites, Cleveland	15 C8	129	
4530 Twin Lakes RV Park, Cumming	20 C5	130	
4540 Twin Oaks RV & Camping, Elko	42 C4	64	
4550 Waterway RV Campground, Richmond Hill	56 A4	36	
4560 Yogi Bear's Jellystone Park at Bremen, Bremen	24 B5	88	•

Hunting

Name	Page & Grid	Acreage	Bear	Coyote	Deer	Dove	Feral Hog	Turkey	Waterfowl	Small Game	Alligator	Furbearers
Alapaha River WMA	52 E3	6,870		●	●	●	●	●		●		
Albany Nursery WMA	50 E3	300			●	●		●		●		
Allatoona WMA	19 B10	6,818	●	●	●		●	●		●		●
Alligator Creek WMA	53 B10	3,086		●	●		●	●		●		
Altamaha WMA	65 A6	30,154		●	●	●	●	●	●	●	●	
Arrowhead WMA	12 E5	400	●	●	●			●		●		
Beaverdam WMA	37 E7	5,500		●	●	●	●	●	●	●		●
Berry College WMA	18 A5	15,029	●	●	●		●	●		●		
BF Grant WMA	28 D2	11,400		●	●		●	●		●		●
Big Hammock WMA	55 B6	7,221		●	●		●	●		●	●	
Big Lazer Creek WMA	34 E3	7,200		●	●	●	●	●		●		●
Blackbeard Island National Wildlife Refuge	65 A10	5,618			●		●					
Blanton Creek WMA	33 E6	4,800		●	●	●	●	●		●		●
Blue Ridge WMA	14 C5	20,900	●	●	●			●		●		●
Broad River WMA	23 D10	440		●	●			●		●		
Bullard Creek WMA	54 B2	15,636		●	●		●	●		●	●	●
Cedar Creek WMA	36 A2	40,000		●	●		●	●	●	●		●
Chattahoochee WMA	15 C9	25,150	●	●	●			●		●		●
Chestatee WMA	15 C7	27,123	●	●	●			●		●		
Chickasawhatchee WMA	59 A7	19,700		●	●		●	●	●	●	●	
Clark Hill WMA	30 B1	12,700		●	●		●	●		●		●
Clybel WMA	27 D9	6,400		●	●	●	●	●		●		●
Cohutta WMA	14 B1	96,503	●	●	●			●		●		●
Coopers Creek WMA	15 B6	30,000	●	●	●			●		●		●
Coosawattee–Carter's Lake WMA	13 D10	6,130		●	●		●	●		●		●
Crockford–Pigeon Mountain WMA	12 C3	20,657		●	●		●	●		●		●
Cumberland Island National Seashore	72 D4	9,800			●		●					
Dawson Forest WMA	14 E5	25,500	●	●	●			●		●		●
Di-Lane WMA	39 C6	8,100		●	●	●	●	●	●	●		●
Dixon Memorial WMA	63 D9	35,559	●	●	●		●	●	●	●		
Elbert County WMA	23 D10	2,500		●	●		●	●		●		●
Elmodel WMA	59 B7	1,600		●	●	●	●	●		●		
Eufaula National Wildlife Refuge	49 A6	11,184			●		●	●	●			
Fishing Creek WMA	31 B8	2,900		●	●		●	●		●		●
Flint River WMA	42 E2	2,300		●	●		●	●		●		
Germany Creek WMA	30 C2	1,200		●	●			●		●		●
Grand Bay WMA	61 E10	8,700		●	●		●	●	●	●		
Griffin Ridge WMA	55 D9	5,600		●	●		●	●		●	●	
Hannahatchee Creek WMA	40 E4	5,095		●	●	●	●	●		●		
Harris Neck National Wildlife Refuge	56 D4	2,824			●		●					
Hart County WMA	23 B8	1,000	●	●	●			●		●		●
Horse Creek WMA	53 C8	8,100		●	●		●	●		●		
JL Lester WMA	18 E5	477	●	●	●	●	●	●		●		●
Joe Kurz WMA	34 B1	3,700		●	●	●	●	●		●		●
Johns Mountain WMA	13 D6	24,849	●	●	●		●	●		●		●
Keg Creek WMA	30 B4	800		●	●		●	●		●		●
Lake Russell WMA	16 D3	17,300	●	●	●		●	●		●		
Lake Seminole WMA	66 A4	8,635		●	●		●	●	●	●	●	
Lake Walter F George WMA	48 C5	923		●	●		●	●	●	●		
Little Satilla WMA	64 B1	18,920		●	●		●	●		●		●
Mayhaw WMA	58 C4	6,300		●	●		●	●		●		
McGraw Ford WMA	20 A3	2,255	●	●	●		●	●		●		●
Oaky Woods WMA	43 B6	12,750		●	●		●	●		●		●
Ocmulgee WMA	43 B7	15,000		●	●		●	●	●	●	●	●
Oconee WMA	28 D5	7,400		●	●	●	●	●		●		●
Ohoopee Dunes WMA	45 B7	3,000		●	●			●		●		
Okefenokee NWR	71 B10	353,981		●	●		●	●		●		
Ossabaw Island WMA	56 C5	9,000			●		●	●				
Otting Tract WMA	12 D2	700	●	●	●			●		●		●
Paulding Forest WMA	19 D7	25,707	●	●	●		●	●		●		●
Paulks Pasture WMA	65 B6	16,600		●	●		●	●		●		
Penholoway Swamp WMA	55 E10	10,546		●	●		●	●		●		●
Phinizy Swamp WMA	31 D7	1,500		●	●			●		●		
Piedmont National Wildlife Refuge	35 B10	35,000			●			●		●		
Pine Log WMA	19 B9	14,134	●	●	●		●	●		●		
Redlands WMA	28 B4	37,500		●	●		●	●		●		●
Rich Mountain WMA	14 B3	19,955	●	●	●			●		●		
Richmond Hill WMA	56 C4	7,400		●	●		●	●		●		●
River Bend WMA	44 C4	3,500		●	●	●	●	●		●	●	
River Creek, The Rolf & Alexandra Kauka WMA	68 A1	2,437		●	●		●	●		●		●
Rogers WMA	64 A2	3,500		●	●		●	●		●		
Rum Creek WMA	35 B9	5,884		●	●		●	●		●		●
Sandhills WMA–West	41 A8	2,498		●	●		●	●		●		
Sansavilla WMA	64 A5	16,867		●	●		●	●		●		●
Sapelo Island WMA	65 A9	9,000			●		●	●				
Savannah National Wildlife Refuge	47 E10	31,551		●	●		●	●	●	●		
Sheffield WMA	19 D8	5,342	●	●	●			●		●		●
Silver Lake WMA	66 A5	9,200		●	●		●	●		●		
Soap Creek WMA	30 A2	1,000		●	●			●		●		
Sprewell Bluff WMA	34 D2	1,330		●	●		●	●		●		
Standing Boy Creek WMA	40 A1	1,580		●	●		●	●		●		
Swallow Creek WMA	15 A10	19,000	●	●	●			●		●		
Tallulah Gorge State Park	16 C3	2,689	●		●							
Townsend WMA	55 D10	32,000		●	●		●	●		●		●
Tuckahoe WMA	32 C2	15,100		●	●		●	●	●	●	●	●
Warwoman WMA	16 A3	15,800		●	●			●		●		
Wassaw National Wildlife Refuge	57 B7	10,053			●							
West Point WMA	33 A6	8,952		●	●	●	●	●		●		●
Wilson Shoals WMA	22 A1	2,800	●	●	●		●	●		●		●
Yuchi WMA	39 B9	7,800		●	●		●	●	●	●		●

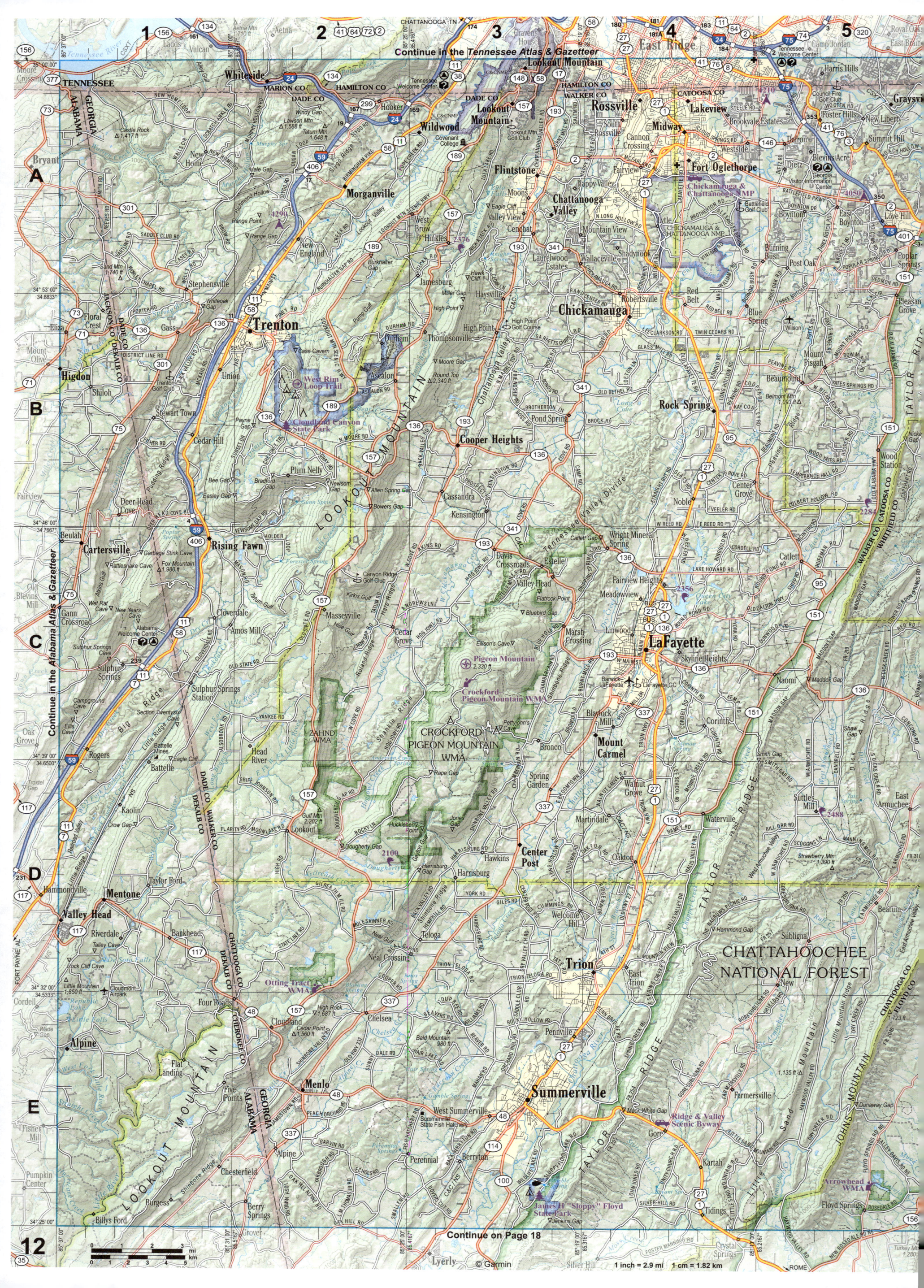

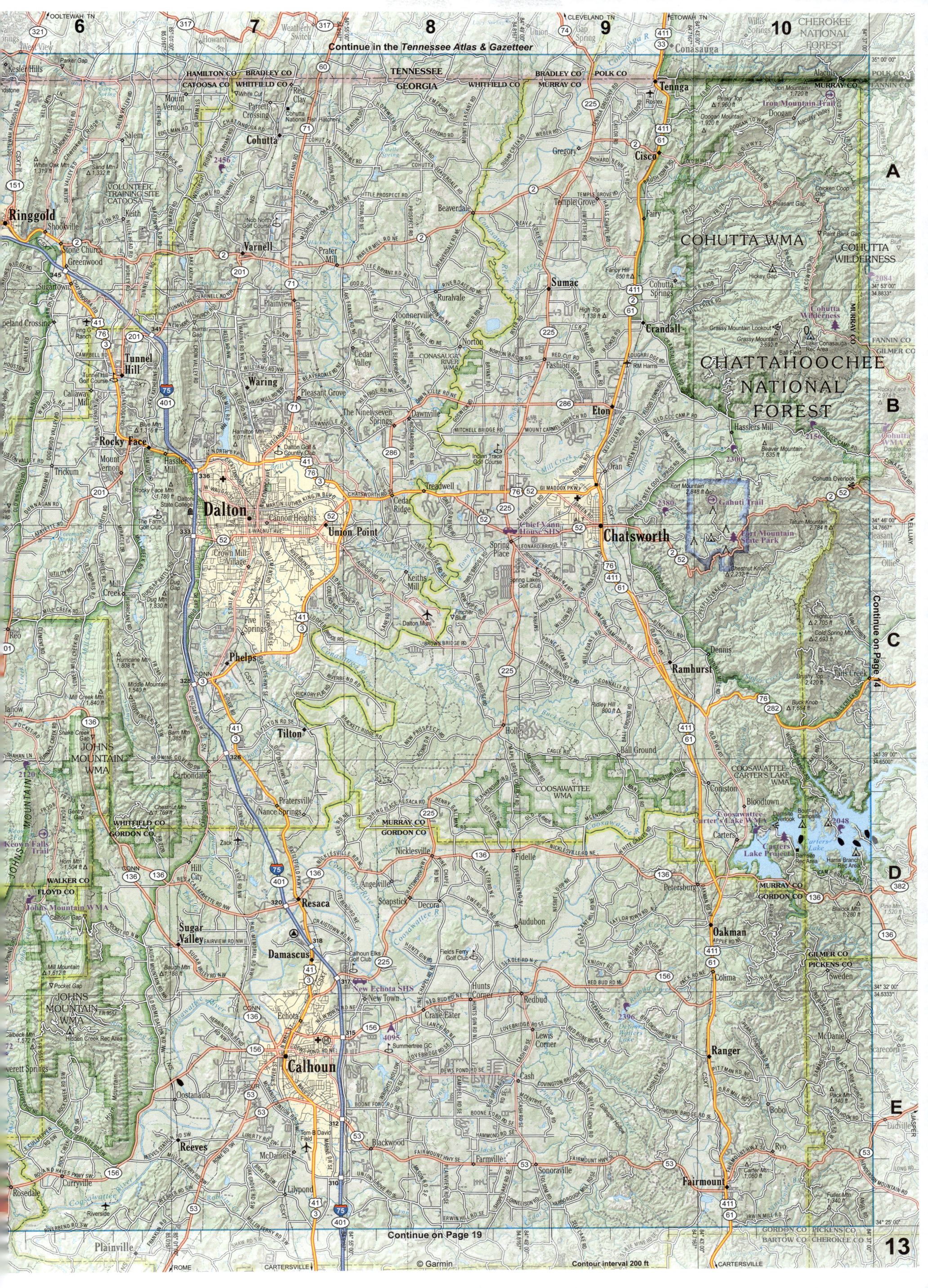

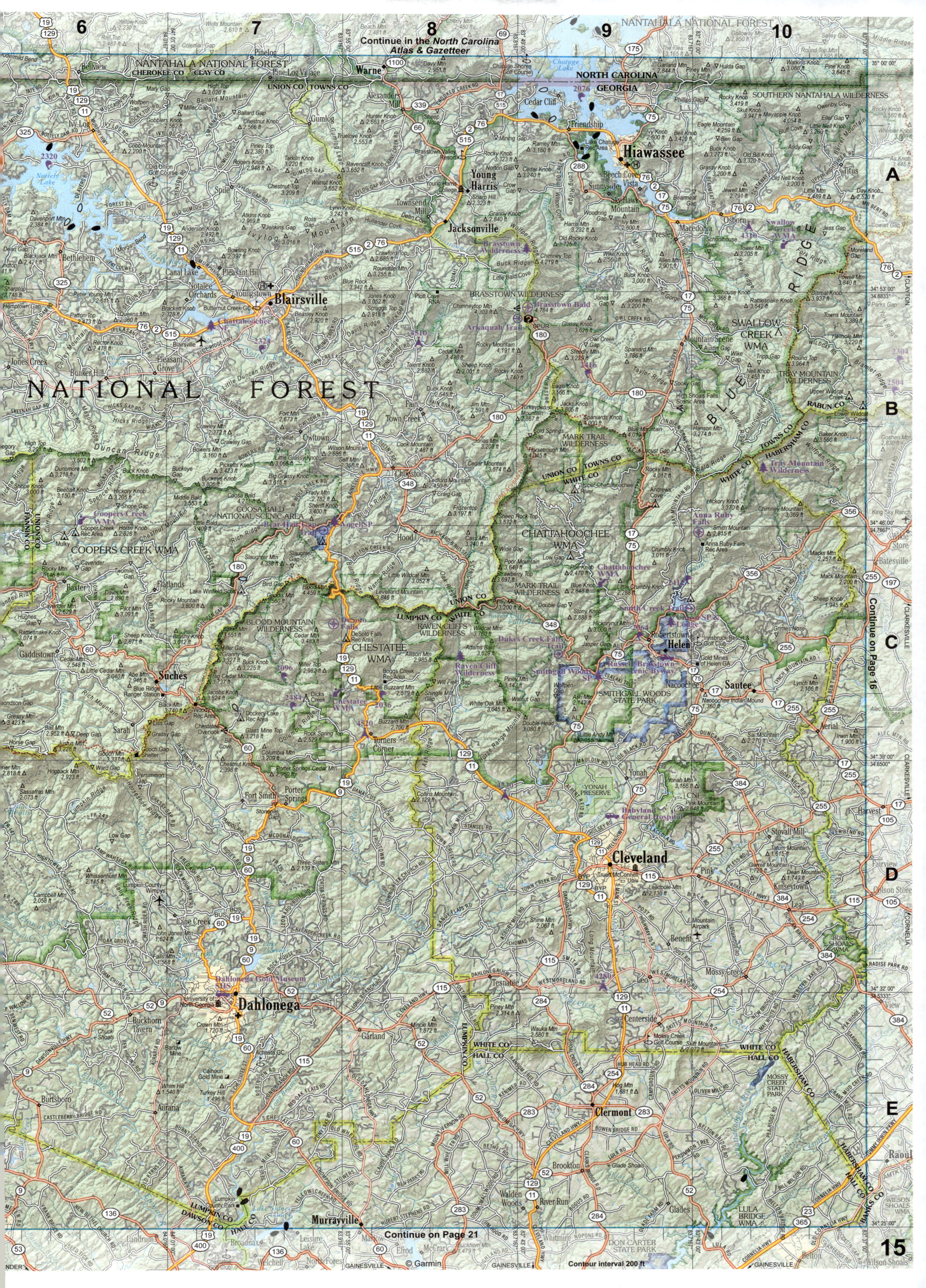

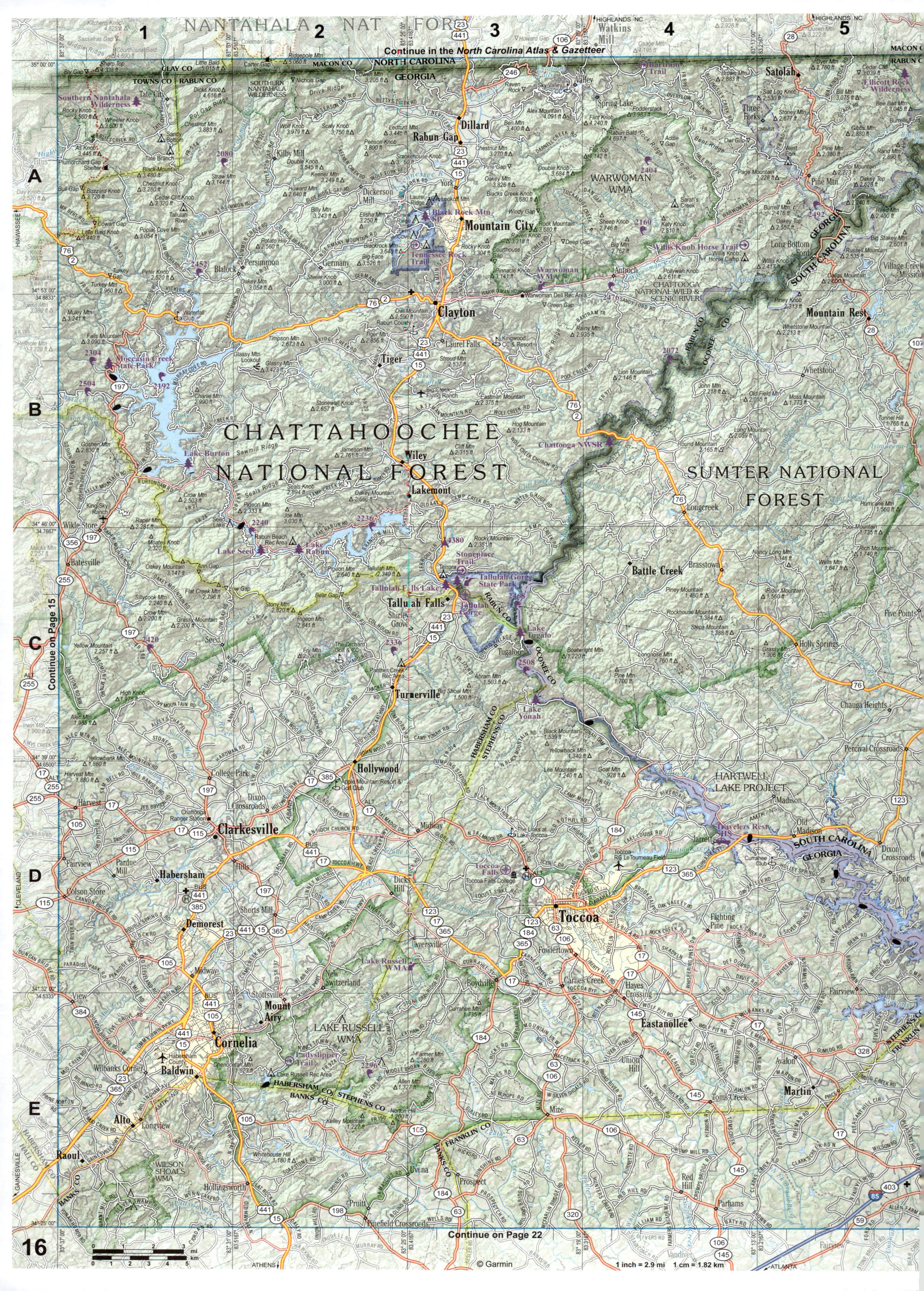

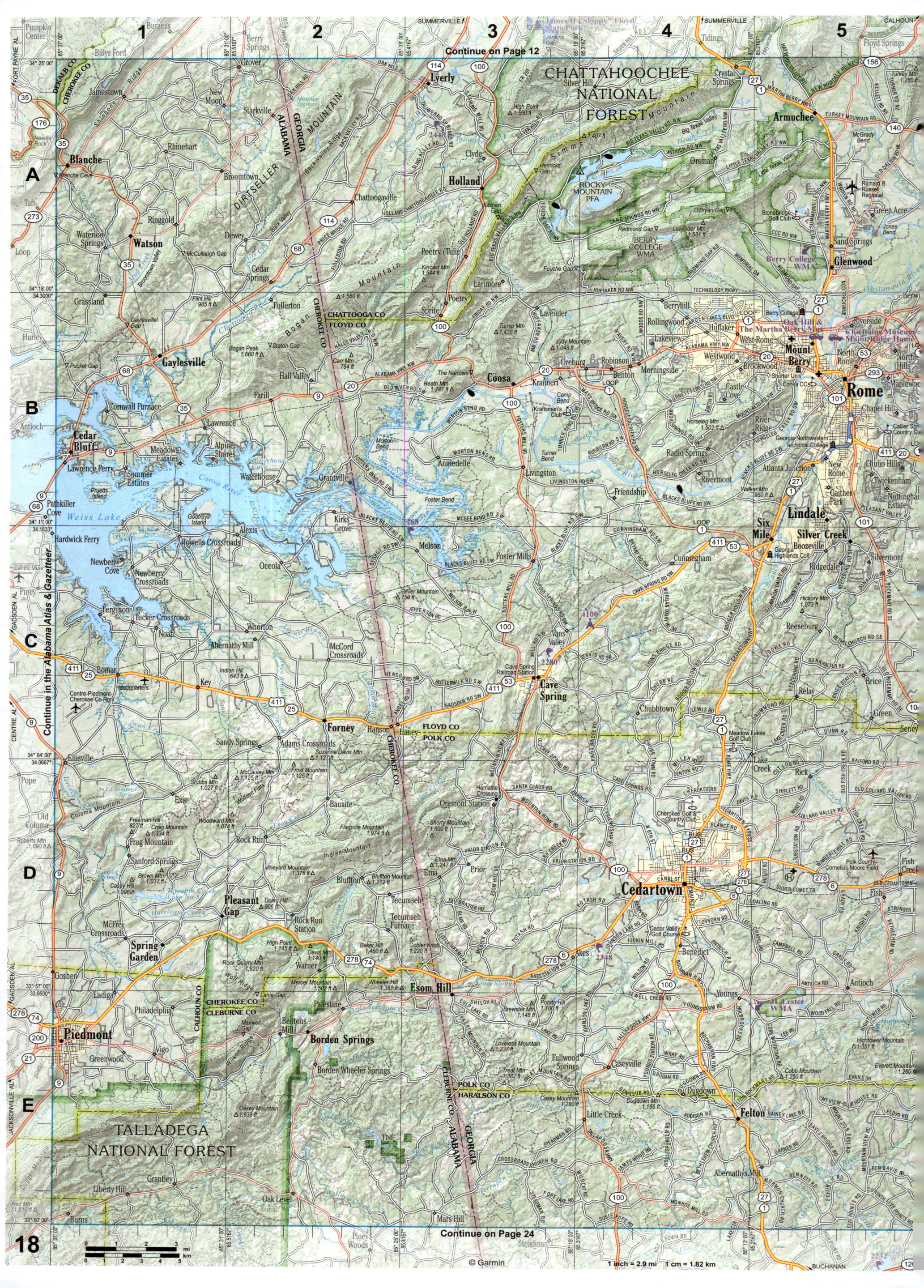

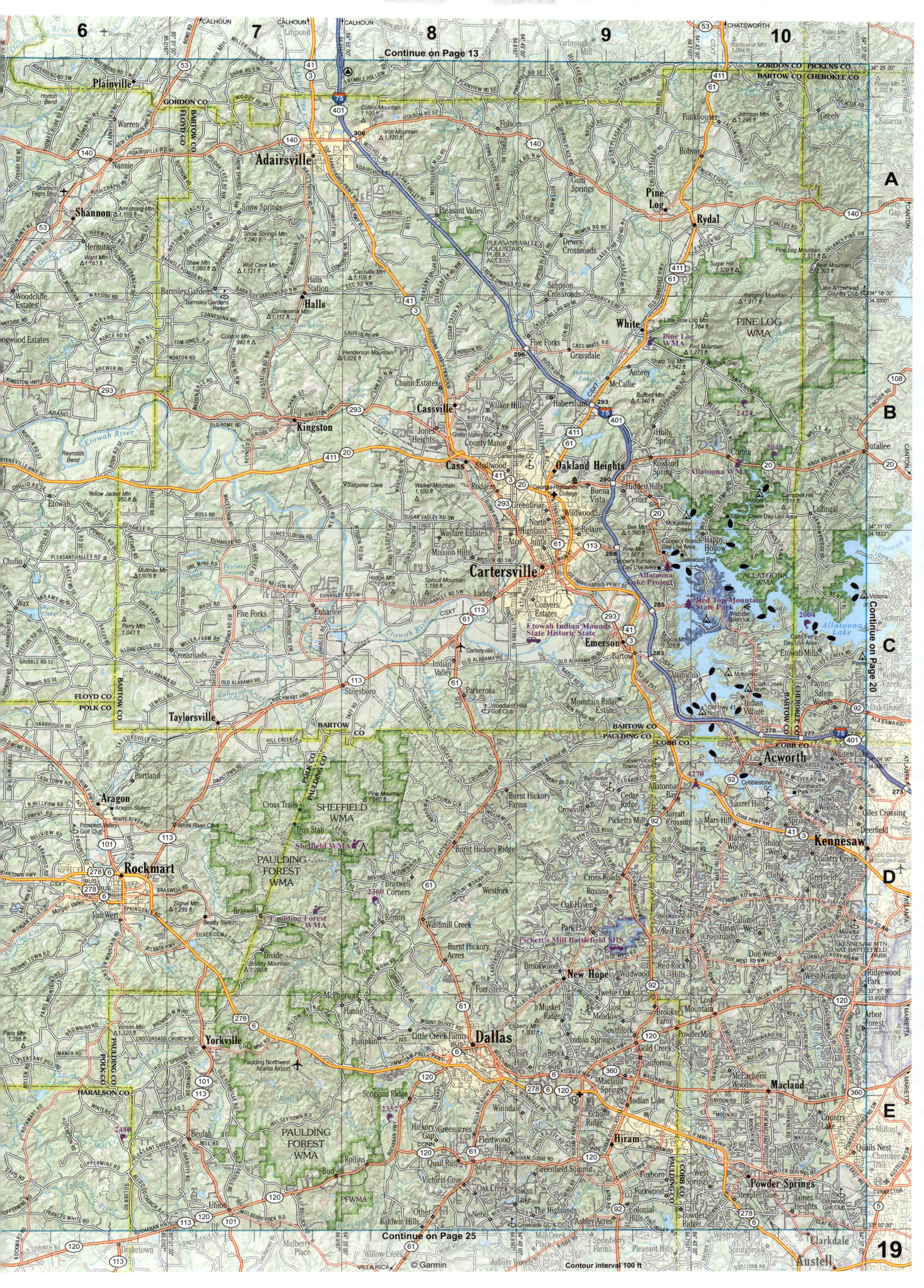

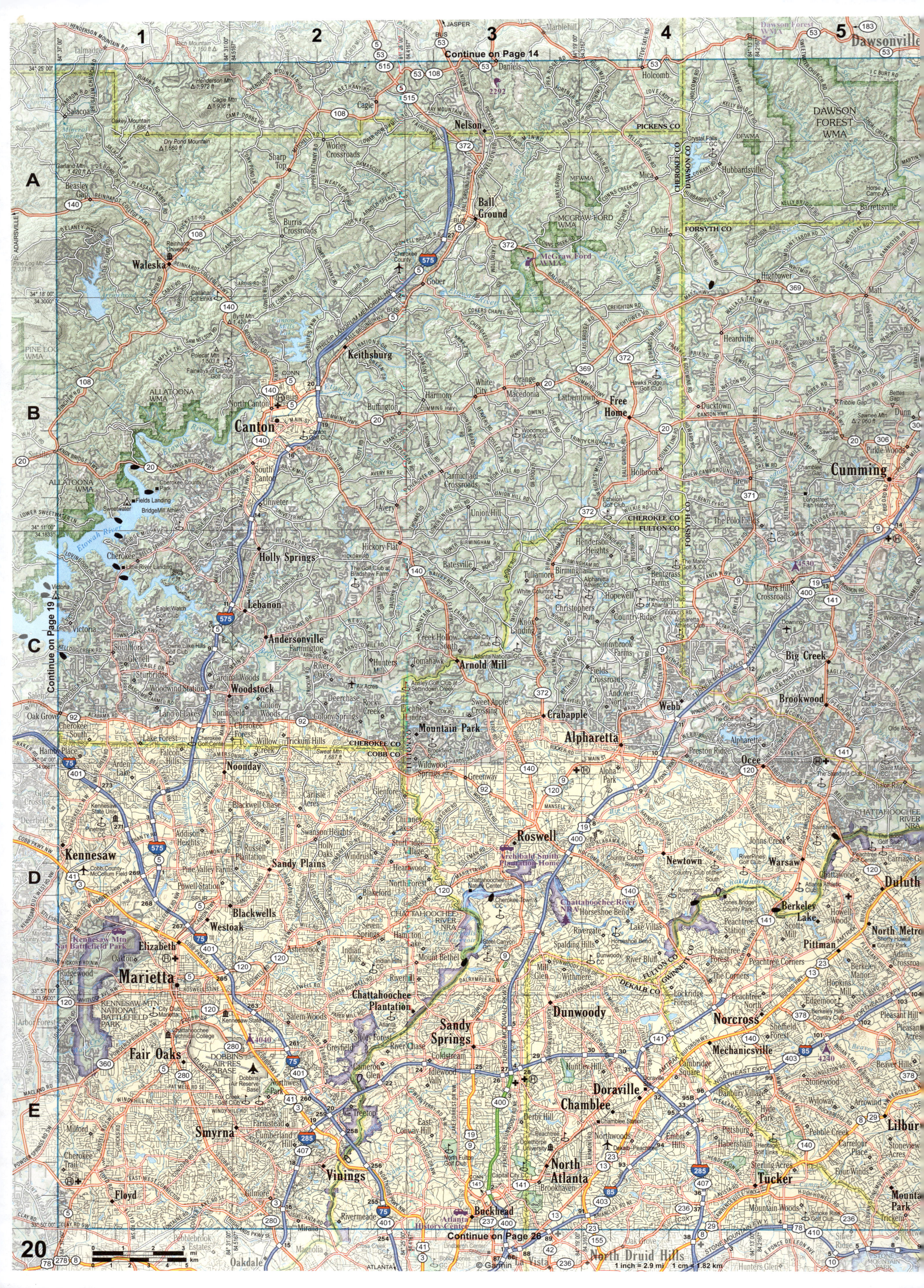

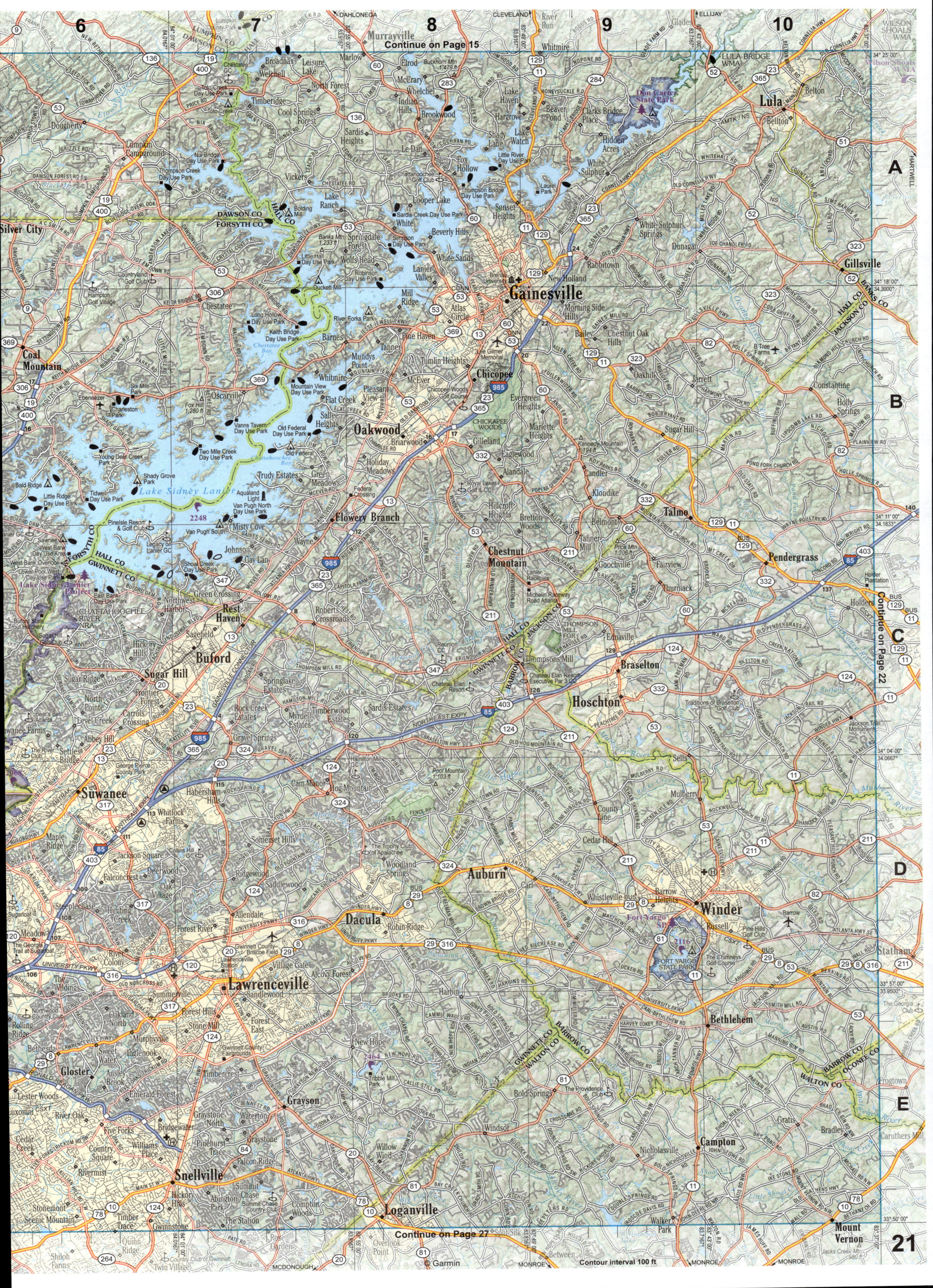

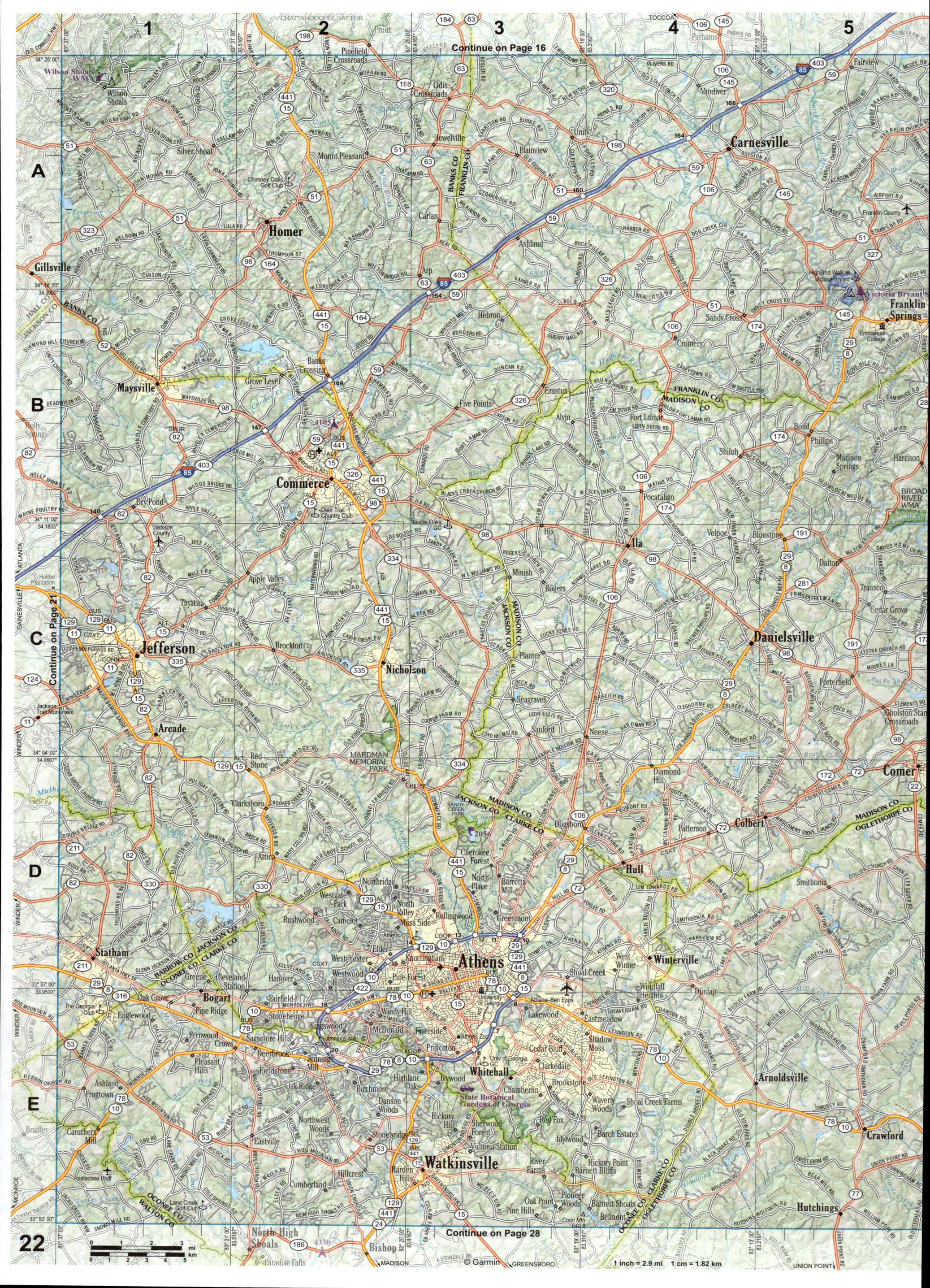

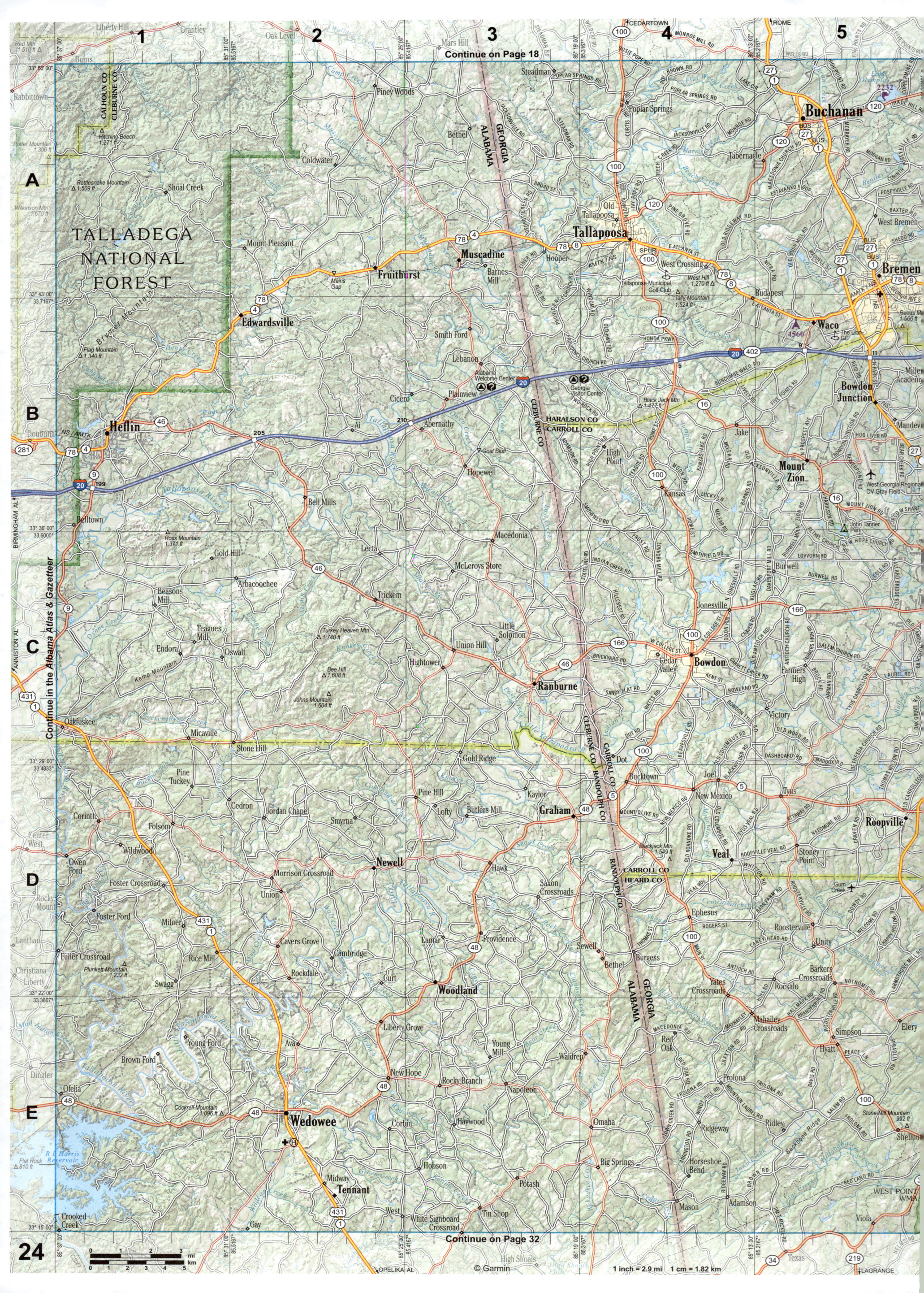

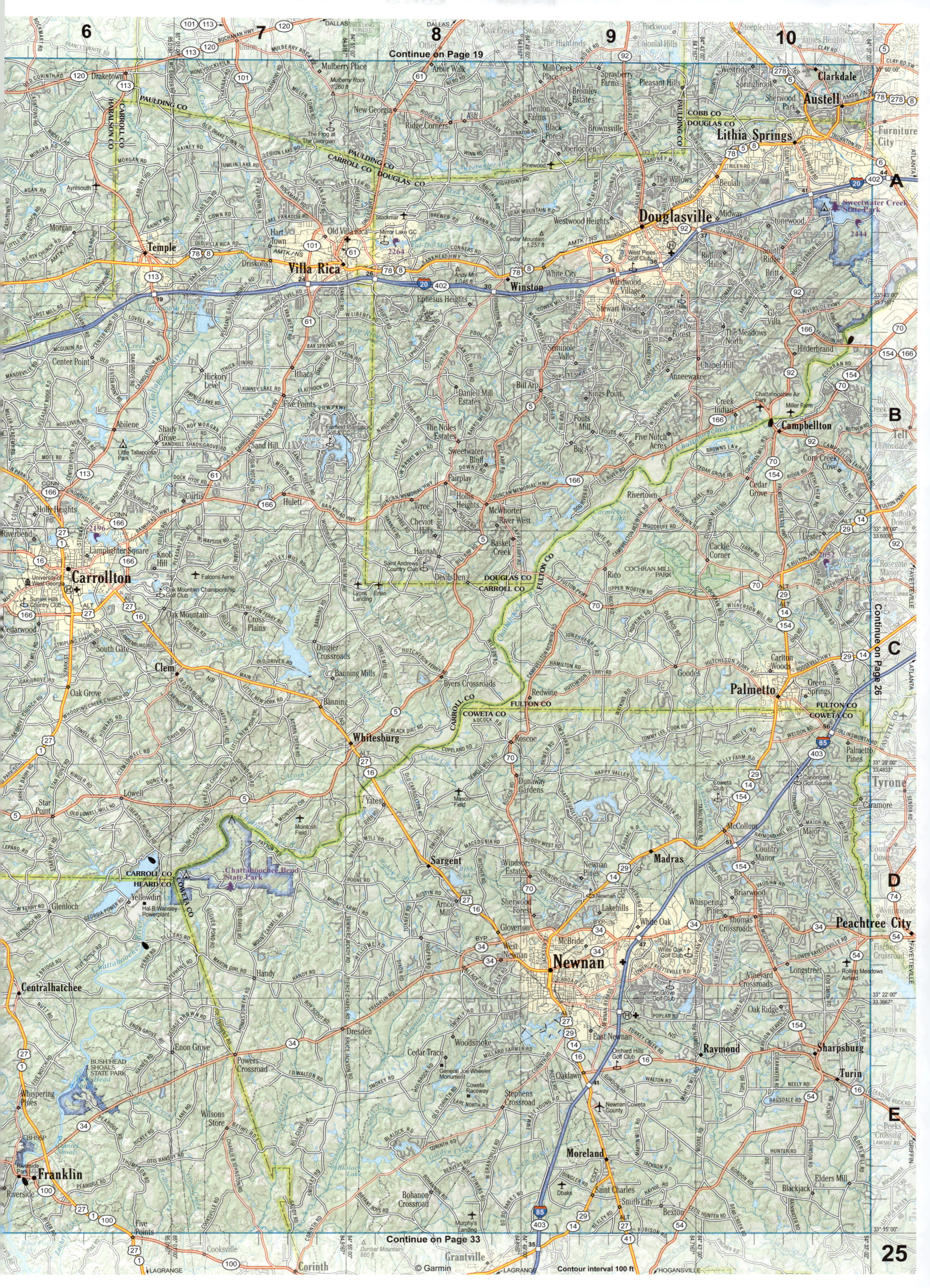

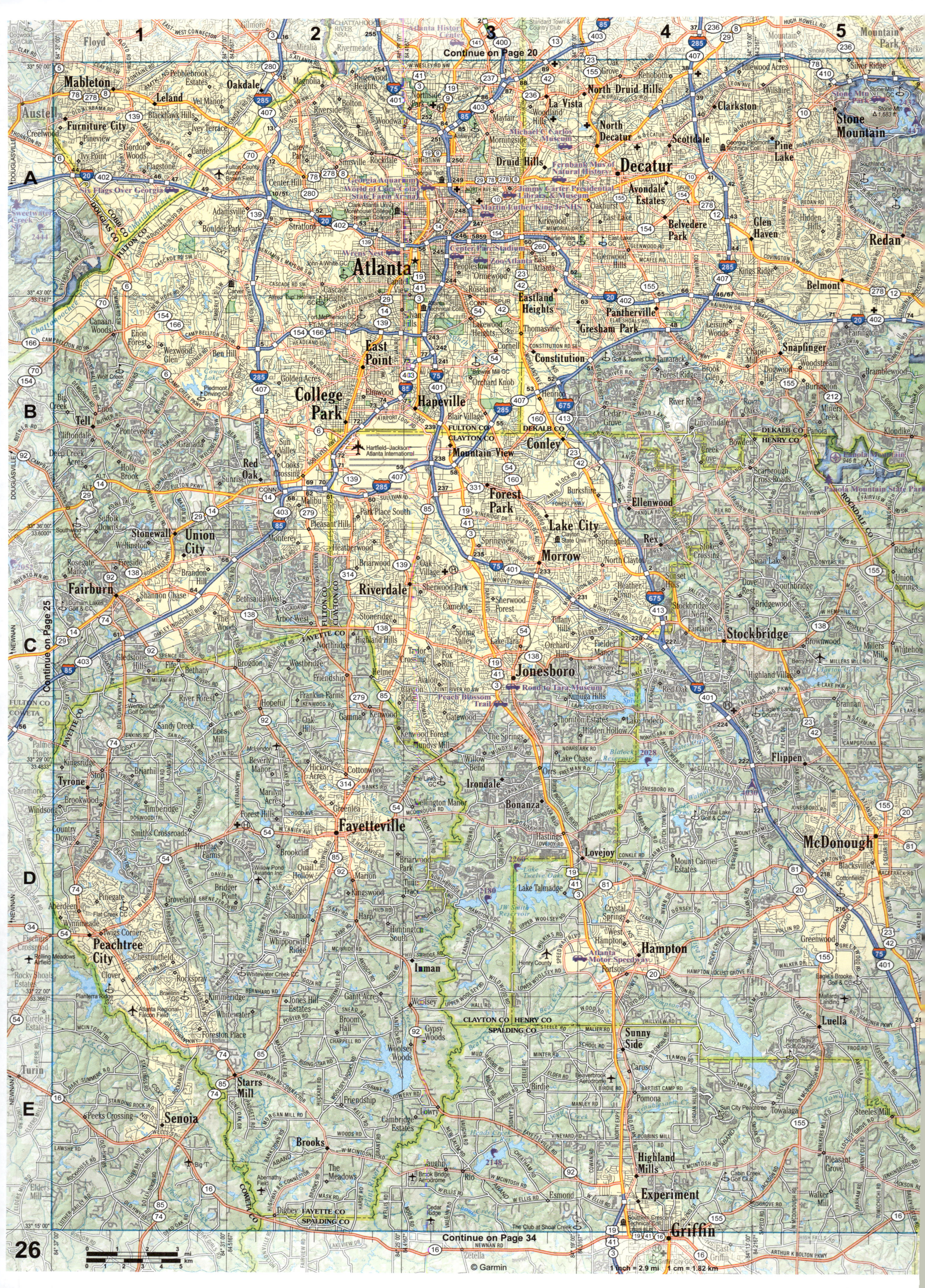

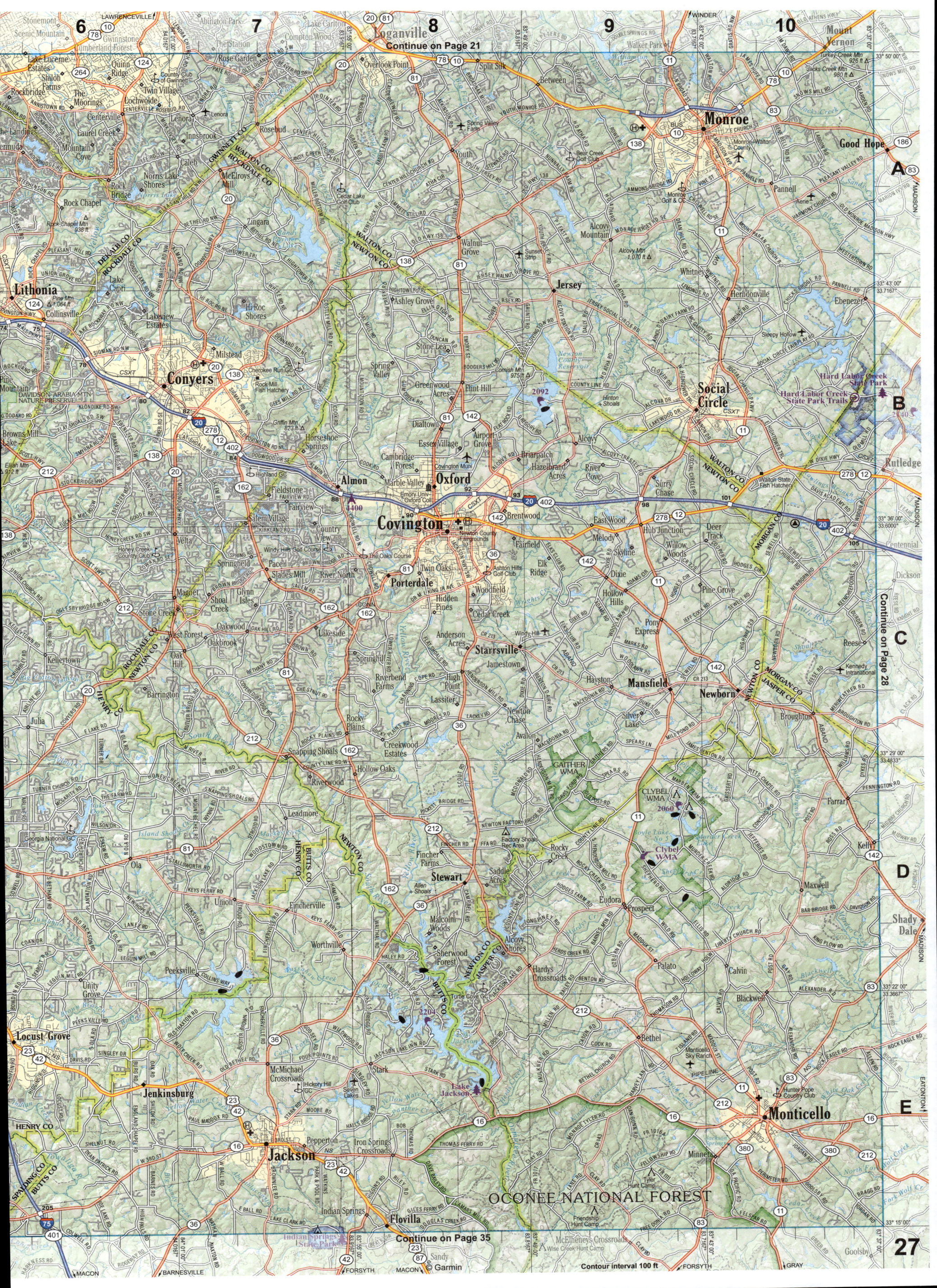

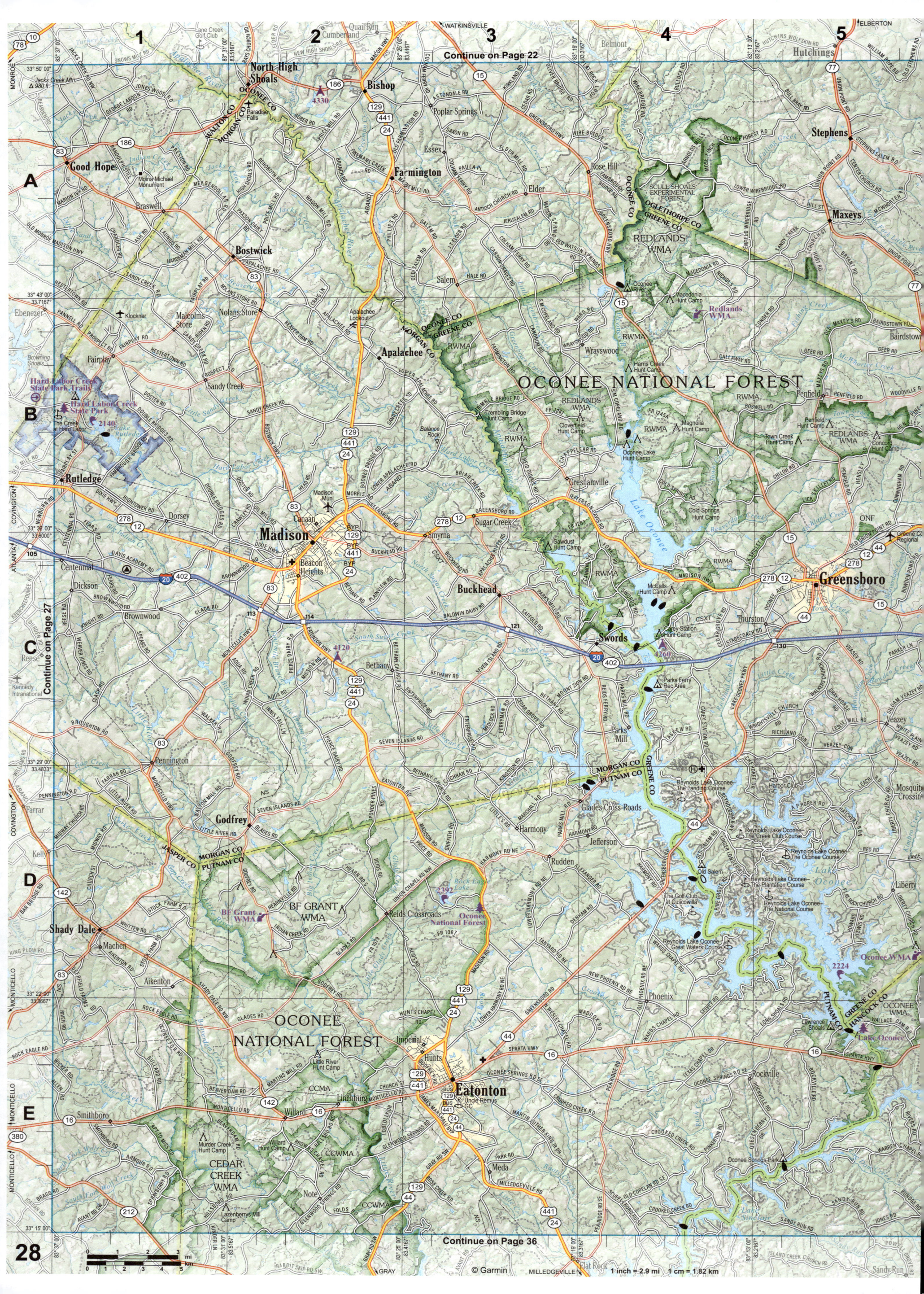

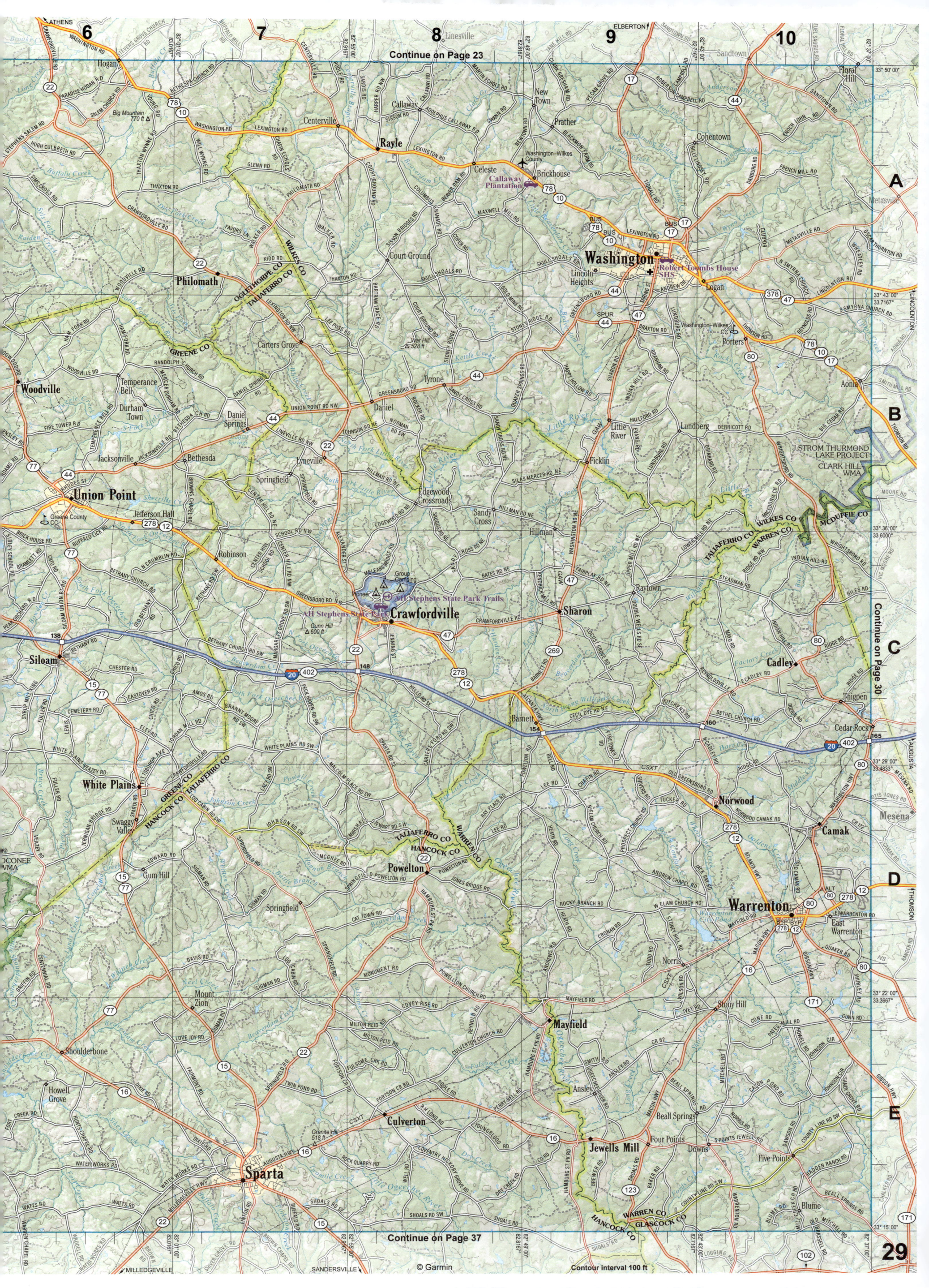

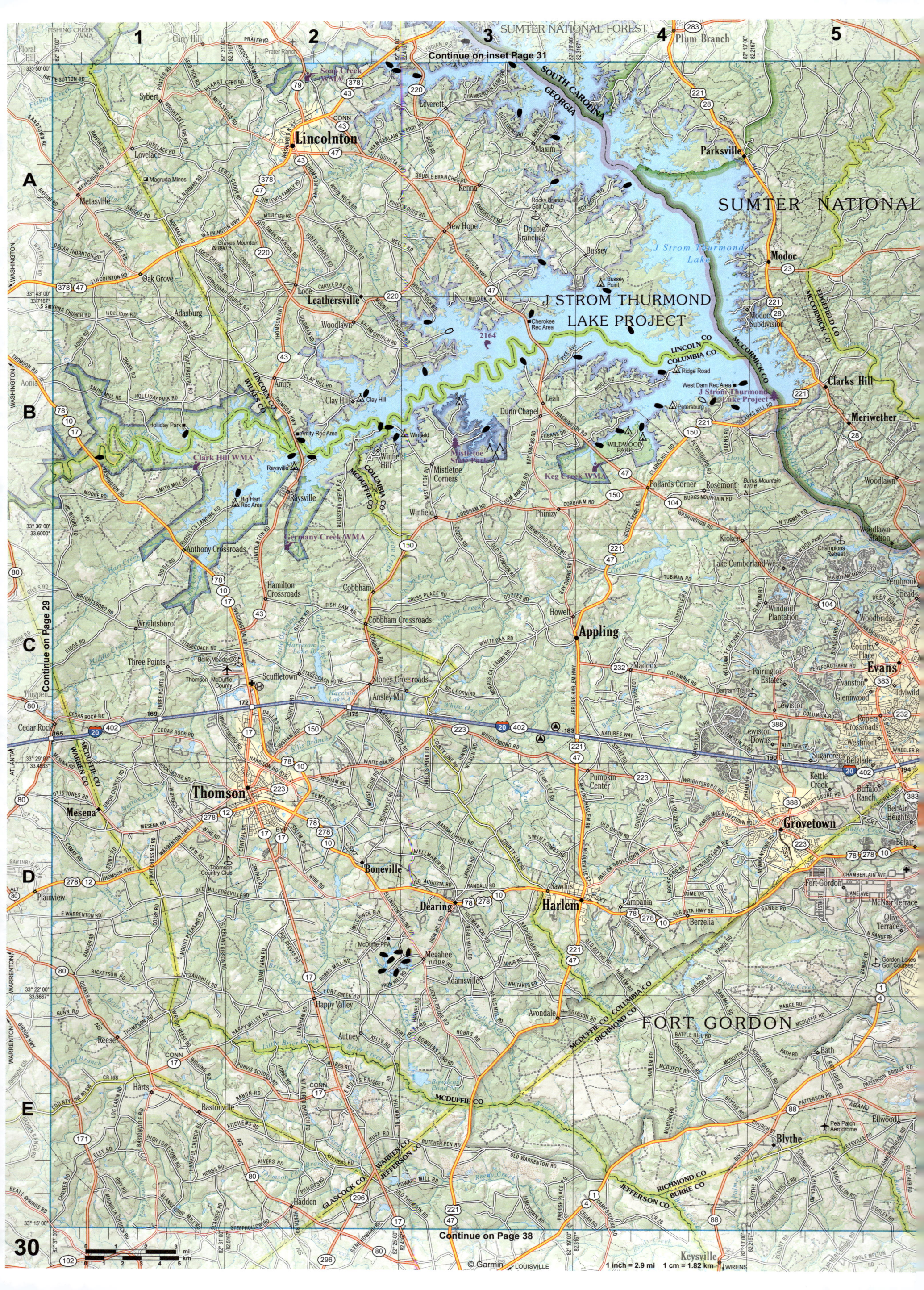

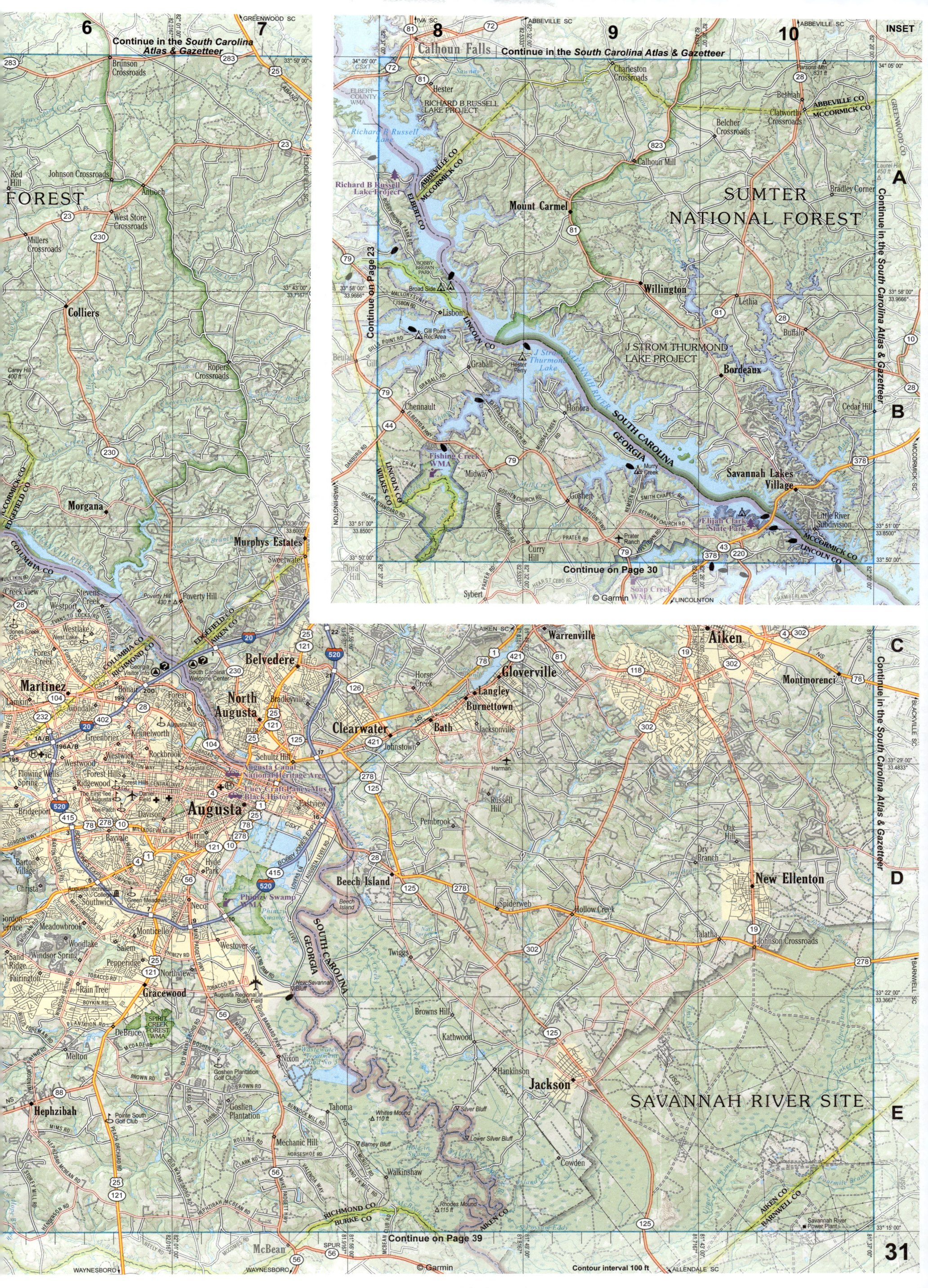

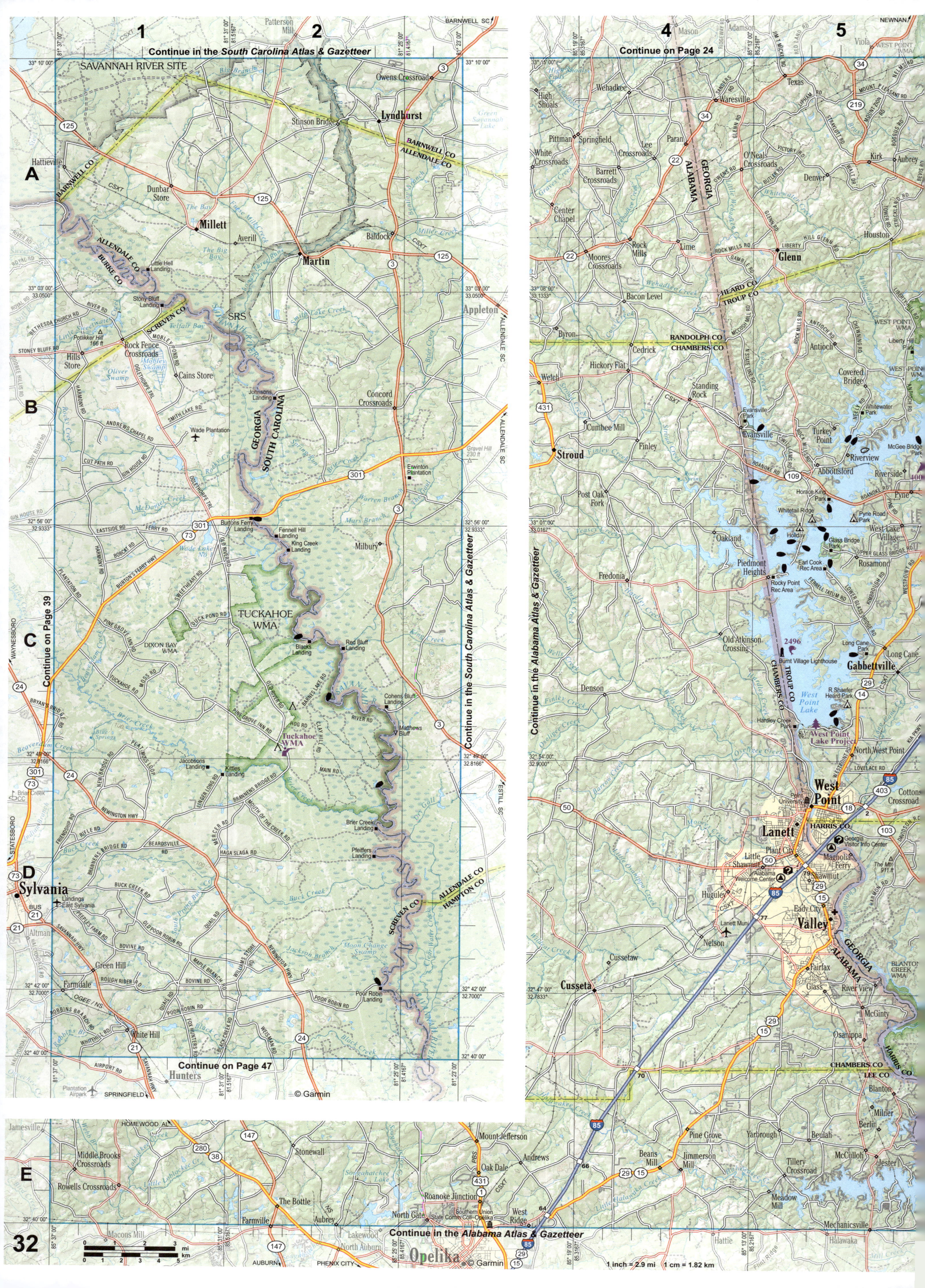

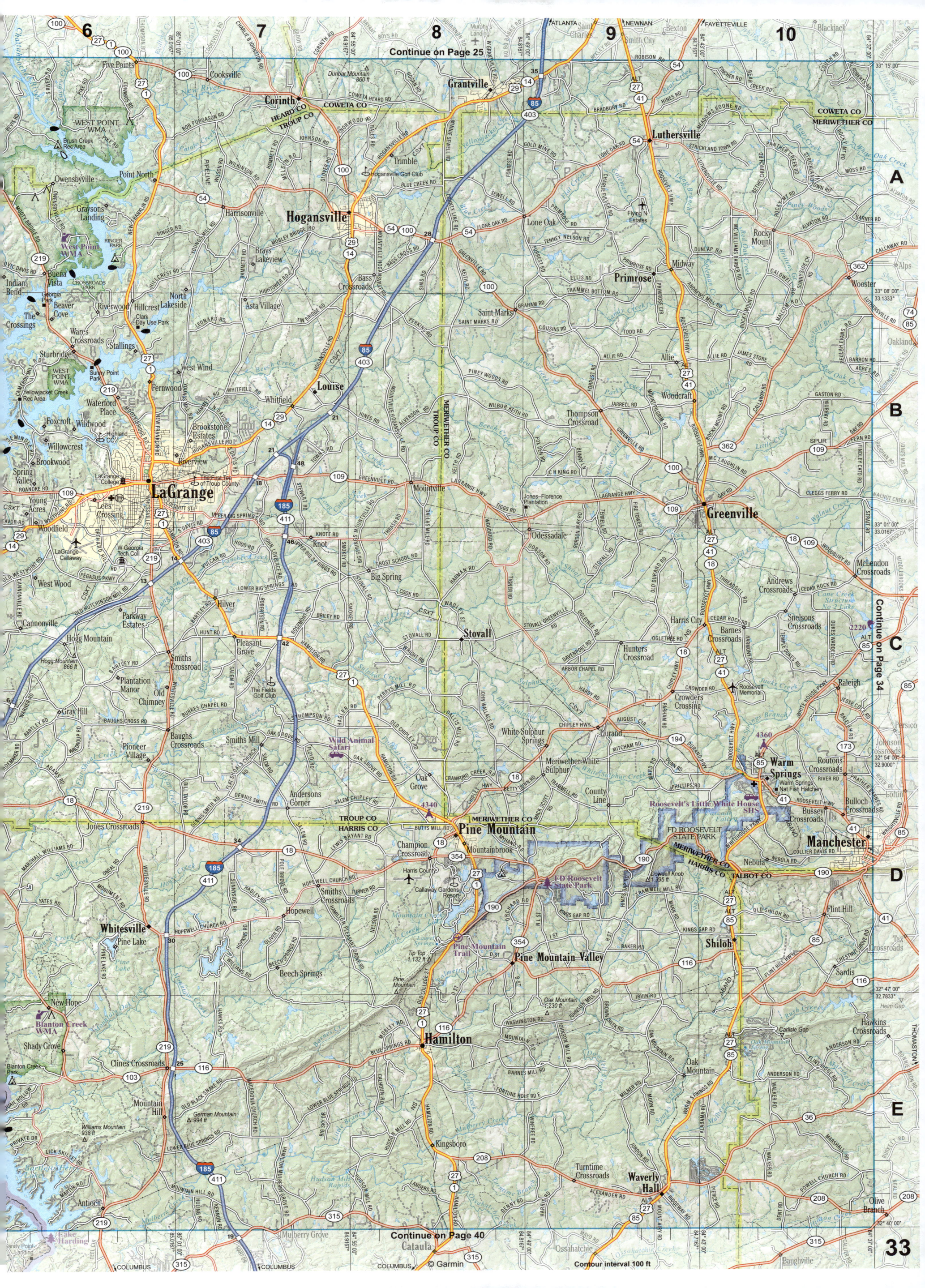

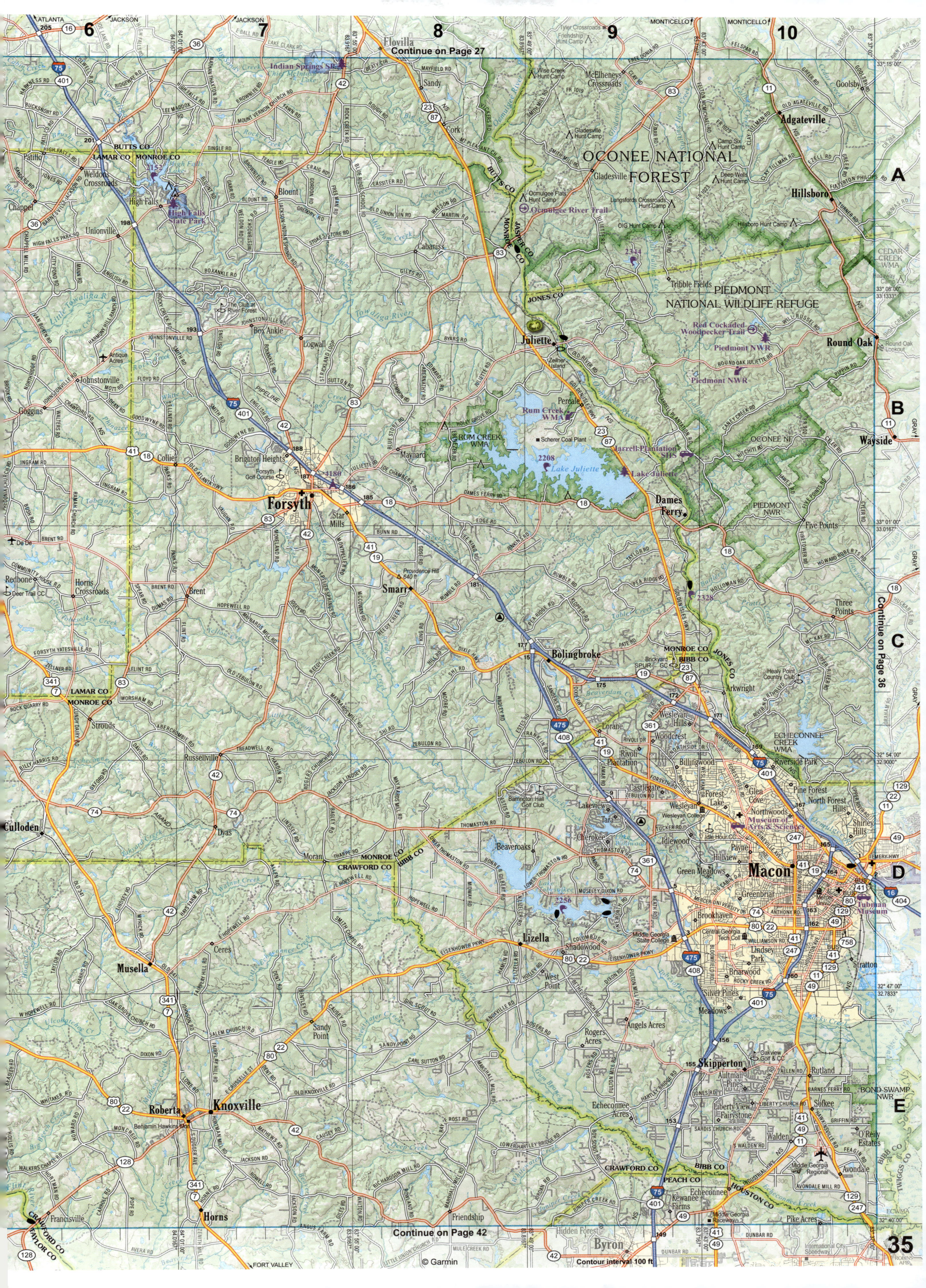

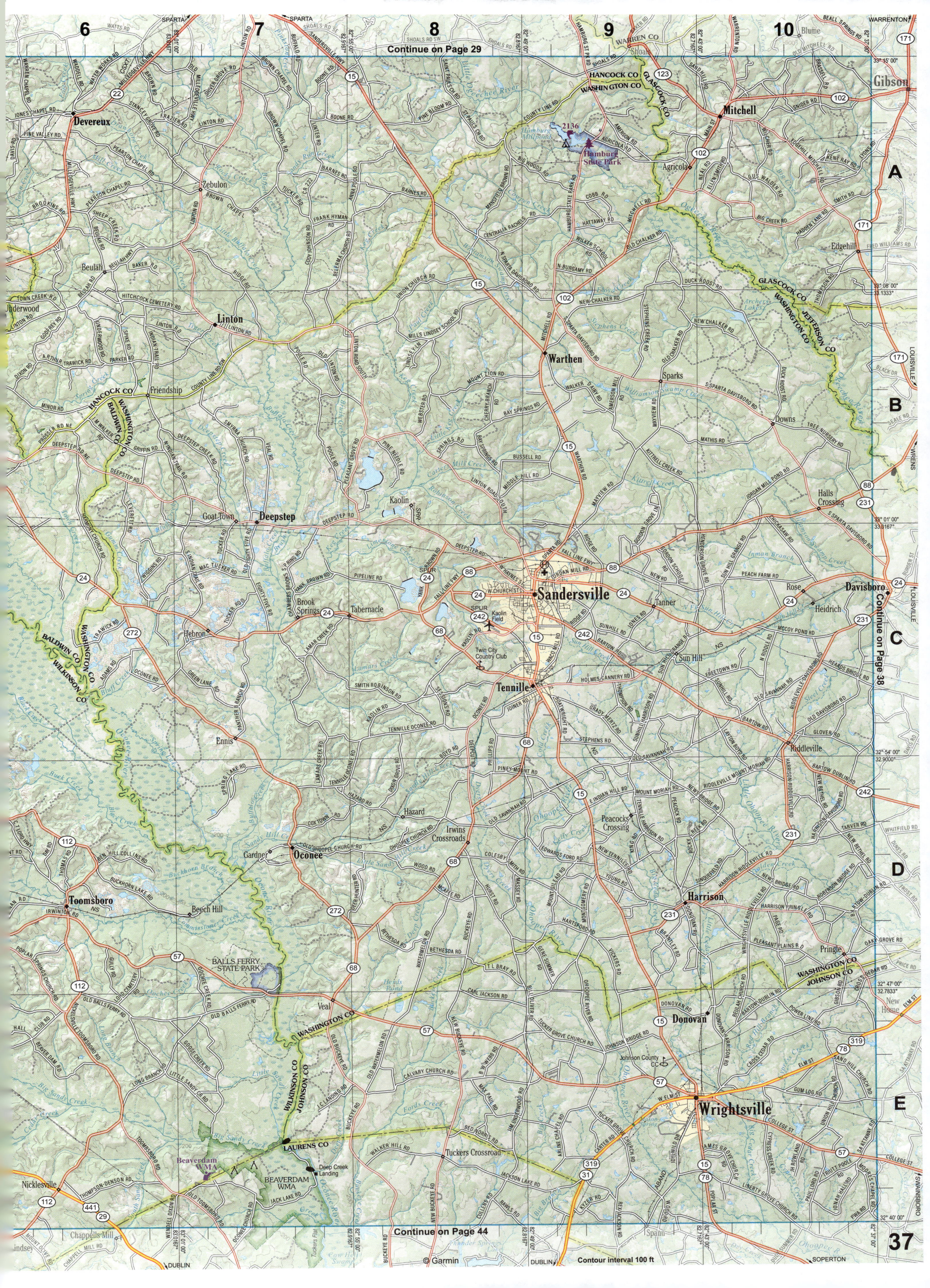

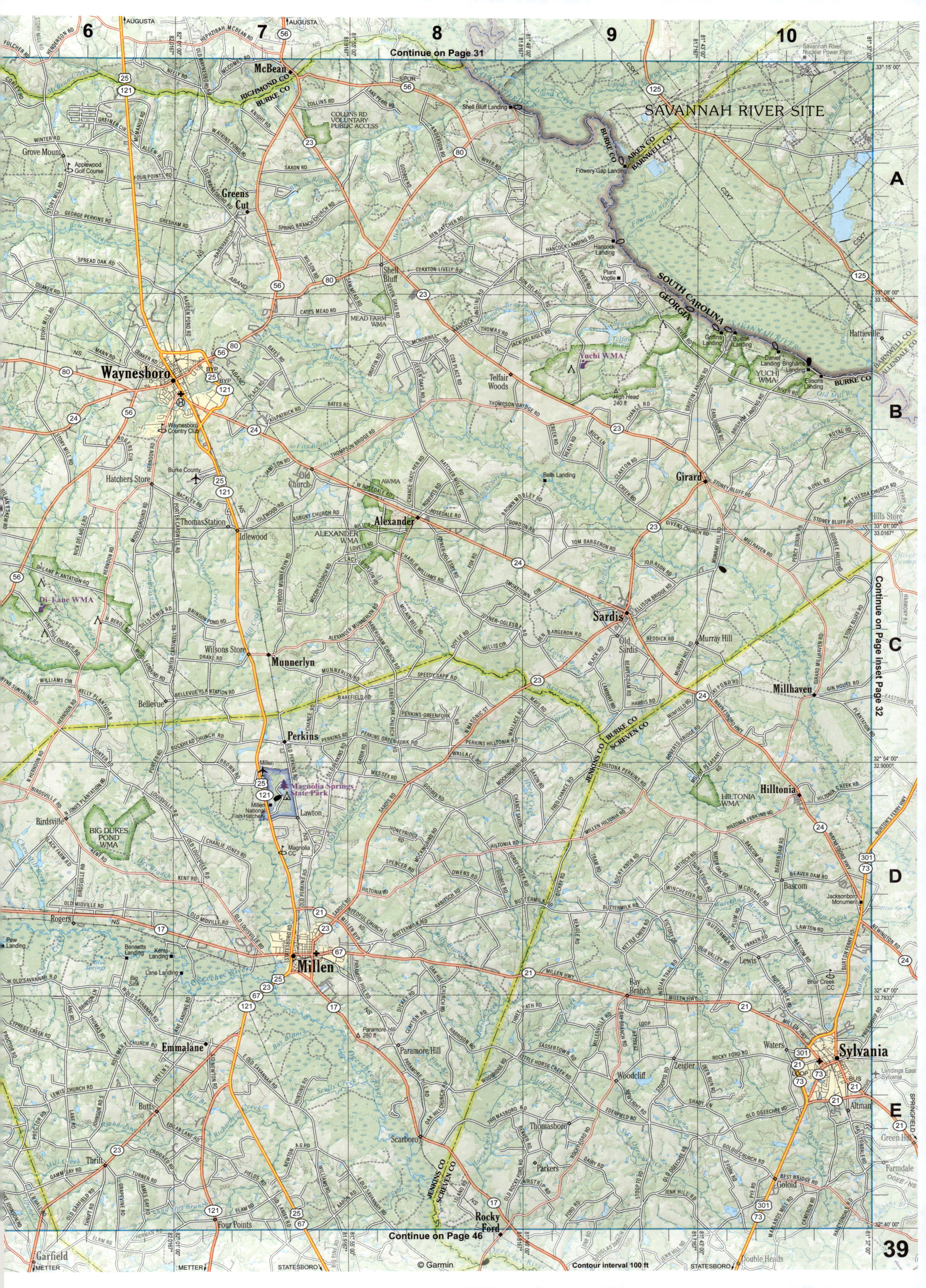

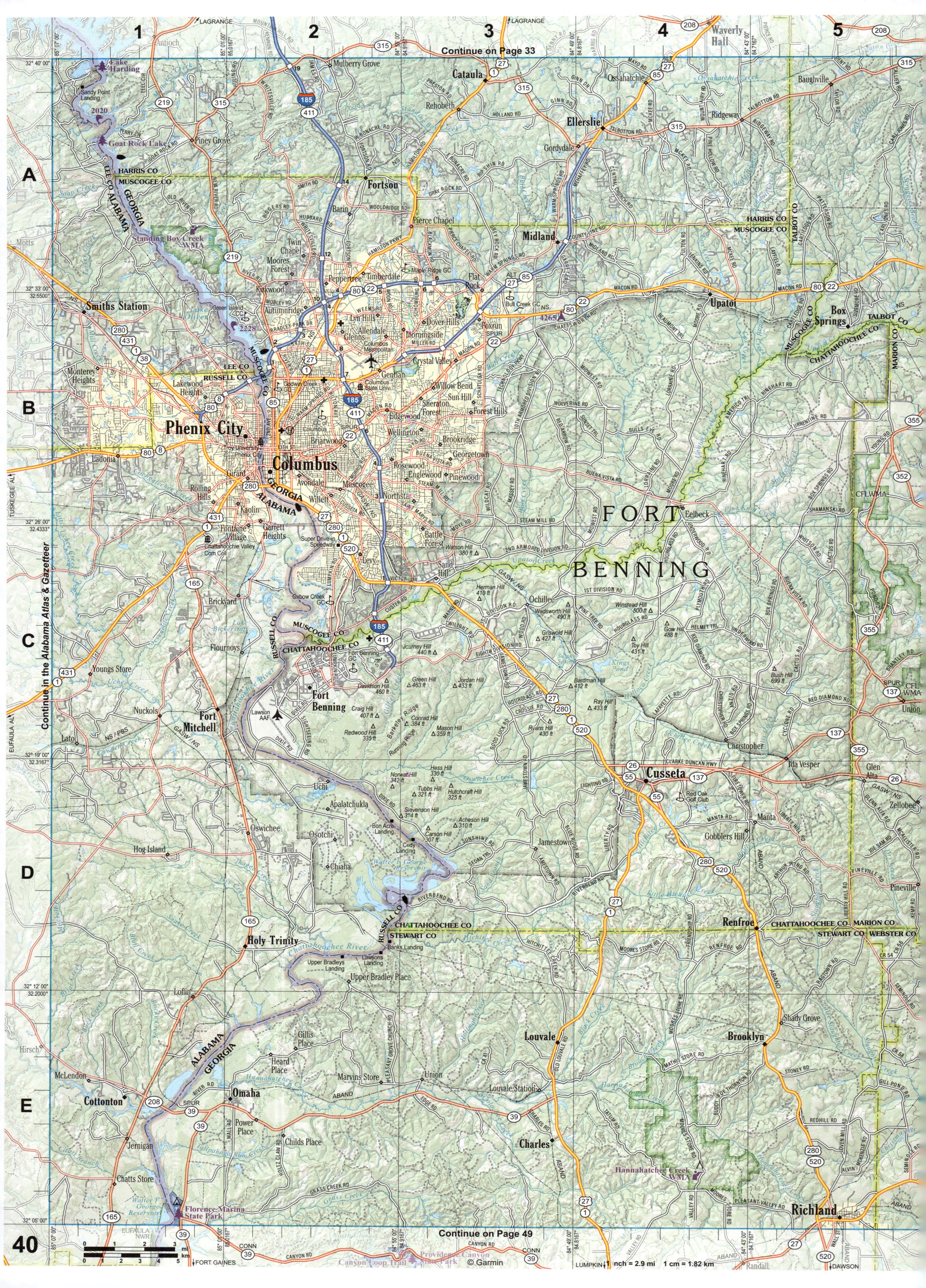

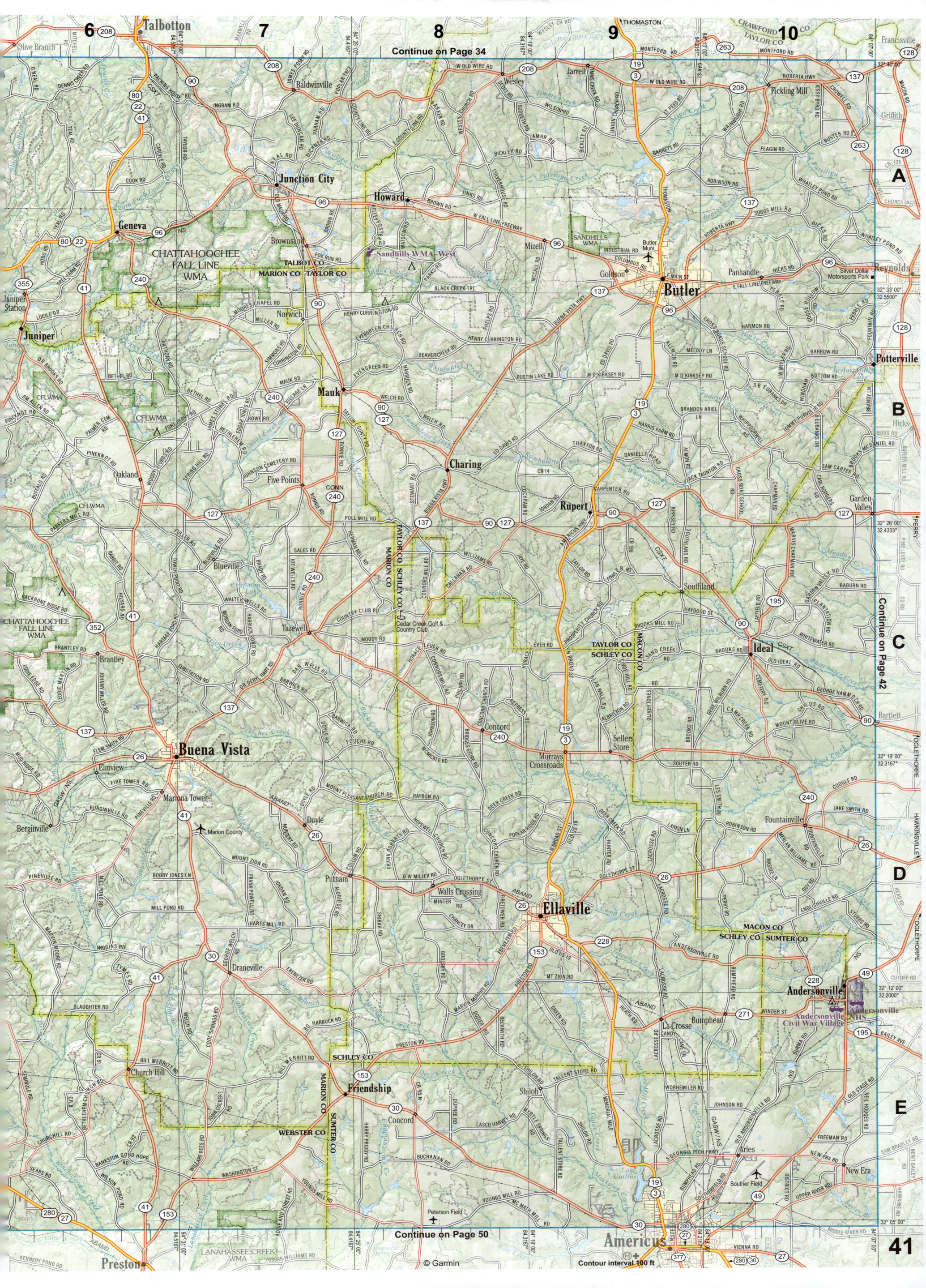

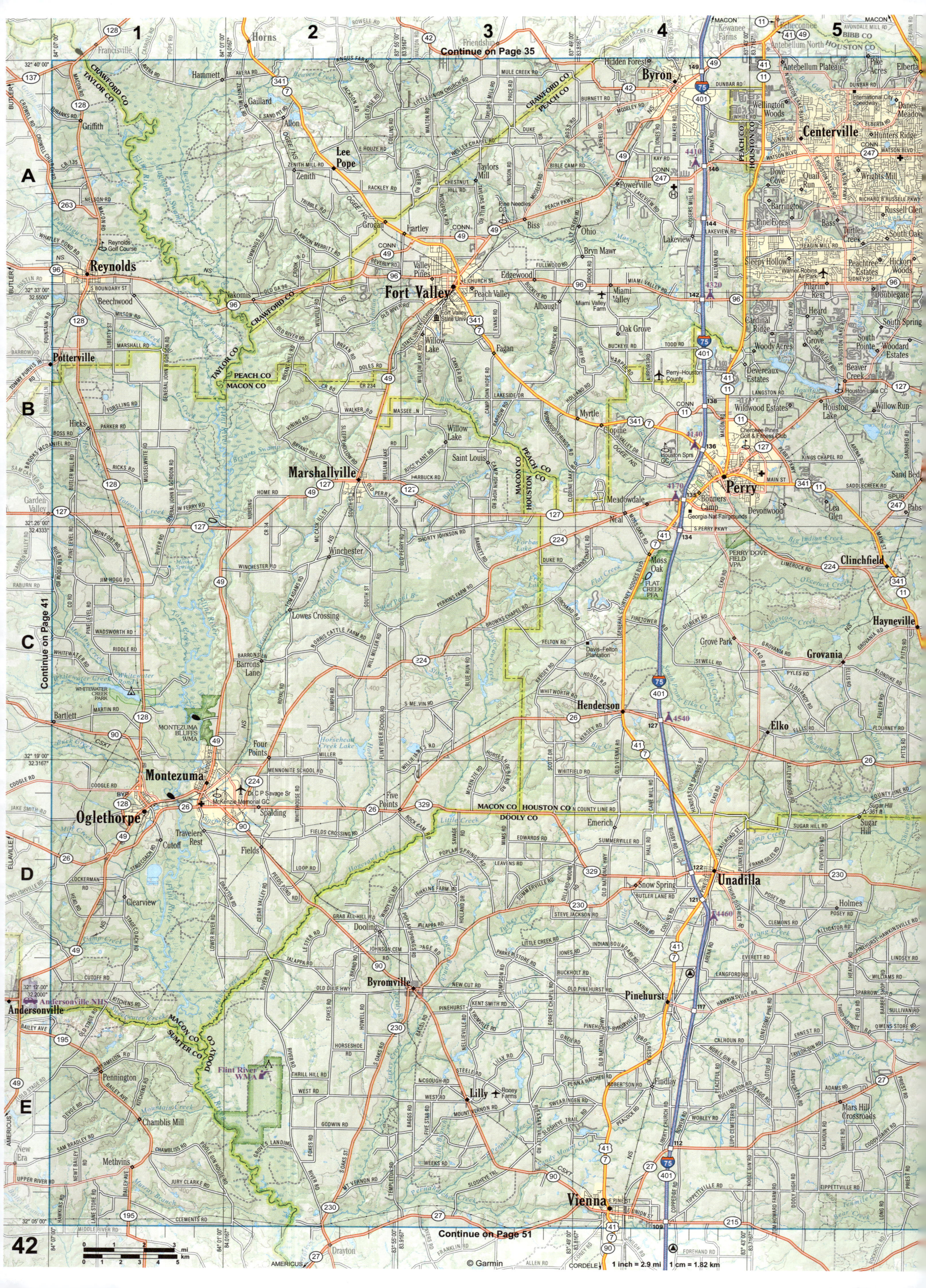

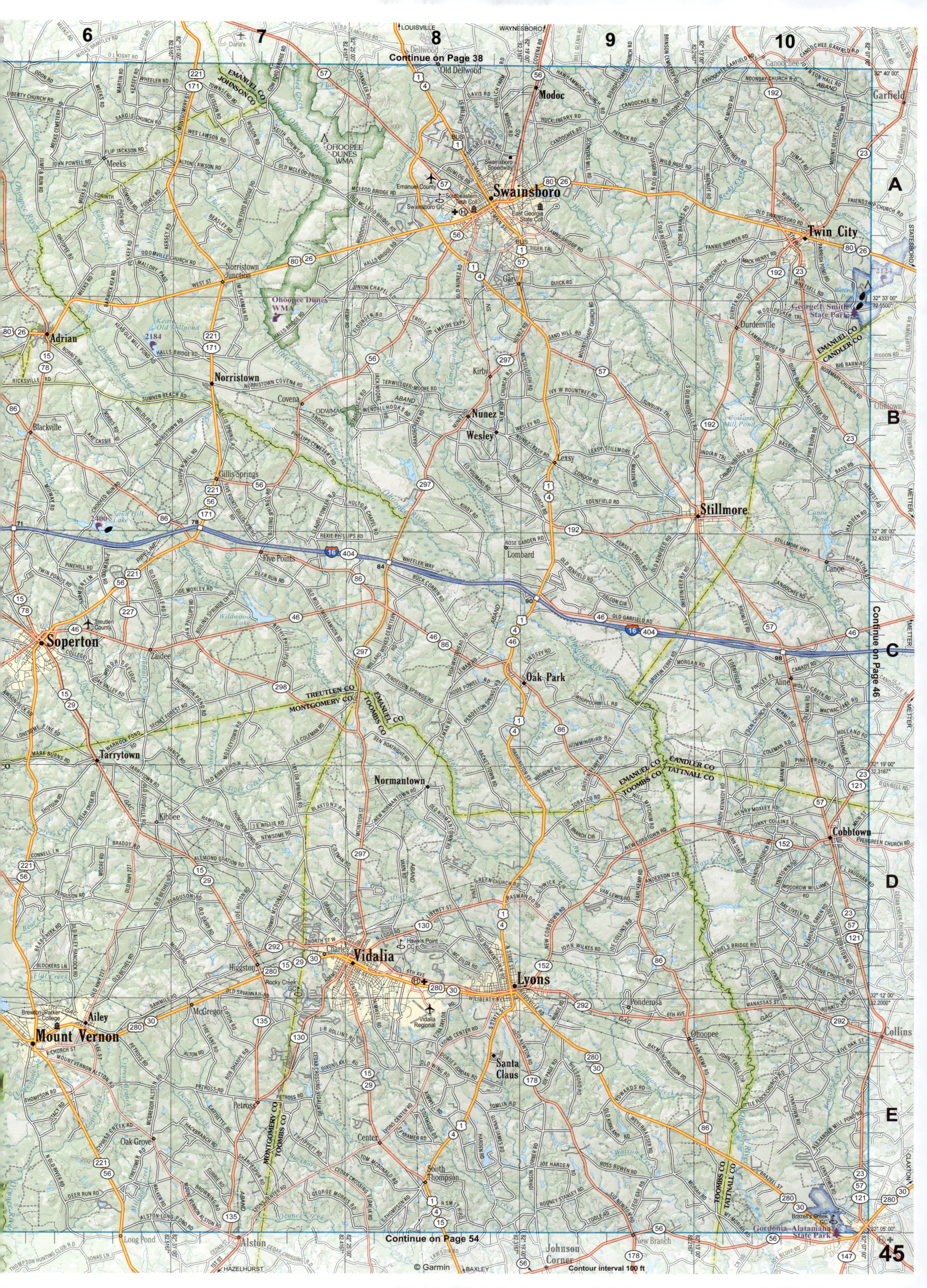

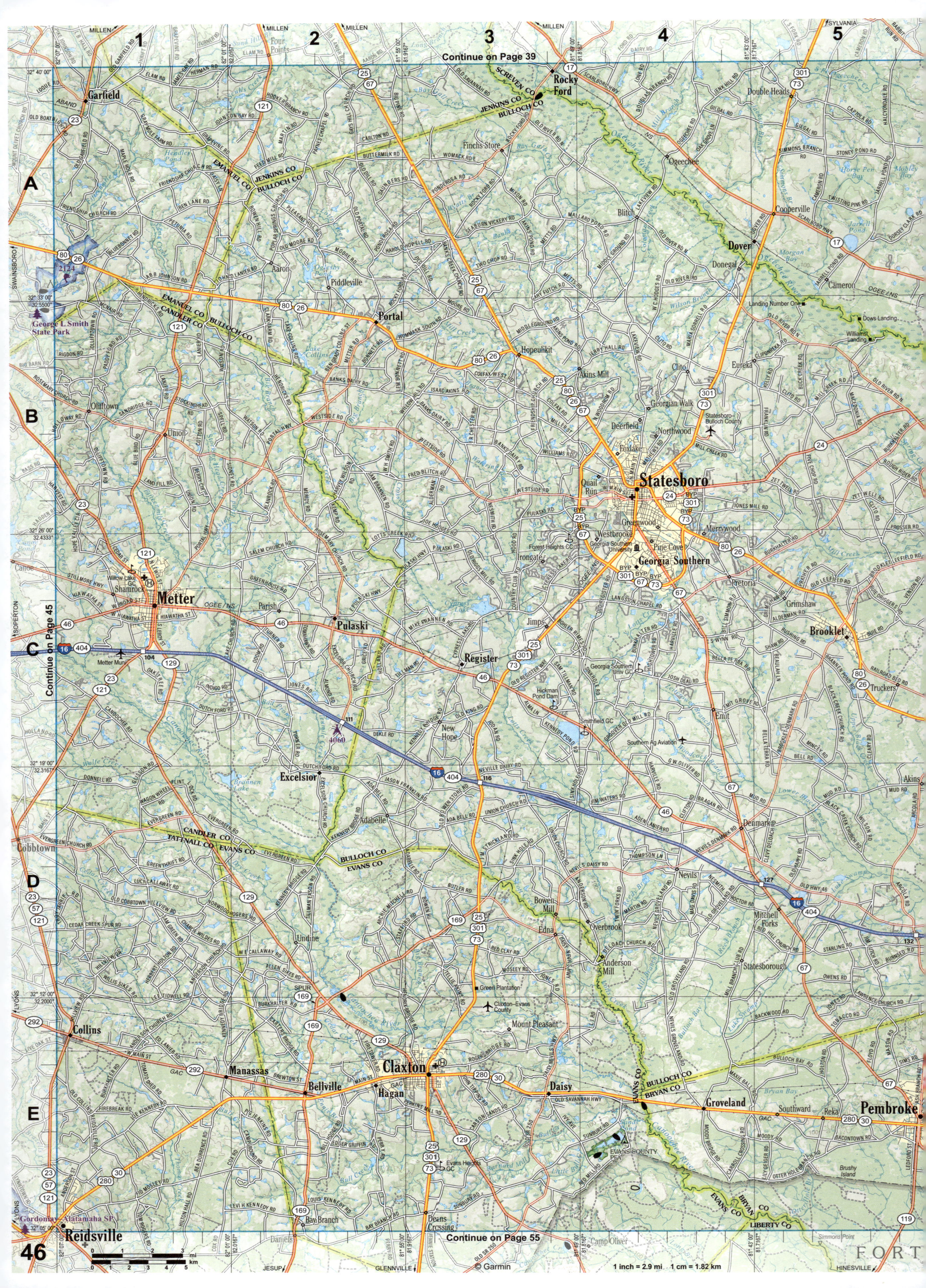

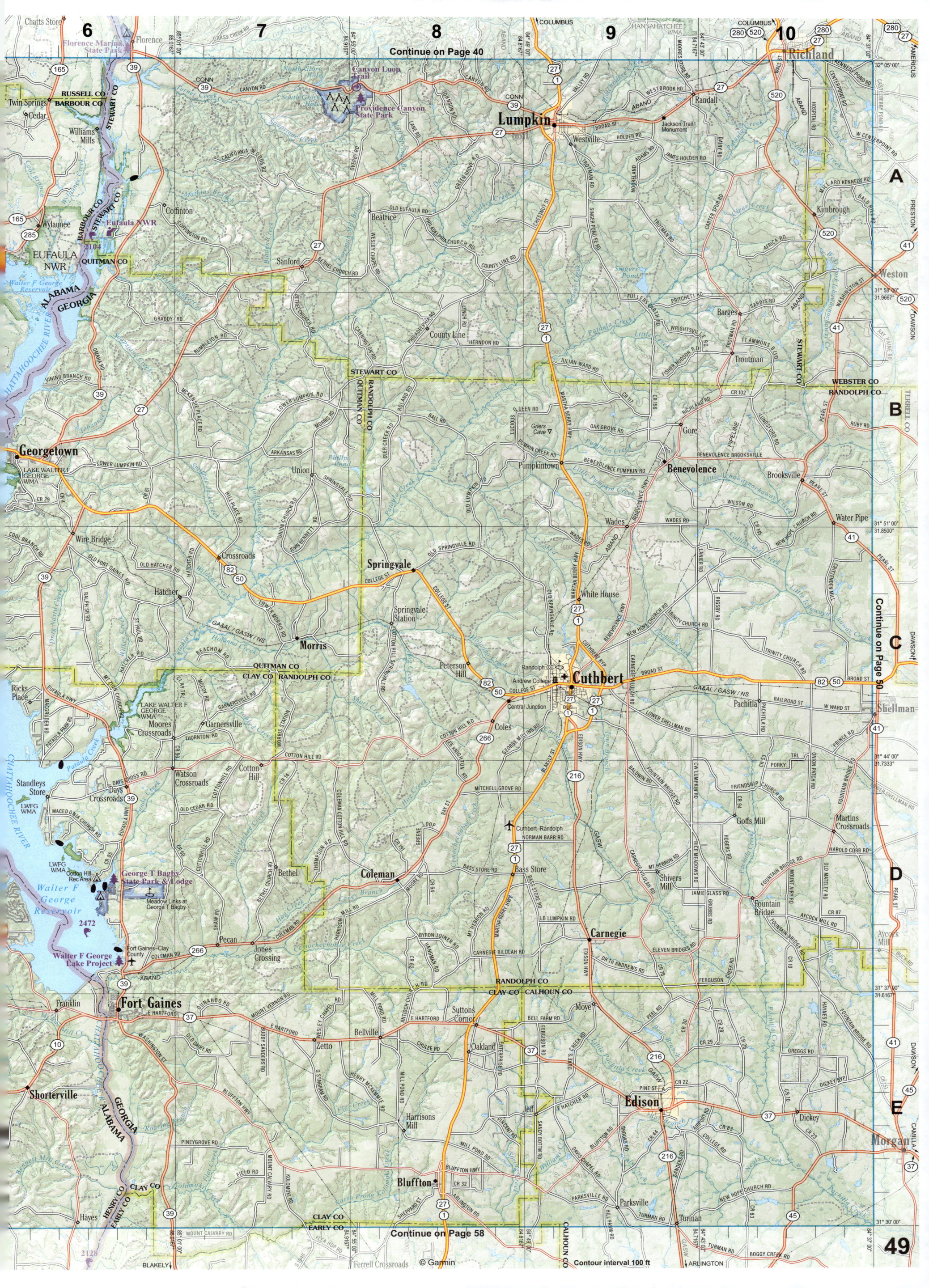

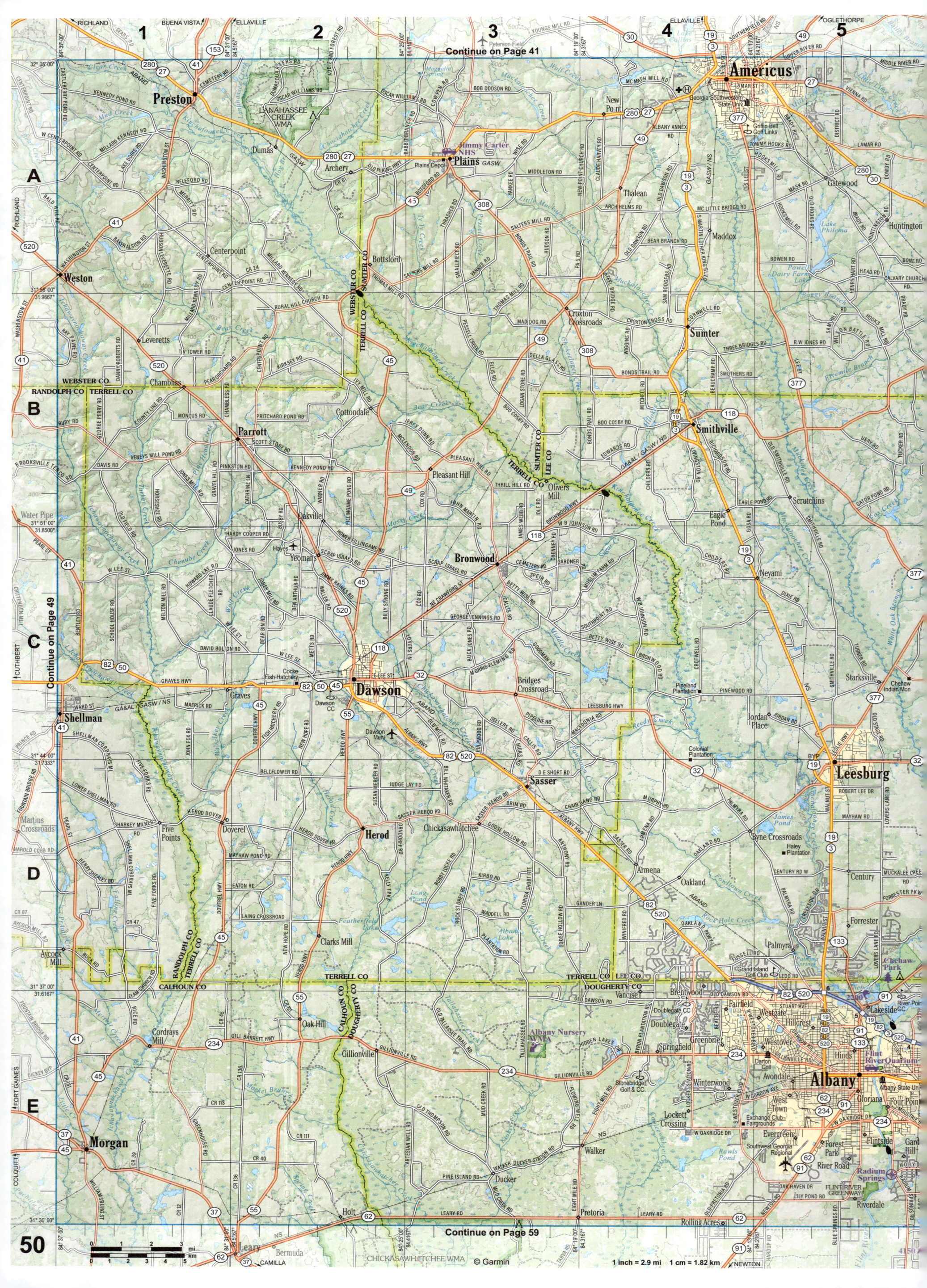

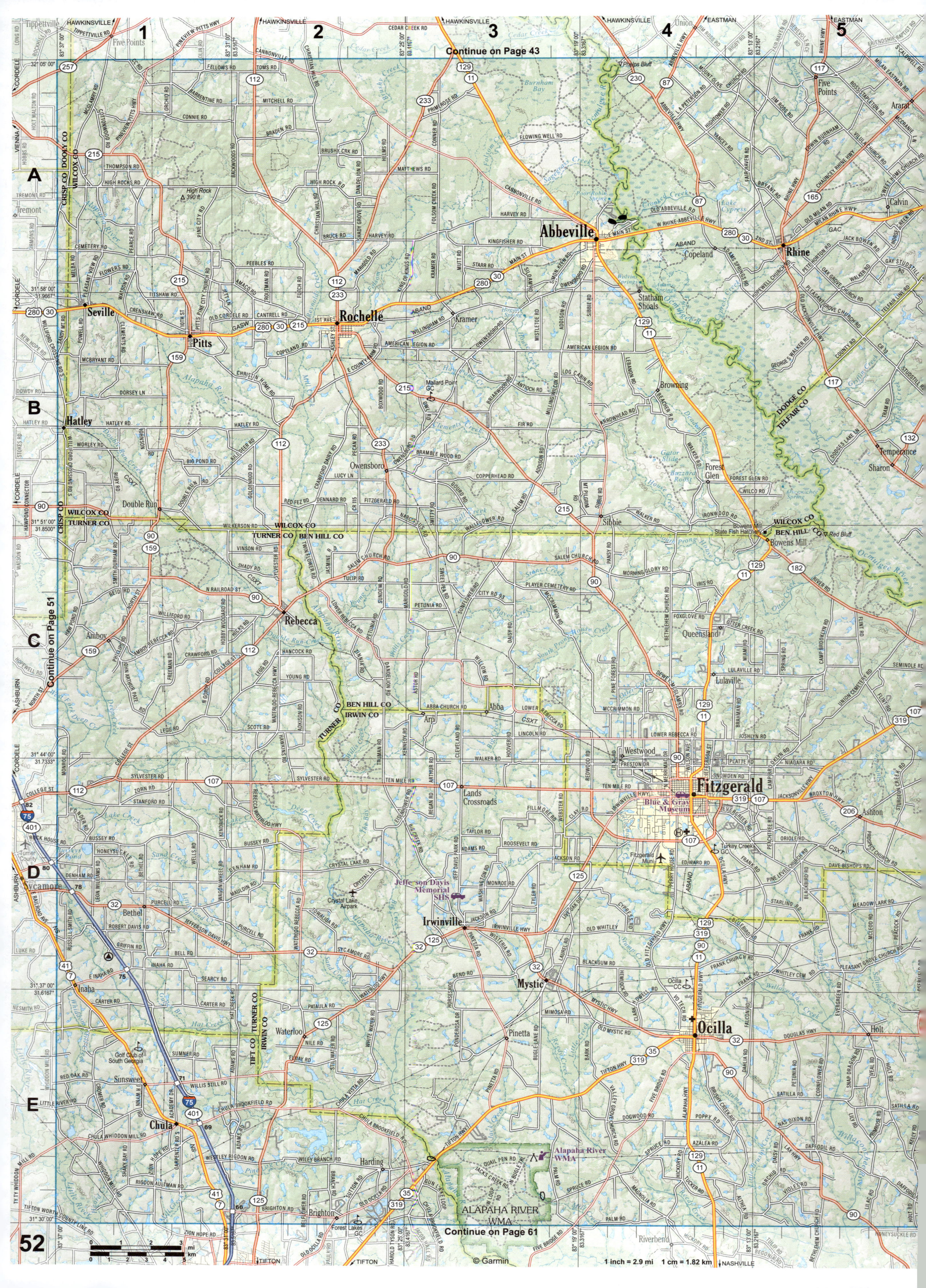

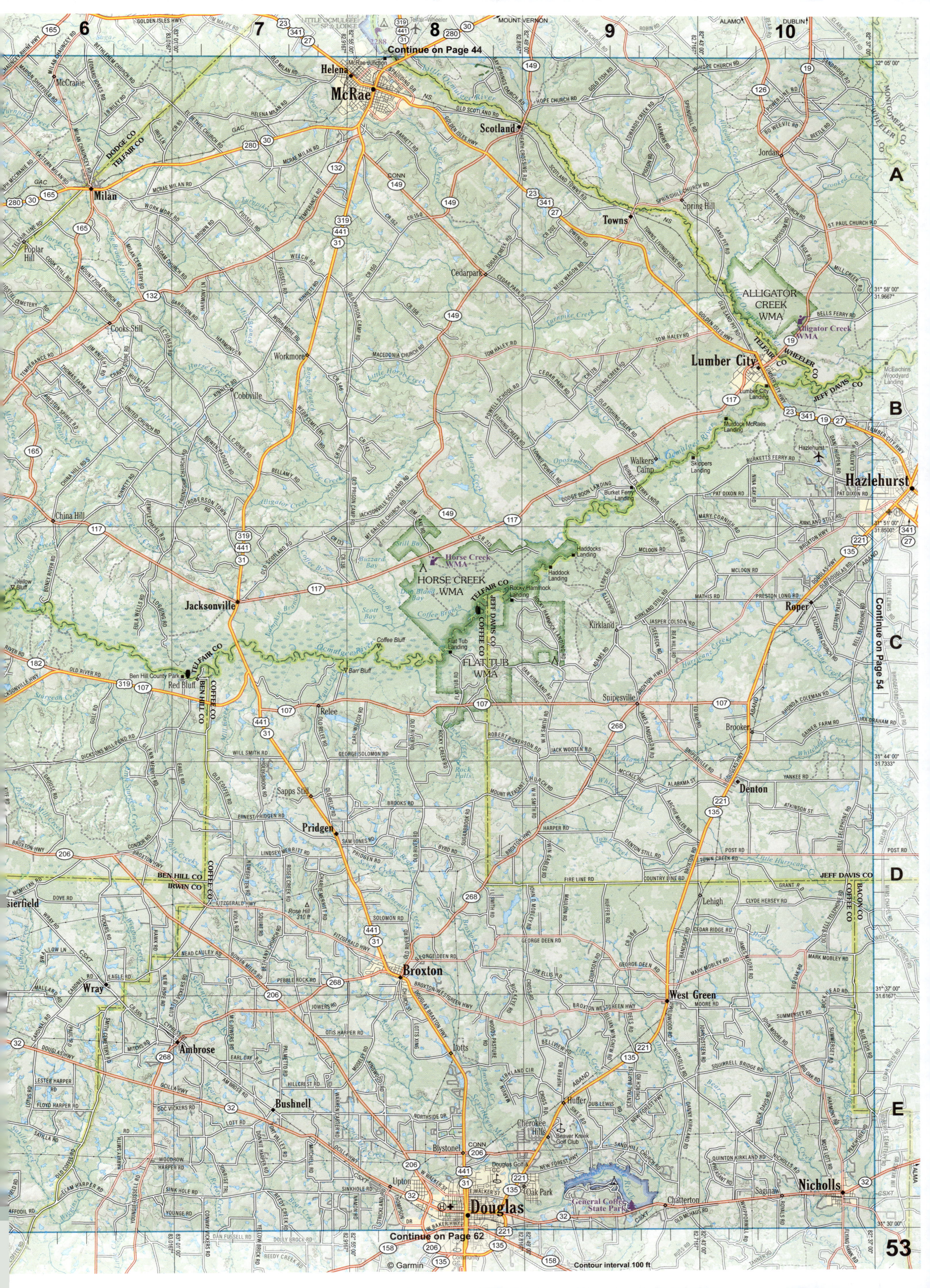

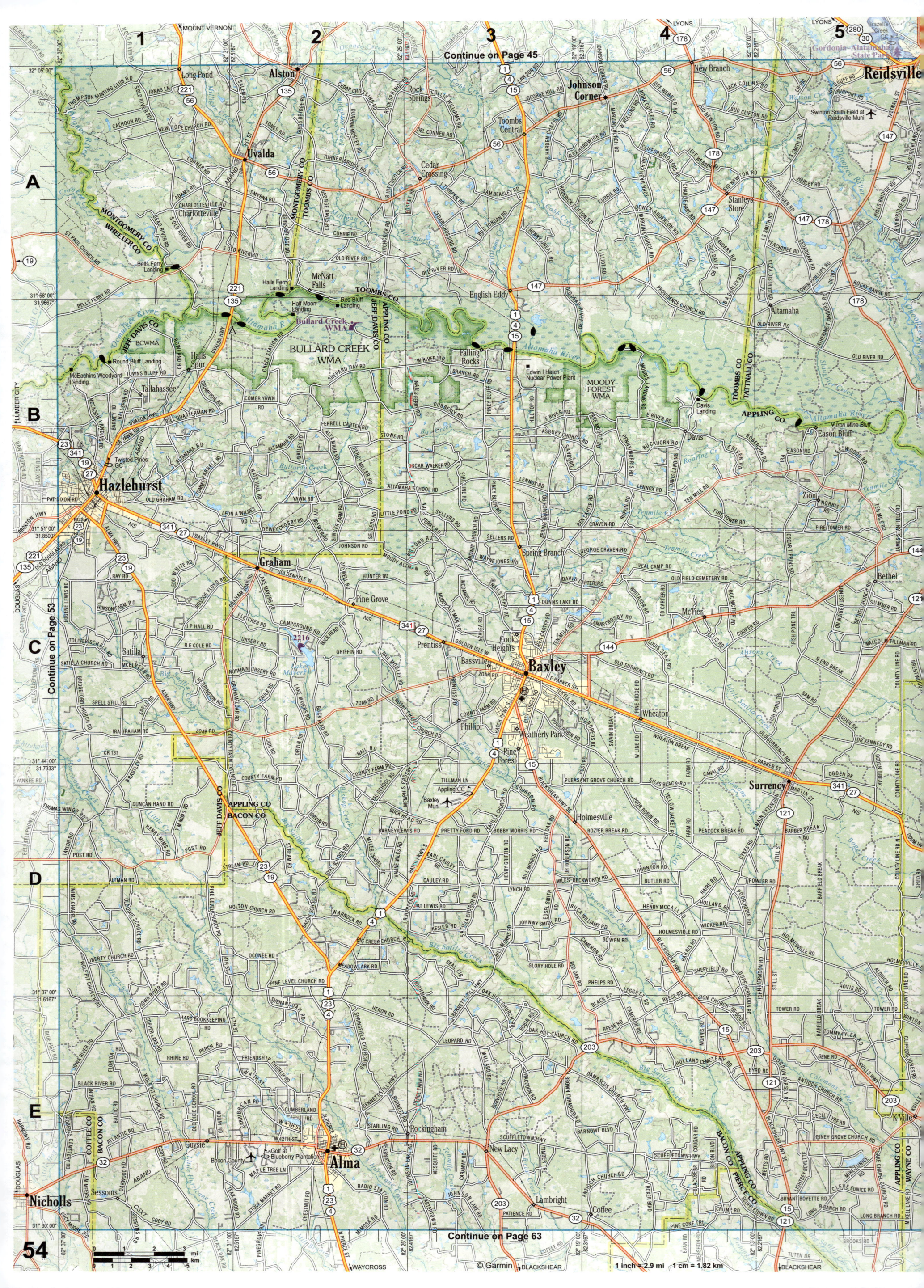

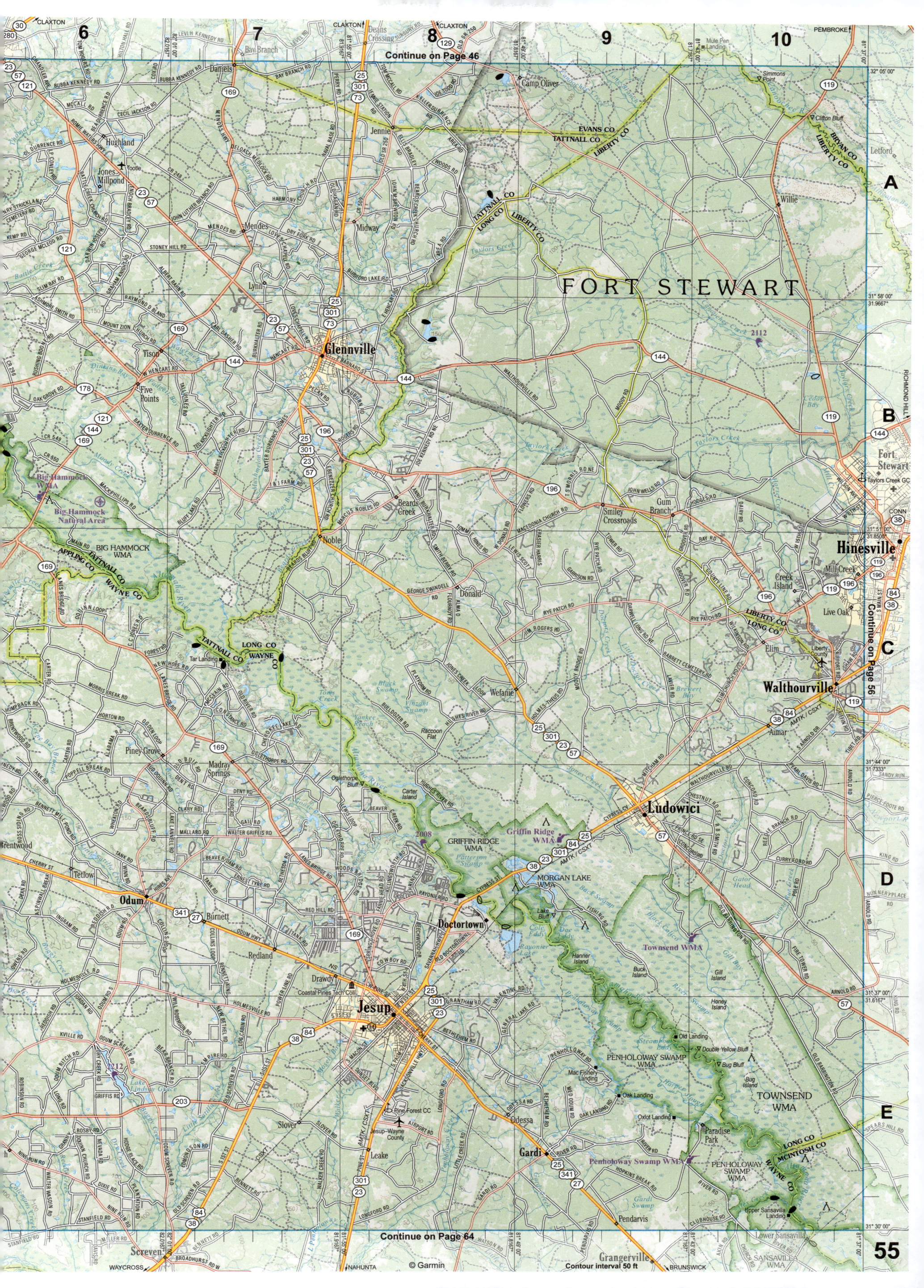

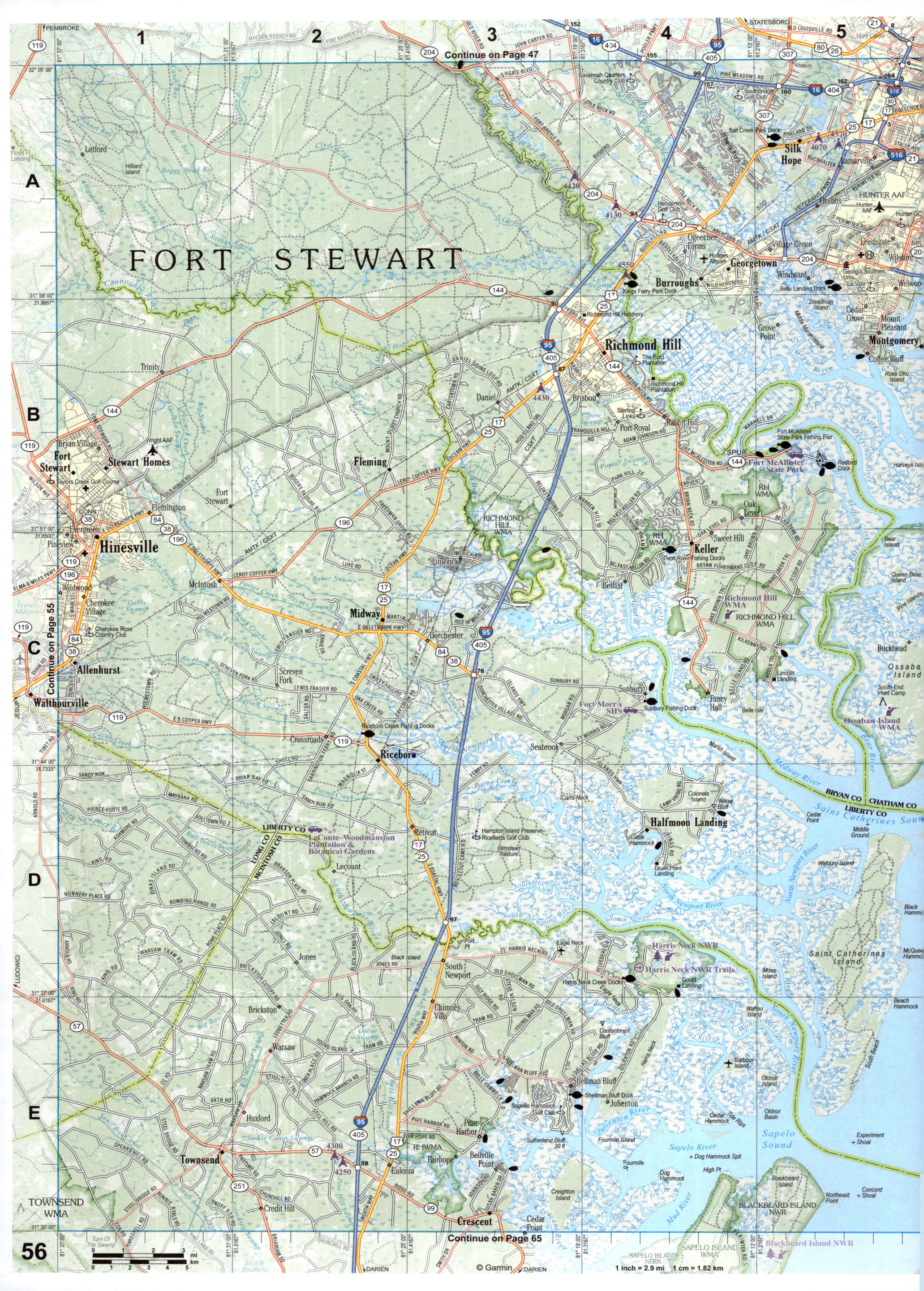

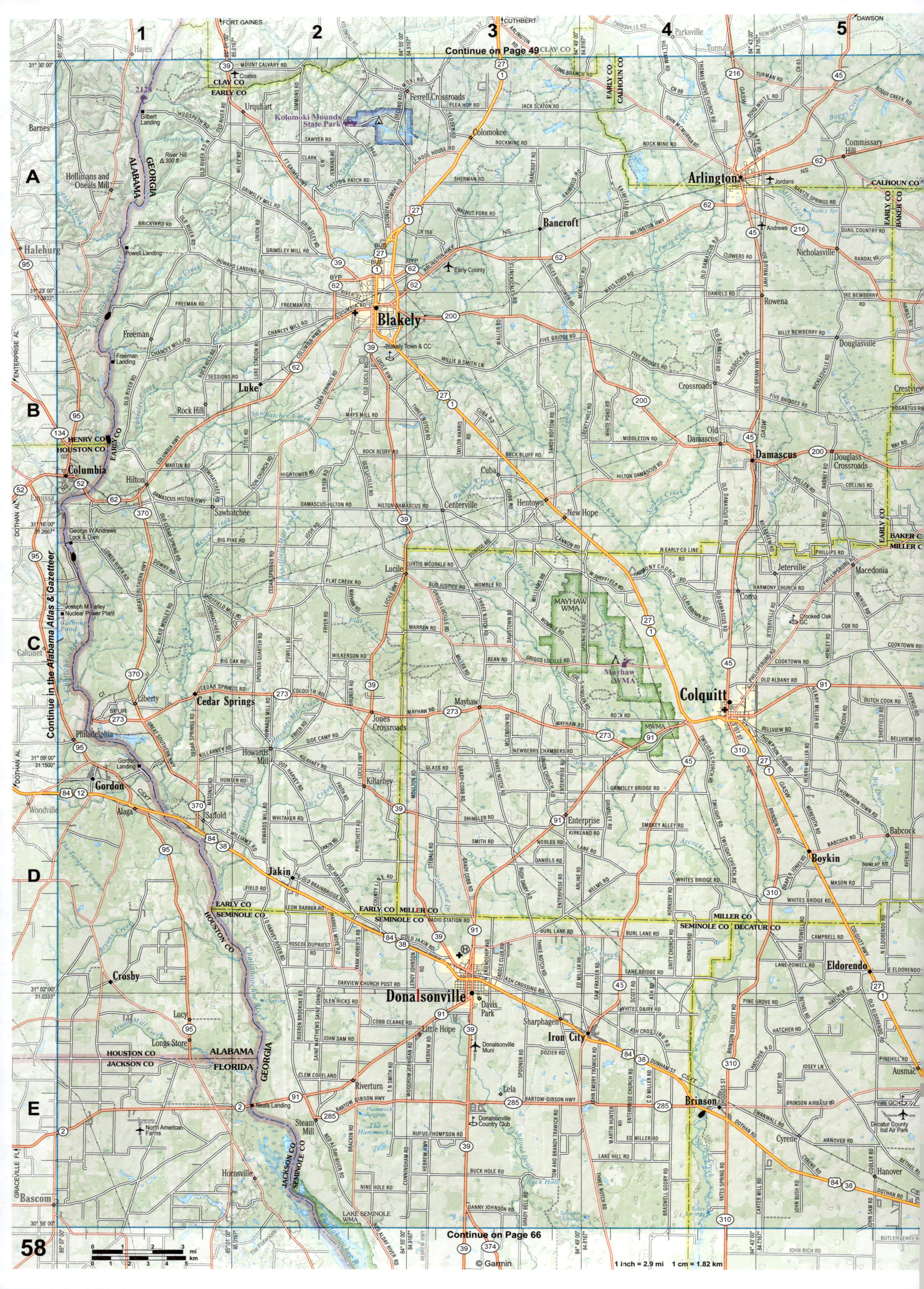

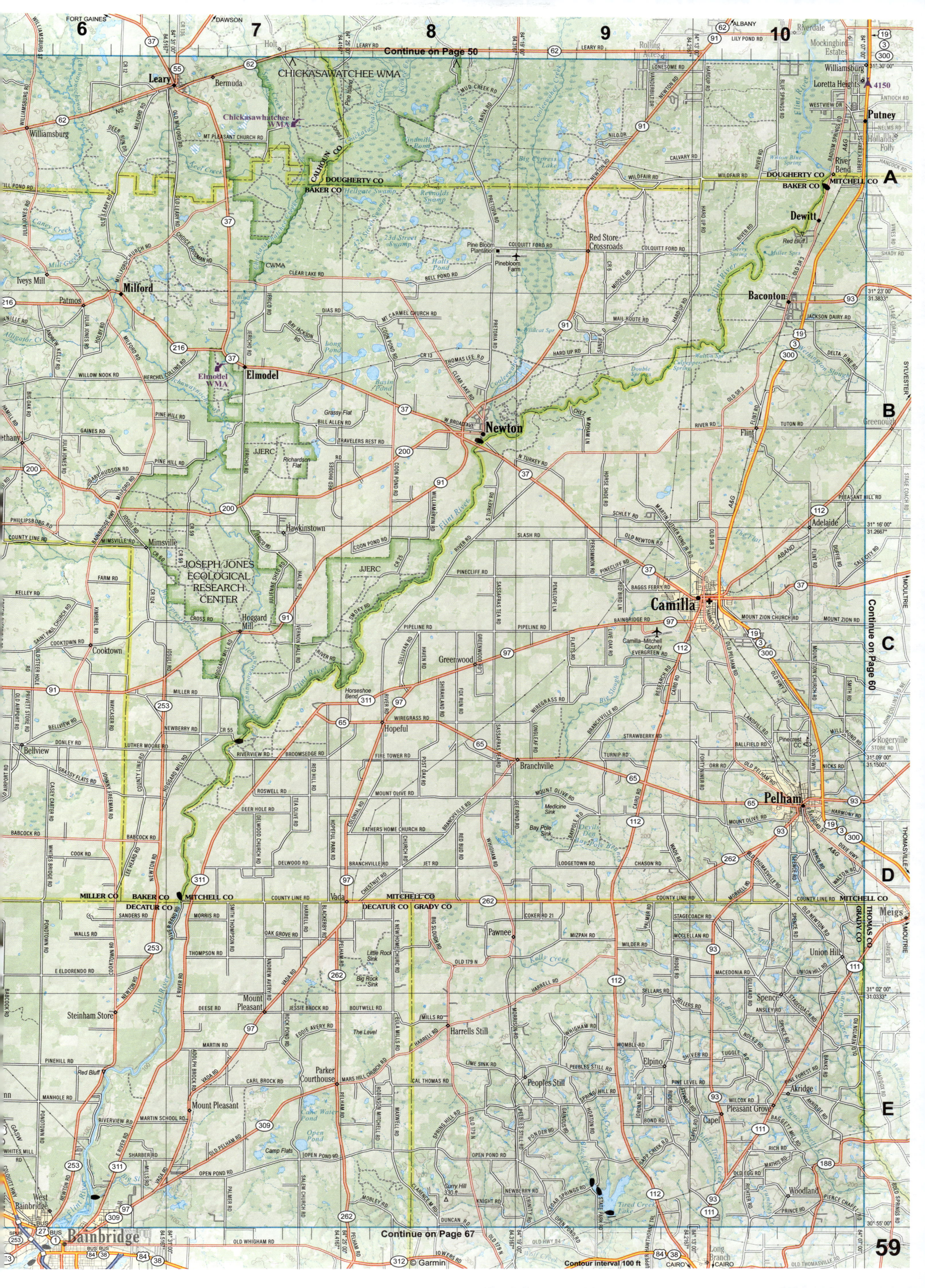

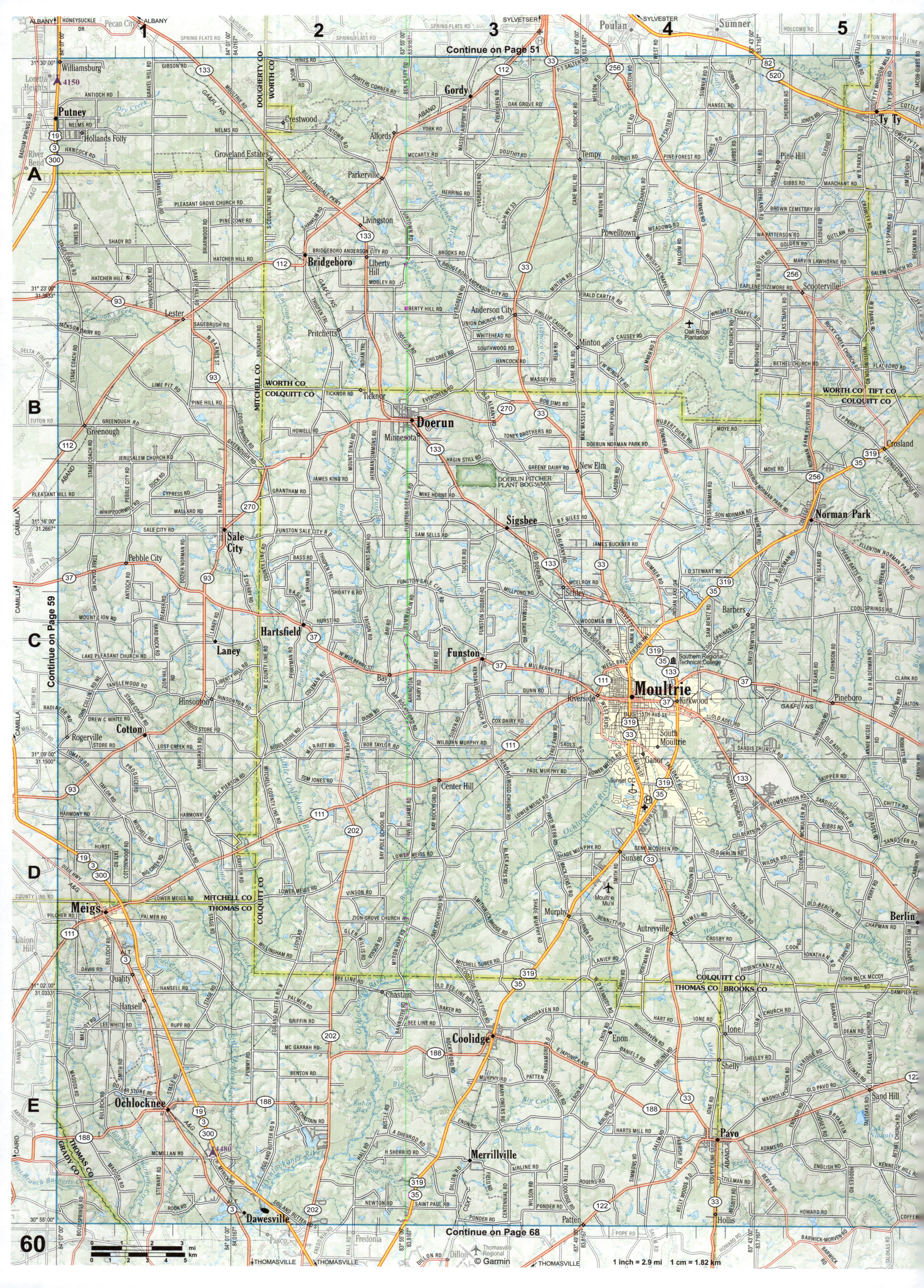

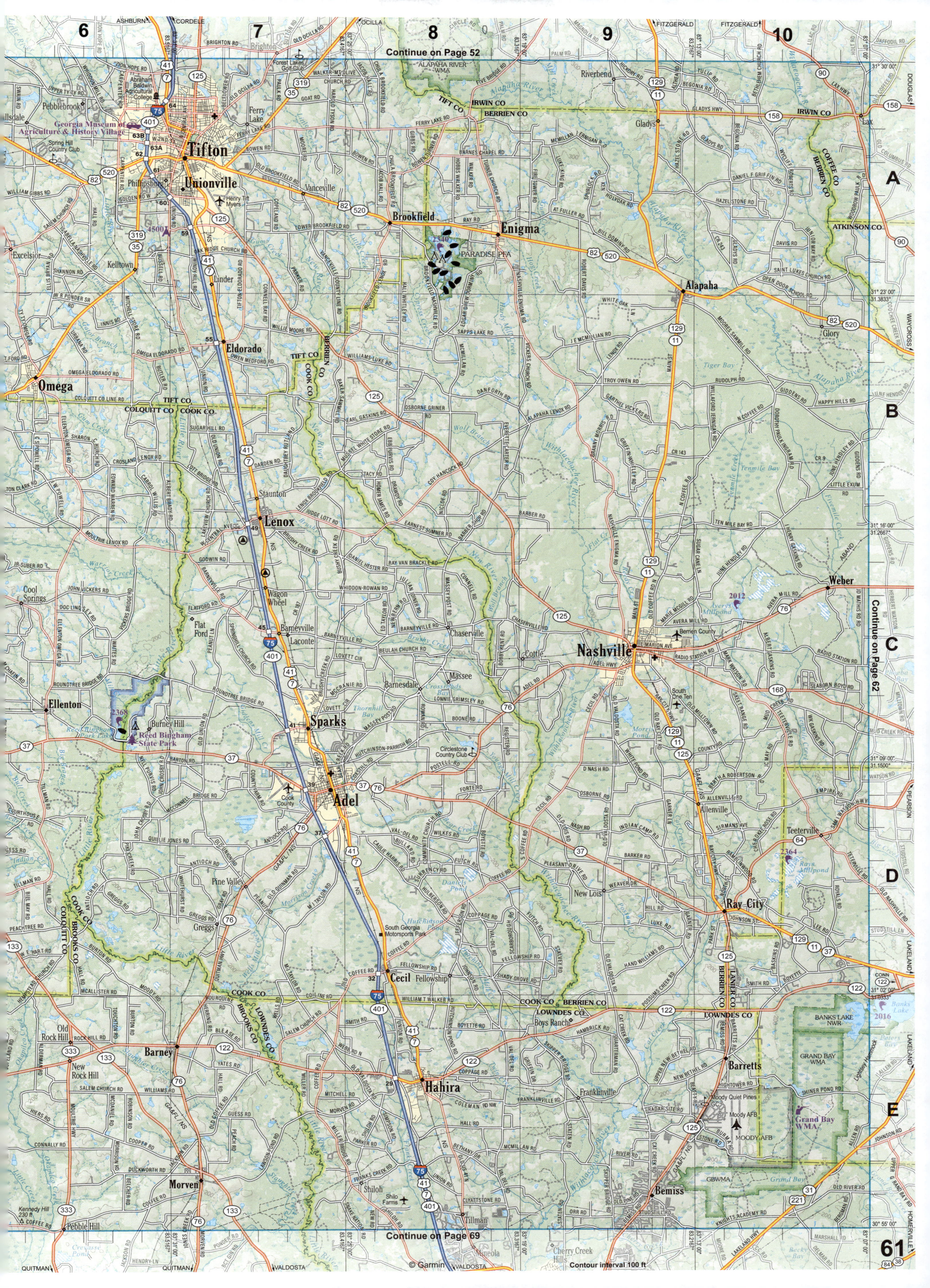

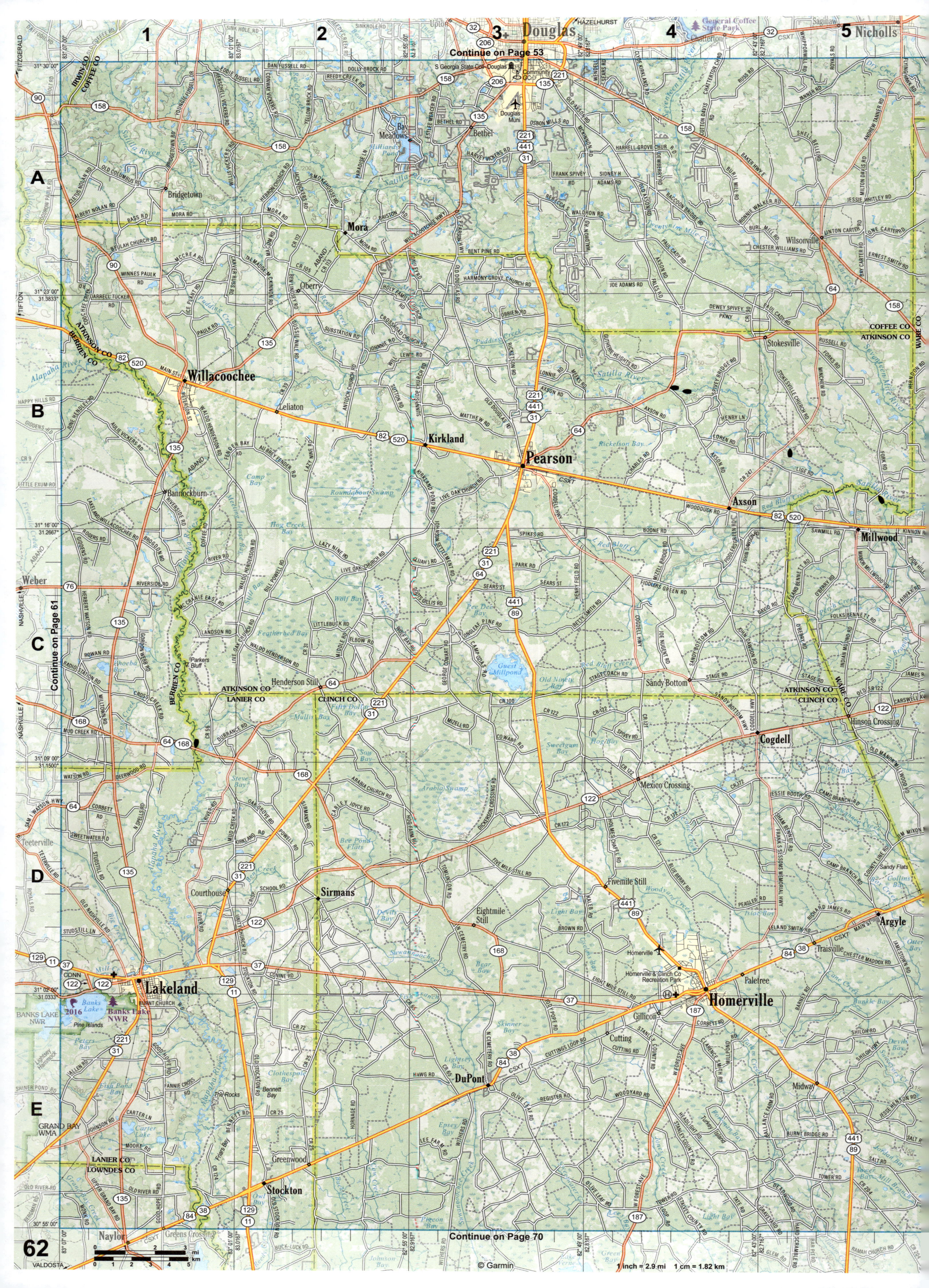

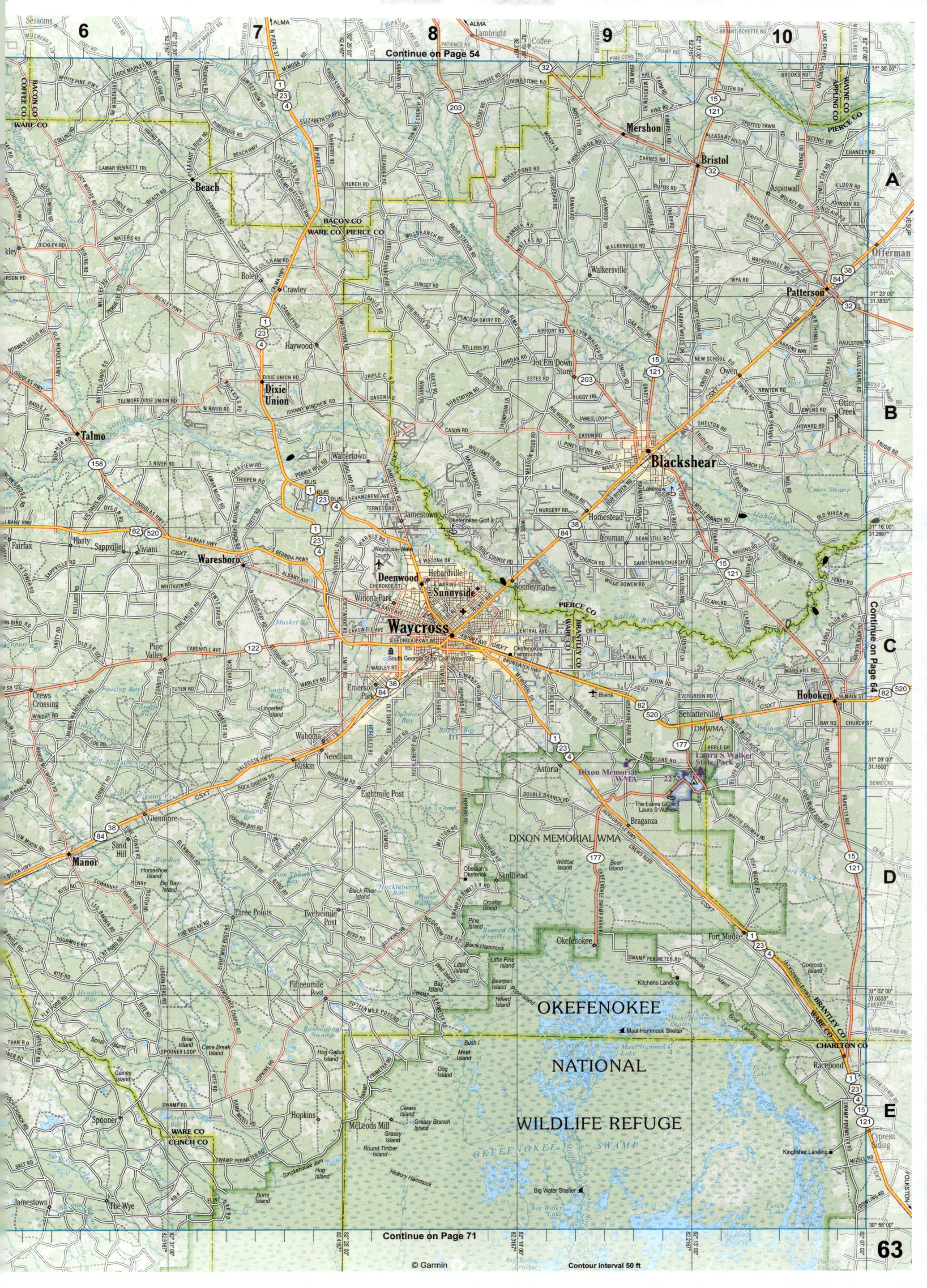

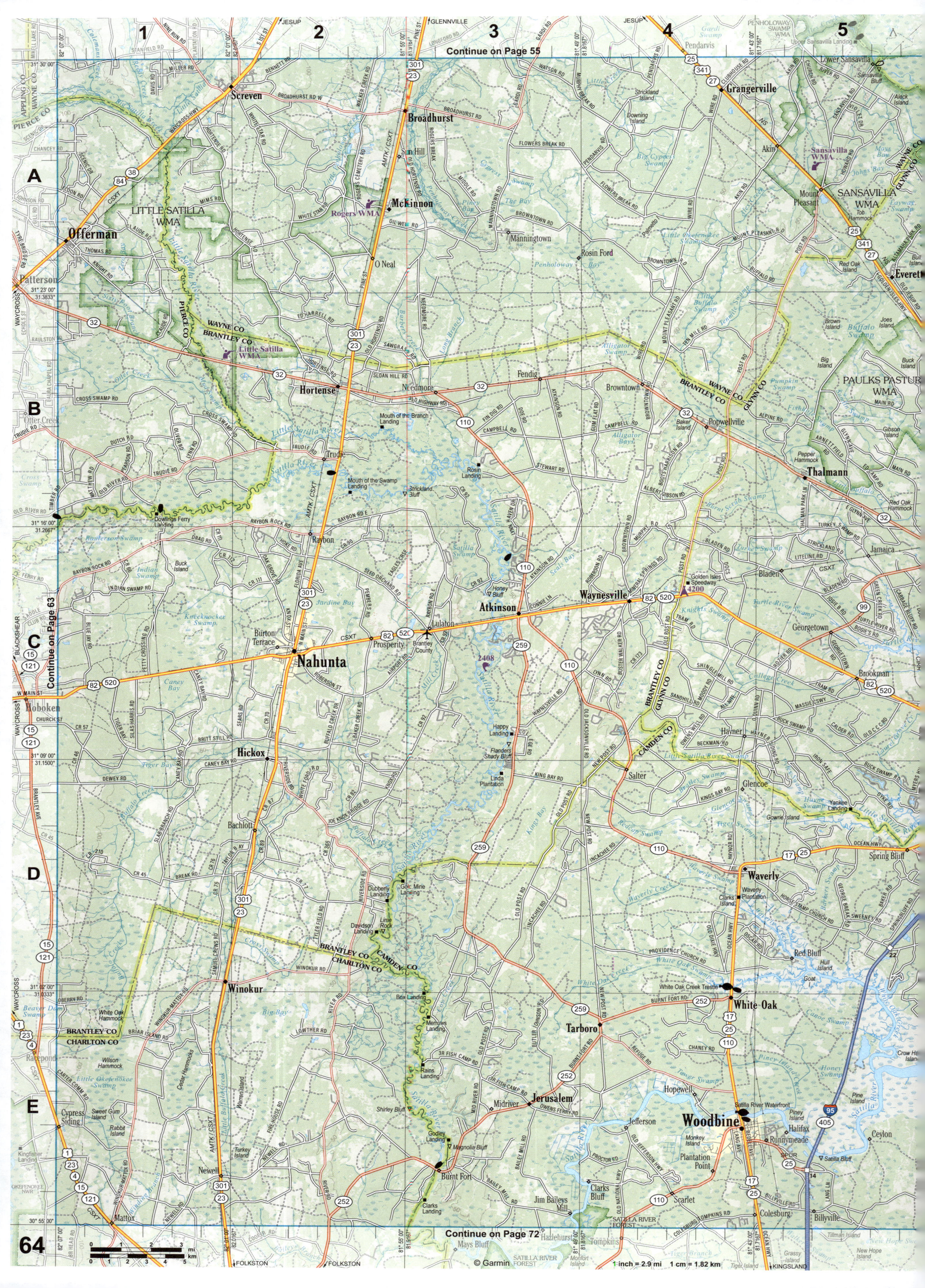

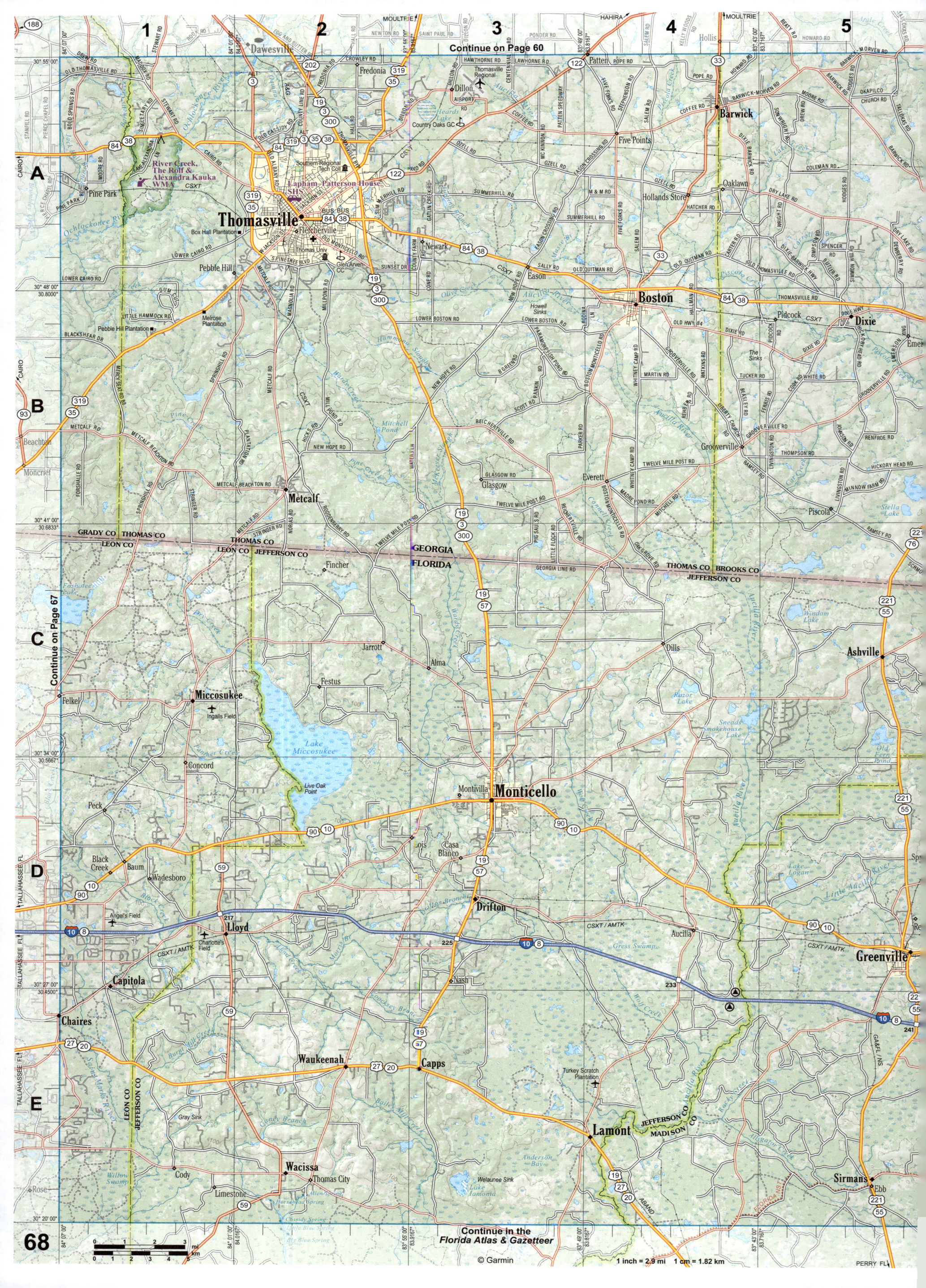

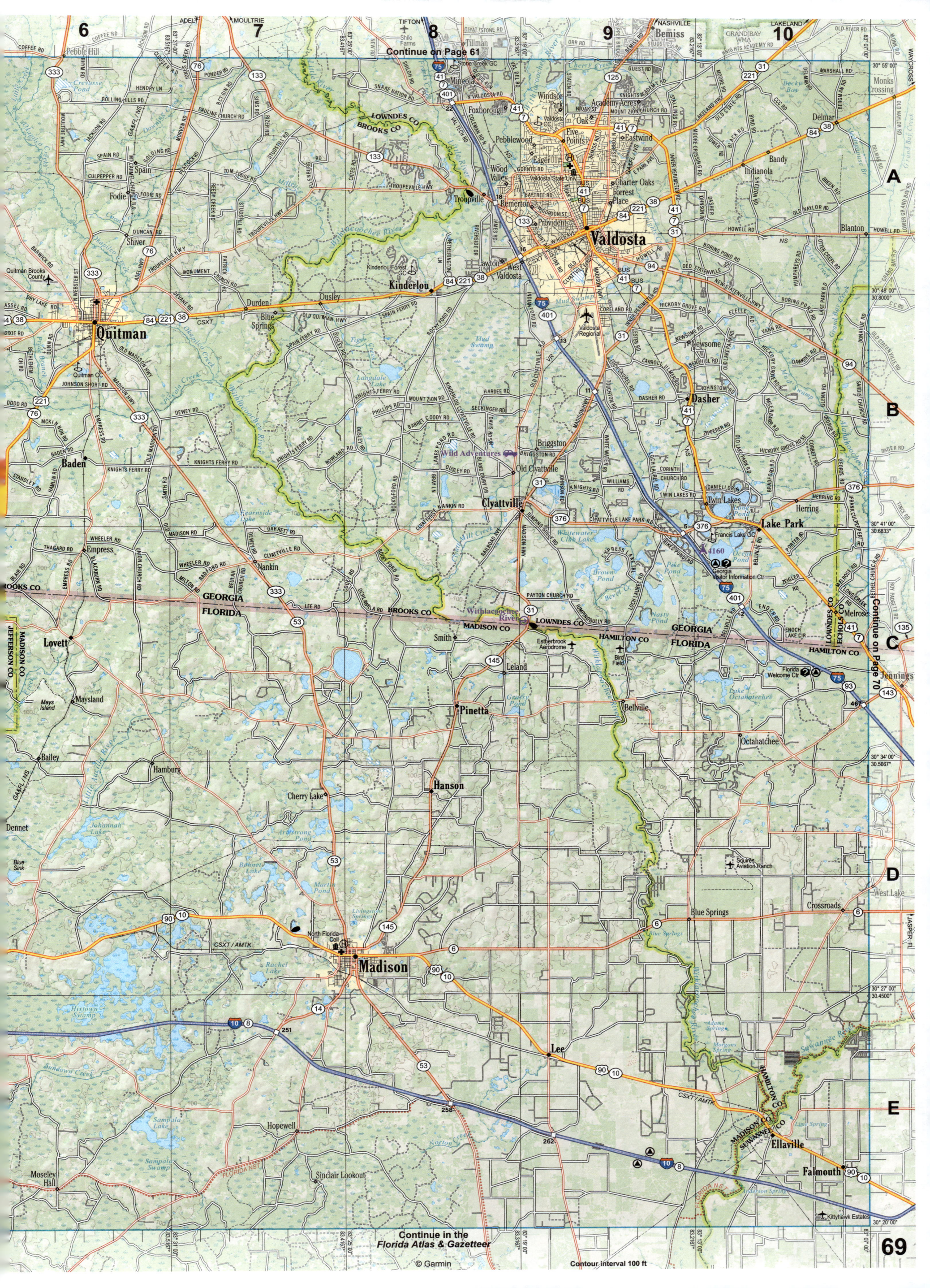

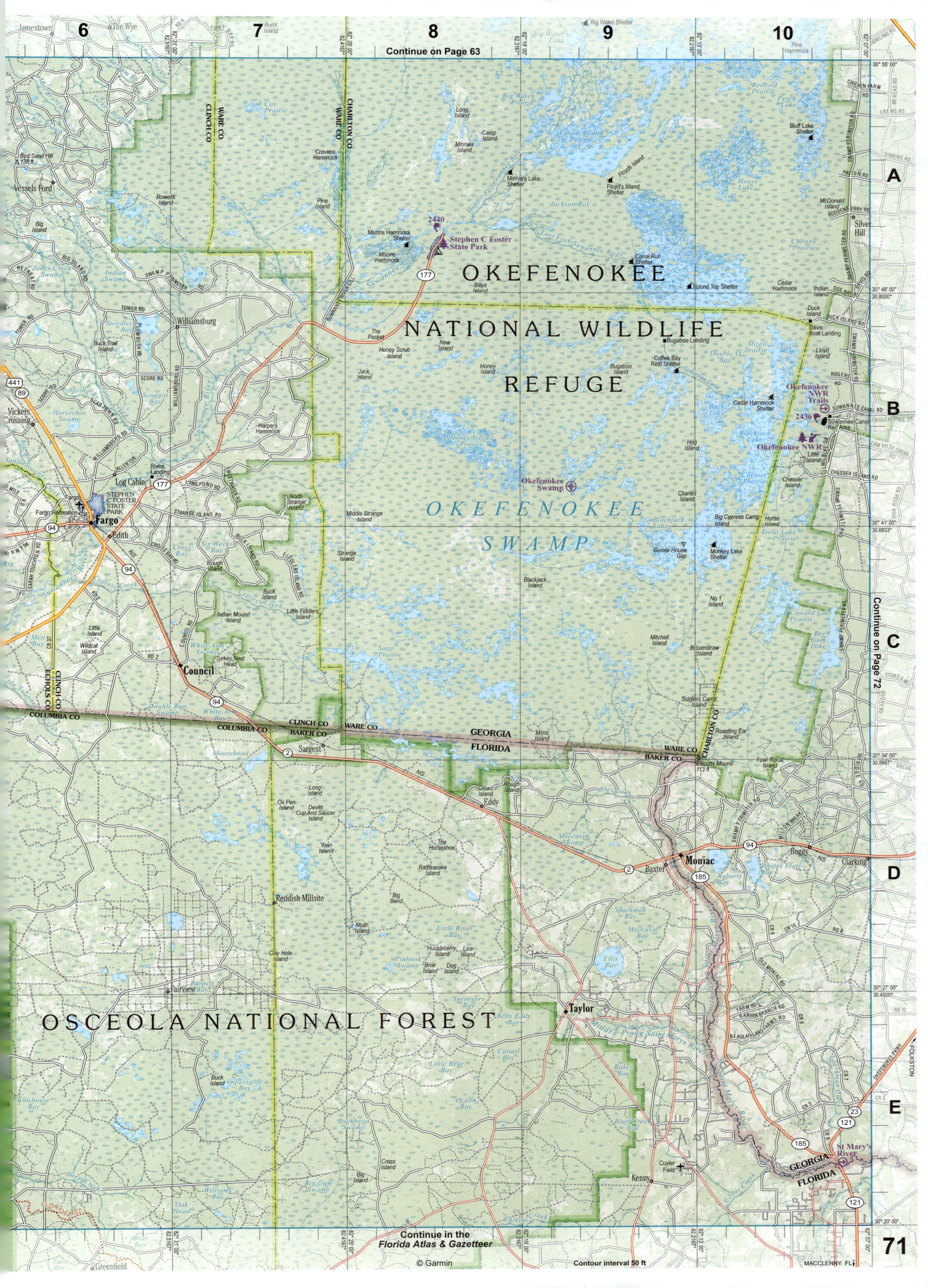